W9-DFM-710

TRIBAL RUGS

TRIBAL RUGS

A BUYER'S GUIDE

Lee Allane

With 93 illustrations, 47 in color

Thames and Hudson

Acknowledgments

I would like to express my gratitude to Hans Christensen (Bickenstaff & Knowles, London), Nash Dan (Anglo Persian Carpet Company, London), Linda E. Dyer (Skinners, Bolton and Boston, MA, USA), Mo Fini (Tumi, Bath and London), Paul Garrod (Chandni Chowk, Exeter), Guri Le Riche (Eastern Artefacts, Edinburgh), Rosalind Price (Chandni Chowk, Barnstaple), Iain Scott-Stewart (Rippon Boswell, London), Nancy R. Skinner (Skinners, Bolton and Boston, MA, USA) and Ron Stewart (Liberty, London) for their considerable help and advice on tribal rugs and artefacts and for supplying the majority of the tribal rugs and artefacts contained in this book. A special debt of gratitude is owed to Sam Wennek (Rippon Boswell International) for his expert knowledge of old and antique items. My appreciation is also extended to Maria Eugenia, Diane Grey, Douglas Robertson, Carlisle Antonio (The American Indian Trust, Bristol), Dori Zdzienski and especially to Glynis Bell and Angela Meidel for providing additional information, translations and support.

Thanks are also due to Glynis Bell, Angela Paine, Frannie Quinnell, James Upton, Steve and Penny Walters and Dorota Zdzienski for allowing me access to their excellent private collections. And finally a very special thanks must be extended to Andrew Daws and Dick Scott-Stewart for their hard work and diligence in producing the superb illustrations and original photographs used in this book.

The sources of the photographs of the colour plates are as follows: Lee Allane 16, 23, 32, 33; Anglo Persian Carpet Company, London 10, 11, 14, 18; Bickenstaff & Knowles, London 8, 9, 30; OCM (London) Ltd 22; Rippon Boswell, London 15, 17, 27, 35; Douglas Robertson 38; Dick Scott-Stewart 1–7, 12, 13, 19–21, 24–26, 28, 29, 31, 34, 36, 37, 40–43; Skinners, Bolton and Boston, MA, USA 39, 44–47

The sources of the tribal rugs and artefacts that appear in the plates are as follows: Anglo Persian Carpet Company, London 10, 11, 14, 18; Bickenstaff & Knowles, London 3, 6, 8, 9, 30; Chandni Chowk, Exeter and Barnstaple, Devon 16, 23–25, 32–34; Guri Le Riche, Edinburgh 38; OCM (London) Ltd 22; Liberty plc, London, and provincial branches 2, 4, 5, 7, 13, 20, 28, 29, 31; Rippon Boswell, London 15, 17, 27, 35; Skinners, Bolton and Boston, MA, USA 39, 44–47; Tumi, Bath 40–43; the private collections of Glynis Bell 1, 12, 36; Angela Paine 21; James Upton 26; Steve and Penny Walters 19; and Dorota Zdzienski 37.

Line drawings by Andrew Daws
Original photography by Dick Scott-Stewart

Any copy of this book issued by the publisher as a paperback is sold subject to the condition that it shall not by way of trade or otherwise be lent, resold, hired out or otherwise circulated without the publisher's prior consent in any form of binding or cover other than that in which it is published and without a similar condition including these words being imposed on a subsequent purchaser.

© 1996 Thames and Hudson Ltd, London

First published in the United States of America in 1996 by Thames and Hudson Inc., 500 Fifth Avenue, New York, New York 10110

Library of Congress Catalog Card Number 96-60258

ISBN 0-500-27897-0

All Rights Reserved. No part of this publication may be reproduced or transmitted in any form or by any means, electronic or mechanical, including photocopy, recording or any other information storage and retrieval system, without prior permission in writing from the publisher.

Printed and bound in Hong Kong

Contents

How to use this book

Tribal rugs are arguably the most confusing of all the hand-made rugs available in the west. They are sold under a bewildering variety of names, and authentic tribal items may be marketed under generic or regional names, or non-tribal, generic or regional items may be attributed to a totally unconnected or even fictitious tribal weaving group. Almost identical items are often sold at vastly different prices, and, due to the absence of independent information, the buyer is often at the mercy of the salesman. *Tribal Rugs, A Buyer's Guide* has been systematically organized to answer all your questions, as well as to provide a comprehensive introduction to the subject.

IF YOU ARE A COMPLETE BEGINNER, turn to Chapter I, which will explain *what tribal rugs are*, *how they get their names* and *where and by whom they are made* and provide an explanation of *essential weaving terms*. It also includes information on *tribal societies* and *a brief history of tribal weaving*.

Chapter II tells you about the *various types of rugs*, *how they are made* and *how the different materials, tools and weaving techniques* affect their quality, character and appearance, as well as explaining the *dyeing and washing processes* and the *origins and meanings of different colours*. It also gives advice on *assessing the age and origin* of a tribal rug, and provides detailed information on *traditional shapes and sizes*.

Chapter III tells you everything you need to know about **BUYING A TRIBAL RUG**, and helps you choose *the right rug at the right price*, whether you want it as an investment, or the start of a collection, or simply to enhance the decorative impact of your home. It explains how to *avoid paying too much*, or *buying something that is unsuitable for your needs*, and helps you to assess *quality and value for money* by telling you what to look for in a rug. *Comparative prices, taxes and import tariffs* are explained and there is information on *where and when to buy or sell*, as well as on the *care and repair* of your tribal rug.

IF YOU WANT TO KNOW MORE ABOUT TRIBAL RUGS Chapter IV provides the **CULTURAL CONTEXT**. It gives information on the *major ethnic groups* and the most important *invasions, migrations and empires*, as well as the *religious influences* that have been integral in the formation of the weaving heritage of the different tribal groups.

Chapter V discusses the *origin, meaning and cultural dispersal of tribal motifs and designs*. This helps in identifying the possible origin of tribal items and enhances your understanding and appreciation of the fascinating cultural, spiritual and historical information often contained in tribal rugs.

Chapter VI contains background information on **THE WEAVING NATIONS, TERRITORIES AND REGIONS**, with cross-references between *ancient and contemporary weaving regions*. The range and *general characteristics of the tribal rugs* produced in each country or region are also detailed.

Comprehensive information on all **THE TRIBAL WEAVING GROUPS** is given in Chapter VII. The tribes have been arranged alphabetically and divided into two sections: the *general ethnic tribes and tribal confederations* and the *specific (or minor) tribal, sub-tribal and regional weaving groups*. In both sections, there is detailed information on the quality, design repertoire, colour schemes, price, size and type of rugs produced by each weaving group, as well as their overall availability and the name (or names) under which they are sold, and, where appropriate, the difference between tribal and non-tribal items marketed under the same name.

Clear cross-references and headings allow you to pursue any line of enquiry to its logical conclusion by moving through the text and referring to the *maps, line drawings and colour plates*.

The *colour plates* have been chosen to illustrate a wide range of rugs, designs and colour schemes available today, and offer instant visual examples to complement the text.

CHAPTER ONE

What is a tribal rug?

The term tribal rug is sometimes used to describe any rug or woven artefact that is essentially tribal in character and appearance, regardless of the function for which it was made or the ethnic origin or lifestyle of the weavers. However, the term should perhaps be more properly applied only to those items that are produced by people living in tribal societies, in a limited number of weaving techniques, and that are primarily used as floor coverings or associated furnishings.

Consequently, rugs woven in a tribal style by non-tribal weavers, whether in small villages or larger urban workshops cannot be properly classified as tribal in origin. Similarly, decorative tapestries, clothes and a number of other woven artefacts, despite their tribal authenticity, cannot be regarded as rugs.

In practice, however, there are exceptions to this precise definition, and some items that cannot properly be described as either tribal or rugs are nevertheless generally accepted as falling into the category of tribal rugs. For example, the term tribal is sometimes applied to all the items woven in the predominantly Kurdish town of Bidjar, Iran, although the vast majority of Kurds in the area live a settled existence as part of the general Iranian population, non-Kurds may have participated in the weaving, and the rugs made in the town have long since evolved their own distinctive regional, rather than tribal, character and appearance.

Similarly, the expression rug is frequently used by dealers as a collective term for a range of items that include tent partitions (*purdahs*), door-flaps (*enssis*), eating cloths (*soufrehs*), stove covers (*rukorssis*) and a variety of bags, animal trappings and other woven artefacts. The same is true of the blankets, ponchos, etc., produced in various parts of North, Central and South America, which, although not strictly rugs, are often considered to have a sufficiently close association with rug weaving to fall under the general umbrella of tribal rugs. It is also common practice for some types of associated items – e.g. *ikats*, *namads* and certain types of tapestry weavings – to be placed under the broad heading of rugs if they originate from one of the traditional rug-weaving areas (e.g. Uzbekistan), but not if they are made elsewhere (e.g. Indonesia).

The term tribal rugs should therefore be viewed as a general, somewhat arbitrary, classification that includes not only items that can be regarded justifiably as both tribal (in origin) and rugs (in function), but also one that contains a number of other items that have traditionally fallen within the bracket of tribal rugs.

However, there are some broad criteria governing the origin and lifestyle of the weavers, the function for which an item is made, the weaving techniques and the region that are generally accepted as fundamental to any definition of tribal rugs. These criteria can be used as broad guidelines to differentiate between authentic tribal rugs and items that are only tribal in character and appearance, although there may be some exceptions.

Names and terms

There are several terms, names and expressions in common usage that may be unfamiliar to people who are relatively new to the subject. Most of these will be explained fully in the appropriate chapters, but there are a few that need to be clarified at the outset.

Spelling and pronunciation
Spelling and pronunciation varies considerably because the spoken languages of the weavers in almost all of the tribal rug weaving regions either do not have a corresponding written equivalent or employ written scripts (e.g. Arabic) whose alphabets do not relate directly to those used in the west. Consequently, most translations are strictly phonetic, and, as yet, there is no universally applied spelling and pronunciation system. One should therefore avoid jumping to the conclusion that an unfamiliar name signifies a

different weaving group or type of rug – it may simply be a variant spelling of a more common name. If in doubt, it is often helpful to repeat both names (preferably out loud) in order to gauge any logical phonetic similarities.

Asia Spelling is mainly phonetic. The only major exceptions are Armenian and modern Turkish, which, in 1927, changed from Arabic to an adapted Latin script. Dealers throughout the world use various spellings, but the following are among the most common. Interchangeable letters or letter combinations: 'q' and 'k', and 'i' and 'y' (e.g. Qashga'i, Kashgay); 'a' and 'e' (e.g. Meshed, Mashad); 'a' and 'eh' (e.g. Khamsa, Khamseh); 'o' and 'u', and 'j' and 'g' (e.g. Khorjin, Khurgin); and to a lesser degree 'g' and 'k', and 'e' and 'i' (e.g. gelim, kilim). Compound consonants not usually found together in European scripts (e.g. 'gh', 'kh', 'qa', etc.) are often used to indicate a specific sound that does not have a direct phonetic translation, although this is sometimes omitted (e.g. Kazakh, Kazak).

Pronunciation is generally straightforward. Each syllable normally has equal emphasis, the English vowel sounds 'eye' and 'ee' are usually represented by 'ai' and 'i', and 'q' is roughly equivalent to the English 'k' (e.g. Taimani and Qashga'i are pronounced 'Tai-mah-nee' and 'Kash-guy-ee'). Some compound consonants (e.g. 'gh', 'kh') use an additional letter (e.g. 'h') to stress the proceeding letters but minor errors in pronunciation are rarely problematic.

North Africa French transliteration and pronunciation is dominant (e.g. Oulad Bou Sbaa is pronounced 'weelad Bwee Sbaa'). A letter, separated by an apostrophe, at the beginning of a name (e.g. Beni M'Tir) is normally pronounced independently (e.g. 'Beni Em-Tir').

The Americas Native phonetic transliterations in North America have been influenced by English, Spanish and French transliterations (e.g. Creek, Navajo and Iroquois, respectively). Spanish and to a lesser degree Portuguese influence dominates Central and South America. However, there is a considerable degree of consistency in spelling (e.g. the Spanish transliteration of Navajo is widely used in English-speaking countries). The spelling of many of the old Mayan, Aztec and Inca names (e.g. Quetzalcoatl) is relatively universal.

Pronunciation is similar to English or anglicized versions of Spanish and French (e.g. Navajo/Navaho and Iroquois/Irokwah). Transliterations of ancient Aztec, Inca and Mayan names, etc., contain a number of unfamiliar consonant combinations. In particular, the juxtaposition of 't' and 'l', as in Tlatoc and Quetzalcoatl, in which the first letter is normally pronounced separately at the beginning of the word (e.g. 'Tuhlatoc') and the second letter at the end of the word (e.g. 'Quetzalcoatel'). Also, the letter combinations 'que' and 'qui' are usually pronounced 'kay' and 'kee' (e.g. Quetzalcoatl, 'Kay-zal-co-at-el' and Quintana, 'Keentana'), and 'x' at the beginning of the word frequently takes the form of 'sh' (e.g. Xinbalba, 'Shinbalba').

Different types of rugs

The term rug may be applied to any item which can be used as a floor-covering, regardless of the weaving technique or the function for which it was made. However, distinctions are often made. (*See* Chapter II)

Pile rugs Generally referred to simply as rugs, and are produced by tying, or knotting, small ribbons of coloured yarn (which forms the pile) around the warps to create the design.

Flatweaves Produced by interweaving individual warp and weft strands to create both the physical structure of the rug and the design visible on the front. The term is used collectively to describe any flatwoven item, regardless of the specific weaving technique or where or by whom it was made.

Kilims A more specific term usually only applied to flatwoven items made using a limited number of techniques, which originate from the oriental rug weaving region. They are known by a variety of local names (e.g. *gelim* in Iran, *palas* in the Caucasus and *bsath* in Syria and Lebanon), but in the west they are generally referred to by their Afghan and Turkish names, respectively, as either kelims or kilims. Flatwoven items made in other parts of the world are rarely, if ever, called kilims.

The relationship between pile rugs and flatweaves It is generally accepted that pile rugs evolved from flatweaves. However, in some areas only flatweaves are produced, while in others, pile rugs predominate and there are some weaving groups whose pile rugs and flatweaves are of equal merit.

Rugs, carpets and runners Terms often used in the west to denote size and shape, for example, a carpet is a rug whose surface area is more than 4.4m^2 and whose length is less than 1.5 times its width, i.e. 9' x 6' (2.74 x 1.83 m).

This distinction is generally confined to Britain and the British Commonwealth and is usually applied only to pile rugs, although large flatwoven items may be referred to as kilims or flatwoven carpets. A runner is a long, narrow rug – whose length is over 2.5 times its width – and is often used for both pile rugs and flatweaves.

Local names denoting size and shape Rugs of certain sizes and shapes are sometimes given specific names by the weavers (e.g. *dozar*) and it is possible to find an item of the appropriate dimensions being sold as a Qashga'i *dozar*.

Names denoting function or weaving technique Sometimes used in place of rug, flatweave or kilim (e.g. a Kazak item woven using the *soumak* technique may be sold as a Kazak *soumak*, rather than a Kazak rug, etc.).

How tribes get their names

The source of tribal names varies considerably, but can generally be traced to a similar range of associations with ancestors, occupations, personal characteristics, environmental factors and political or religious allegiances to those used in the west for allocating place or family names. For example, Johnson, son of John; Chicago, place of the skunk; Chandler, boat builder; Bronwyn, white breasted. The meanings and origins of several tribal names are totally obscure, although they possibly stemmed from one of these sources.

Common ancestors Frequently encountered among Turkic tribes (e.g. the Uzbeks take their name from their former leader, Uzbek Khan).

Place of origin and environment Fairly common across a wide range of tribal groups, e.g. Firozkohi (which means 'mountains of turquoise') is believed to be a reference to the real or mythological origins of the Aimaq tribe of that name. Some tribes are also named after, or give their name to, the village or region in which they live (e.g. Alti Bolagh).

Occupation and lifestyle Especially common among pastoral nomads, e.g., the Yuruk and the Belouch are both named after local expressions for nomad or wanderer. The Maldari Belouch derive their name from the word for sheep owner, and the Kara Qoyonlu (black sheep owners) and the Ak Qoyonlu (white sheep owners) are rival Turkoman sub-tribes.

Characteristics, appearance and allegiances Found most often in Iran and the Americas, e.g., the Kyzylbash (or red-headed) federation take their name from the red turbans they used

to wear; and the Aztecs (which means 'crane people') derive their name from the crane feathers in their head-dresses. Certain tribal confederacies are named after the number of tribes they contain (Khamseh, the Persian word for five, is applied collectively to the five tribes of the Khamseh confederacy).

Sub-tribes, clans or sections Most tribal groups are composed of various sub-groups, which often have their own individual name. For example, the Turkomen are divided into a number of major tribal groups (e.g. Ersari) who are in turn made up of a number of sub-tribes, clans and sections that may be known by a traditional name (e.g. Jangalarik), the name of the town or district in which they live (e.g. Barmazit) or the type of *gul* they use in their designs (e.g. Waziri, so called because it was developed by a government official, or Wazir, during the late 19th or early 20th century). Consequently, if an Ersari weaver was asked to define her tribal identity, she might refer to her general ethnic/cultural origins (i.e. Turkoman), her major tribal affinity (i.e. Ersari), her individual tribal allegiance (e.g. Jangalarik, Barmazit, etc.) or even the head of her extended family group.

Western versions of tribal names Not always the same as the weavers' own names for themselves, e.g., certain nomadic tribes in Turkey call themselves Turkomen, the Lurs sometimes refer to themselves as the 'Kuhi' (mountain people) and the Navajo as the 'Dineh' (human beings). Dealers often prefix a tribal name with the name of the town in which a tribe has traditionally marketed its rugs (e.g. 'Meshed' Belouch) to identify stylistic variations, although the tribe would not necessarily refer to themselves in the same way.

How rugs get their names

There are a number of criteria used for naming tribal rugs, which mainly relate to where or by whom a rug was made, but may also refer directly to the weaving technique, design or designated function of certain items.

Weaving tribe The most common method is to give rugs the name of the weaving tribe. Consequently, a rug woven by the Belouch confederacy would be called a Belouch.

Place of origin The second most popular method is to name items after the place where they were made. This is often the preferred practice when classifying items woven by settled tribal weavers or when the exact tribal attribution is unclear. For example, rugs made by settled Kurdish weavers in the Iranian town of Bidjar are known as Bidjars.

Tribe and place of origin Both names may be used to indicate that a rug was made by a tribe, who inhabit one particular area, rather than by their kinsmen who live somewhere else. For example, a rug sold as a Kerman Afshar indicates that it was made by the Afshar tribesmen living in Kerman Province, southeast Iran, rather than Afshar tribesmen who inhabit the Azerbaijan or Khorassan regions.

A double tribal name Sometimes employed to indicate that a rug was produced by a sub-tribe, clan or section of a larger tribe or tribal grouping. For example, a Taimani Aimaq would be woven by the Taimani tribe, who are part of the Aimaq confederacy.

Name of the weaving technique, function or design Normally only used if a more exact attribution is unclear or in place of the term rug or kilim. Consequently, an unattributed item woven in the *soumak* technique may be marketed as a *soumak* and an Afshar made as an eating cloth may be sold as an Afshar *soufreh*.

Name of the marketing centre Tribal rugs may also take their name from the town in which they are collected and marketed. For example, Bokhara in Turkmenistan acted as a marketing centre for Turkomen tribesmen and it became common practice for all Turkoman rugs to be referred to collectively as Bokharas.

Generic names Normally used to categorize a general type of rug that may be produced by a number of weaving groups, but which do not refer to any actual tribe. For example, *gebbeh* is the name given to thick-piled, sparsely patterned items woven by Lurs and other tribes in southern Iran. Similarly, some Turkoman-style rugs are prefixed by names that refer to the style and quality of their manufacture (e.g. Andkhoy, Mauri) or the name of the *gul* used in the design (e.g. Pendi). Also, the names of certain towns or villages may be used to define a specific type or style of items produced in a number of neighbouring centres (e.g. Labijar).

The relationship between rug names and weaving groups Normally synonymous if the rug takes its name from an actual tribe or weaving village, e.g., a rug made by Belouch tribesmen would normally be called a Belouch and would be classified as belonging to the Belouch weaving group. However, the relationship is less exact if rugs are named after their weaving technique or design, or are sold under a generic name.

Tribal origins of the weavers

The word tribe is derived from the Latin for three and was first applied by the Romans to a group of autonomous primitive clans as a method of defining their three major political divisions. It is now used to describe any independent or semi-independent social group – especially those who live a nomadic, semi-nomadic or primitive hunter-gatherer existence – who occupy (or lay claim to) a specific territory and share a common ancestry, social structure, culture or set of customs. A tribe can also be defined as a group in which the people govern their own affairs as independent (usually localized) communities without reliance on central government organizations, and whose primary allegiance is to the tribe, rather than the state. The people share in the production of food and other basic necessities, are governed by their own laws and customs and learn the traditional skills needed to perpetuate the tribal way of life through direct participation in tribal activities, rather than formal schooling.

In the context of tribal weaving, the term is loosely applied to any socially cohesive nomadic, semi-nomadic or village group who are either of the same ethnic origins or belong to a long-standing political confederation, and who conform to a common cultural weaving and design heritage that underpins the character and appearance of their rugs.

The terms tribal or ethnic Often used interchangeably, but each term has its own precise definition, i.e., tribal implies a particular lifestyle or social structure, whereas ethnic merely refers to homogeneous racial origins. Shahsavan rugs can therefore be described as tribal, despite being made by people of different ethnic origins, whereas rugs made by racially homogeneous Armenians should perhaps be more properly referred to as ethnic.

Classifying tribal origins
Most tribal groups can be broadly divided into formal tribal confederacies, ethnic tribes or informal tribal confederacies. However, it is advisable to view these divisions in relative, rather than absolute, terms – e.g. a Kurdish tribe would be composed primarily of ethnic

Kurds, but may also contain people of other ethnic origins. Tradition and convenience also play a part in classification, and – if the exact composition of a tribal group is unknown – it is common practice to accept their cultural assimilation as historical fact or focus on the largest or most easily identifiable ethnic group.

Ethnic tribes Share the same racial, as well as social and cultural heritage, and normally trace their lineage back to an identifiable common ancestor or through a set of unifying historical events to the same real or mythological roots. However, it is quite probable that some tribal groups, who are generally considered to be of the same ethnic origin, are in reality an amalgamation of people of different ethnic ancestry, who banded together for political or social convenience at some point in the past, and have gradually evolved into a relatively homogeneous social and cultural unit. For example, the Afshar are generally considered to be descendants of Turkic tribesmen – themselves a mixture of quite diverse racial groups – who invaded Iran between the 11th and 15th centuries, and subsequently people from other ethnic groups would probably have been absorbed, either by marriage or cultural osmosis, into Afshar society.

Informal tribal confederacies Culturally, rather than ethnically, homogeneous tribal groups that have evolved a common identity over the centuries, but whose sub-tribal divisions often retain a significant degree of ethnic and cultural independence. For example, the Belouch are composed of a number of sub-tribes, clans and sections, who are quite clearly from a variety of racial backgrounds, but are generally viewed as a collective tribal group because of the similarity in their lifestyles, allegiances, customs, and the common characteristics of their rugs.

Formal tribal confederacies Usually trace their origins to a specific point in history, or to the individual responsible for their formation. For example, the Shahsavan ('those who are loyal to the Shah') was formed by Shah Abbas at the beginning of the 17th century from ethnic Turkic, Kurdish, Tajik and Georgian nomads in order to protect the northern border of the Persian Empire against the rebellious Kyzylbash (Dervish) movement. Subsequently, a fusion of the cultural, social, religious and weaving divisions (that existed at the time of their formation) gradually took place and, allowing for minor sub-tribal differences, the Shahsavan are generally viewed as a homogeneous tribal group. Consequently, their rugs may be marketed as Shahsavans of Mogan or Bidjar, but never as Turkic or Georgian Shahsavans.

Consistency in tribal classifications Variable because of the different criteria employed by historians and dealers. Consequently, the three classifications used in this book are not applied universally throughout the trade and should be treated as a useful means of clarifying the complexity of tribal divisions, rather than as hard and fast divisions.

Classification by weaving characteristics Sometimes the character and appearance of rugs produced by a specific weaving group, rather than the ethnic origins or cultural affinity of the weavers, are the deciding factor in classification. For example, rugs made in the village of Firdous by settled Arabs are normally classified as Belouch (or Firdous Belouch) because of their close affinity to the rugs produced by Belouch tribesmen.

Tribal societies and lifestyles

Environment and lifestyle Normally closely connected because all human social groups, at some point in their history, were faced with the simple choice – in order to survive – of either adapting their way of life to suit the environment, or modifying their environment to suit their way of life. Generally, people have followed the line of least resistance – those occupying densely forested or fertile delta regions usually adopted a sedentary, village lifestyle, whereas tribes living in vast semi-desert, tundra or grassland areas generally opted for a nomadic or semi-nomadic existence.

Transition from tribal to national societies It is clear that many modern nations, as their names suggest, have evolved from the traditional territories of their indigenous, or early, tribal inhabitants – e.g. Germany (territory of the Germanic tribes). However, it is extremely difficult, if not impossible, to identify precisely when these transitions from tribal homeland to independent nation took place. In all probability, they were gradual progressions – including a variety of changes to borders and ethnic mix – rather than single events. Similarly, several of today's rug-producing nations (e.g.

Azerbaijan) are still in a transitional state between being arbitrarily defined 'homelands for homogeneous tribal people', and clearly defined 'countries' in the general sense of the term. It is therefore advisable to treat some of the more recently formed countries as if they were still essentially tribal territories.

Geographical dispersal of weaving tribes Tribal societies exist to varying degrees throughout most parts of the world. However, the majority either do not produce rugs, or their items do not possess the uniqueness of character and appearance necessary to distinguish them from those woven by other ethnic or tribal groups. For example, weaving is not a traditional craft of the Australian Aboriginals and, although practised throughout sub-Saharan Africa, Indo-China and the Pacific islands, it is mainly confined to clothes and items that cannot be defined as rugs. The European Gypsies still weave rugs, but they are generally viewed as being synonymous with the country or region they inhabit, rather than the tribe.

Tribal weaving is generally confined to the traditional oriental rug weaving area, which stretches from North Africa, through Turkey, Iran and other parts of the Middle East, the former Soviet Caucasian and Central Asian republics, Afghanistan, western Pakistan and East Turkestan. There is no tribal weaving in the Balkans (if we discount the European Gypsies), central and eastern China, India and eastern Pakistan. However, a few tribal items are produced in some of the Indian Himalayan provinces (e.g. Sikkim, Ladakh), Mongolia, Bhutan and Tibet; there are isolated pockets of tribal weaving throughout the Americas, especially in the south-west of the USA, Mexico, Ecuador and Peru.

Different types of tribal societies

Nomadic societies Can be applied to any tribal group that moves constantly from place to place in search of work, food, water, shelter or grazing for their animals, and can be applied equally to the hunter-gatherer Aboriginal tribes of Australia, the Bedouin 'horse and camel traders' of the Sahara Desert and the European Gypsies (musicians, entertainers, fortune tellers, seasonal workers and itinerant labourers, etc.). However, in the context of rug making, the term is normally reserved for pastoral herdsmen whose migrations are dictated by the need to follow the

natural cycle of available pasture, water and shelter. They are found primarily in North Africa and Asia, especially Morocco, Iran, Afghanistan and Central Asia.

Semi-nomadic societies Essentially the same as nomadic societies, except that they spend part of the year (usually the winter) in, or near, villages on their migratory routes.

Settled or village societies Normally based around former nomadic or semi-nomadic tribal people, who have opted for a more settled way of life, but have retained their tribal customs, allegiances and weaving traditions and can be found throughout the entire weaving region. Settled tribal societies have increased steadily over the last few decades as people have rejected the nomadic way of life.

The decline of tribal societies

Very few tribal societies have been able to resist completely the pressures to modify their way of life and conform to the dominant national culture of the countries in which they live. Consequently, there has been an accelerated decline, throughout the 20th century, in both the number of people living in tribal societies and the range and variety of the tribes themselves. It is now a definite possibility that many traditional tribal societies will become extinct during the first few decades of the 21st century, partly owing to the lure of urban living, but also as a direct result of government policies.

War Has almost become a way of life for many tribal people (especially those, like the Kurds, who are still fighting for a homeland), and even those not directly involved are often caught up in national conflicts. For example, the Afghan–Soviet War and the numerous smaller ethnic and territorial disputes that have continued to flair over the last few decades, especially in the former Soviet Caucasian and Central Asian republics, have devastated many tribal groups. Similarly, during the Iran–Iraq War, the Iranian government adopted the policy (used extensively by the Safavid Shahs during the 16th and 17th centuries) of forcibly employing tribal people as its first line of defence, and if future conflicts arise, it is probable that this policy will be used again.

Environmental damage Caused primarily by war, government-sponsored industrialization and military weapons testing. For instance, many of the traditional migratory routes of tribes in Afghanistan are still unsafe because of the plethora of land-mines and unexploded bombs left behind after the Afghan–Soviet War. Similarly, the Soviet policy of draining the Aral Sea for irrigation and urban usage has resulted in it shrinking to between 50% and 60% of its former size, causing the surrounding Aralkum Salt Desert to be extended, and creating an environmental disaster for the tribal groups in Kazakhstan and Uzbekistan. Remote tribal areas have also been used to test nuclear and chemical weapons – e.g. the Soviet Union in parts of Central Asia, China in East Turkestan and the USA in the deserts of Arizona and New Mexico – and there is no guarantee that all the countries concerned will put environment protection before industrial and military advancement.

Persecution and forced resettlement Has included the systematic slaughter or wholesale expulsion of any tribal (especially nomadic) people whose loyalty to the State cannot be guaranteed. For example, the Iraqi government used chemical (as well as conventional) weapons on Kurdish and Marsh Arab villages and encampments throughout the 1980s and 1990s, and, during the same period, Turkey continued to ban the Kurdish language and enforce settlement on a number of nomadic Kurdish tribes. Ethnic cleansing has also occurred throughout the former Soviet Caucasian and Central Asian republics and, in Afghanistan, military pacification of the country's more independent tribal groups has been continued by the post-Soviet Afghan regime.

The attitudes of western governments Generally apathetic and occasionally complicit, e.g., the day-to-day destruction of tribal societies is rarely mentioned in the western press, and, even something as widely reported as Iraq's use of chemical weapons on Kurdish villages did not stop Britain and other western governments from continuing to sell arms to the Iraqi regime. Regrettably, short-term self-interest rules, and most western governments are unlikely to interfere in, or even condemn, the internal policies of offending countries if it might lead to a disruption of trade, a reduction in company profits or a decrease in their political influence in the region. It should also be remembered that governments are in the business of control and the presence of independent groups – whose primary loyalty is to the tribe, rather than the state – undermines their authority. This is equally true in the west where we have largely eradicated our tribal societies, and the few that remain are either isolated in remote reservations (e.g. Navajo) or pressurized into adopting a non-tribal way of life (e.g. European Gypsies and New Age Travellers).

Classifying tribal rugs

Tribal rugs cannot be classified according to one comprehensive, universally applied criterion because they are influenced to varying degrees by their country of origin, their weaver's lifestyle and weaving group.

Country of origin
It is necessary to classify tribal rugs according to their country of origin because production costs, exchange rates and import/export tariffs and regulations sometimes vary considerably, which may result in discrepancies between the prices and availability of almost identical items. For example, during the Afghan–Soviet War (*c.* 1979–89) Belouch rugs woven in Afghanistan were generally more expensive and harder to obtain than comparative items woven by their kinsmen in Iran and Pakistan. This was partly due to the conflict itself and partly as a consequence of some western governments, most notably the USA, levying punitive or favourable import tariffs on the goods produced in each country, depending on their attitude to the regime. Consequently, an Afghan Belouch imported into the USA would attract a 40% tax levy on top of its purchase and export costs while an almost identical item made in Pakistan was zero rated and could be sold in the shops for at least 40% less.

However, tribal rugs do not conform to the same degree of stylistic uniformity as regional and workshop rugs from the same country. For example, although there may be some shared national characteristics, the rugs woven by Kurdish tribesmen in Iran, Iraq and Turkey are often closer to each other than to items woven by their non-Kurdish neighbours.

Weaving groups
The term weaving group can be applied to any ethnic tribe, tribal confederacy, village, town or geographical region, whose rugs possess an overall uniformity of character, weaving structure, appearance and design. An ethnic,

cultural or regional connection on its own is not enough – the weavers must also produce items that conform to the same broad characteristics. For example, there are several pockets of ethnic Arab weavers throughout Turkey and Iran but their rugs are rarely, if ever, classified under the collective umbrella of an Arab weaving group because they are usually closer in character and appearance to other localized weavings than to the rugs woven by Arabs elsewhere. In contrast, the Belouch, despite their diverse ethnic origins, produce rugs in a number of different countries, which, allowing for some local variations, are sufficiently similar as to warrant classification under the same weaving group. The term may be used either specifically or generally and is normally applied in accordance with a sliding scale of attributions, based on the degree of certainty about the exact origins of each individual rug.

General weaving groups Collective groups of weaving people who may be composed of a number of smaller, specific weaving units (e.g. sub-tribes), but whose rugs conform to an overall uniformity of characteristics.

Specific weaving groups Individual weaving units (e.g. tribal groups, sub-tribes, villages) that produce their own distinctive rugs and may or may not be part of a larger general weaving group. Some specific weaving groups (e.g. the Ersari) can be further divided into smaller sub-tribes (e.g. Jangalarik, Kazan, Dali), each of which produces their own subtle variations on the rugs. Consequently, a Jangalarik rug can be classified under its general ethnic/cultural (Turkoman), its specific (Ersari) or sub-specific (Jangalarik) weaving group. In contrast, some weaving groups are generally viewed as unconnected independent units (e.g. Kutchis).

A localized diversity of weaving groups Fairly common for a number of weaving groups to coexist in the same location. For example, Bidjar in Iran is a major centre for non-tribal items that conform to a distinctive regional style, as well as acting as an important marketing centre for a number of tribal weaving groups. Consequently, rugs sold as Bidjars may be non-tribal regional items, or tribal rugs made by one of the indigenous or migrating tribal groups (e.g. Shahsavan, Afshar, Kurds).

Normal marketing practice Rugs are usually sold under the name of the specific weaving group, if known, and the general weaving group if a more precise attribution is unclear.

Weaving in tribal societies

Weaving in nomadic societies Vitally important because in order to survive nomads must maintain a degree of flexibility in their movements, including the capacity to break camp, travel to an alternative location and establish a new encampment in the shortest possible time. This is achieved partly by living in tents and partly by having rugs and other woven artefacts which provide readily transportable floor-coverings, tent flaps, blankets, table cloths and a wide variety of storage bags and other functional artefacts. Weaving also reinforces a socially stable division of tribal duties between the sexes, allowing the men to tend the herds and protect the tribal unit, while the women maintain the household and make most of the artefacts and wares that the tribe need both for personal use and trade.

Weaving in semi-nomadic societies Almost identical to nomadic societies except that during these periods of settlement the women may have access to larger, upright looms that enable them to weave larger and wider rugs.

Weaving in settled societies Similar to nomadic weaving, but villagers generally have a greater access to dyes and other materials, as well as being able to use vertical looms. Consequently, their rugs are often larger, wider and sometimes more sophisticated than those woven by their nomadic kinsmen.

Who are the weavers In North Africa and Asia women are responsible for all tribal rug production. Young girls are taught from childhood and it is customary for them to display their early solo works as a part of their rite of passage into womanhood when their weaving skills will be seen as an essential ingredient in establishing their marriageability. They gradually learn to weave from memory most of the tribe's repertoire of traditional designs, adding new ones that reflect current experiences or changes in the tribe's structure or fortunes (e.g. the Afghan–Soviet War or assimilation into another tribe). Their role is both as artisan and artist, providing functional artefacts for personal use and trade, and also preserving the tribe's history, culture, religious beliefs and separate identity in the rugs they produce.

In the Americas, weaving is undertaken by both men and women. However, in South and Central America women are more likely to weave rugs on the traditional horizontal and backstrap looms, and men are more closely associated with vertical and treadle looms.

Rugs as 'high art' Rug weaving is the chosen, and often the only, medium for recording the religious, social and cultural beliefs of several nomadic and semi-nomadic tribes in Asia. As such, it represents the only current example of 'high art' as a totally female preserve.

The character and appearance of tribal rugs

Tribal rugs vary considerably in size, shape, colour, design and quality. Some are loosely woven, uneven in shape, and limited in design to a few bold, sometimes crudely articulated, motifs executed in two or three primary colours, whereas others are as finely knotted and intricately articulated as the rugs produced in all but the finest workshops. The type of loom and the weaving conditions place some limitations on the size, quality and appearance of the rugs that can be easily produced. It is a mistake to assume that rugs woven in villages will necessarily be finer or more intricately designed than nomadic items – and, in many instances, the reverse is true – but there are some differences between the rugs made by weavers with different lifestyles.

Nomadic rugs Generally either relatively small or long and narrow, sometimes with a rough-hewn or folk-art quality that may be enhanced by the inclusion of animal hair, beads, shells, etc., and are often made with a specific function in mind. Nomads also produce a wide range of bags, animal trappings and other woven artefacts, which they often use before selling or trading them in the bazaars. Designs vary considerably in their overall style, complexity and execution, but they are frequently based on relatively bold primary motifs, sometimes with intricate infill patternings, which are usually angular, rather than curvilinear, in form. Heraldic and totemistic elements (often of plant or animal origin),

which range from identifying tribal insignia to a variety of talismen aimed at warding off the evil eye, are also extremely common. The entire design is frequently achieved using only two to four primary hues. However, even the most basic, crudely executed nomadic rugs often possess a vibrancy and primitive charm that defies the simplicity of its design and manufacture.

Semi-nomadic rugs Largely indistinguishable from nomadic items, but because semi-nomads have access to vertical looms and a more extensive range of materials during their periods of settlement larger, wider and more thematically diverse items may be made.

Settled or village rugs Generally conform to the characteristics of the traditional items produced by other members of the same tribal group, but bags, animal trappings, etc., are less common. Access to vertical looms enables larger, wider and sometimes more sophisticated items to be made and they may also possess a degree of regional influence (seeping in from other local weaving groups) that may modify their characteristics. (However, if the rugs are closer to those woven by other local weaving groups than to the ones produced by other members of the same tribe, they may be classified as belonging to a separate specific regional weaving group.)

Assessing tribal rugs Always take into account their overall character and appearance, rather than their level of technical or compositional perfection. Allowances should also be made for variations in colouring (abrashes), the occasional lack of symmetry in the composition (or even the rug's physical shape) and individual motifs that may be strangely articulated, omitted altogether, or even replaced by something entirely different. These imperfections, if not too severe, often enhance a rug's uniqueness, character and tribal authenticity.

A brief history of tribal weaving

It is impossible to pinpoint exactly when, where or by whom the first tribal rugs were made. The raw materials of rug weaving (wool, cotton and silk) are easily perishable and rarely survive for more than a few centuries, unless safeguarded from the elements. Consequently, only a handful of fairly complete rugs and several fragments made before the 16th and 17th centuries have so far been discovered – mainly in the last hundred years –

in different locations, as far apart as East Turkestan (China) and Peru. This makes it impossible to chronicle either the evolution of rugs in general or their specific development and dispersal throughout various parts of the world. However, there are certain factors that played an important role in determining whether a tribal culture produced rugs and also in dictating the type of rugs that they were able, or motivated, to weave.

Climate and environment Rug weaving generally flourished in either the cold, reasonably dry climates of the uplands and mountains, or in the hot and dry semi-desert regions. In these environments, rugs provided an ideal form of insulation from the cold or heat (striking upwards from the ground) and also protection (as door-flaps) from the wind and wind-blown dust or sand and, because the climate in these areas was predominantly dry, the rug-making materials were less susceptible to the accelerated rotting that frequently accompanies excessive damp or humidity. In contrast, rug weaving did not develop in the cold, damp regions of northern Europe (where animal furs or straw provided more practical insulation for stone floors or bare earth), nor in the hot and humid conditions of Amazonia, equatorial Africa and parts of South-East Asia, where the humidity would ensure quick disintegration.

Availability of materials Societies inhabiting areas where there is an absence of rug-making materials (e.g. wool) either have no weaving tradition or have developed only those techniques that are suitable using their local materials. For example, the Amerindian tribes of the coastal regions of North America developed basic interweaving techniques (e.g. twining, netting) and produced blankets and wall-hangings from a variety of grasses, cedar bark, feathers and animal hair. But, the innate limitations of these materials made it almost impossible for them to progress to more sophisticated flat- or pile-weaving techniques. In contrast, the Pueblo Indians – in the south-west of the USA – had access to cotton, and produced authentic flatwoven rugs.

The origins of weaving

Flatwoven rugs Have been produced for over three millennia by a variety of geographically separate cultures, which do not appear to have had any contact, either with each other or with a common source (e.g. the Turkic tribes of Central Asia, the Paracas culture in Peru). It therefore seems probable that flatweaving evolved independently over a similar timeframe in different parts of the world. This is hardly surprising considering that basic flatweaving and cloth-weaving techniques are almost identical and, given the right conditions, it is a small step from weaving clothes to producing rugs. Today, flatweaves are made throughout the entire rug-weaving area, and in the Americas are the only type of rugs made.

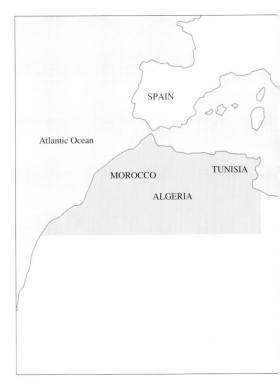

Pile rugs Generally accepted that they were first made by nomadic Turkic or Mongol tribesmen – living somewhere in Central Asia, East Turkestan or Mongolia – prior to the beginning of the 1st millennium BC. Their lifestyle (as nomadic herdsmen) and the prevailing climate (dry and hot in the deserts, dry and cold in the mountains) were both conducive to rug weaving and the region had an ample supply of other raw materials (e.g. cotton, plants for dyes). Physical evidence supporting this theory was uncovered, in 1947, by a Russian archaeologist, S. J. Rundenko, during his excavations of a 5th-century Scythian (or possibly Turkic) tomb – located in the Altai Mountains in southern Siberia. It contained a number of flatweaves, felt rugs and an almost entirely preserved hand-knotted carpet (now known as the Pazyryk carpet), which had been preserved for over 2,000 years because the tomb had been broken into shortly after it was sealed, allowing in water that had subsequently frozen during the Siberian winter.

If this theory is true, it can be assumed that the various nomadic tribes in the region gradually spread their weaving skills throughout the rest of Asia through migration, trade, intermarriage, and, perhaps most importantly, via the numerous conquests and invasions. These began with the Huns (4th century) and reached their climax (11th to 15th centuries) as a succession of Turkic and Turko-Mongol

Weaving region of Asia and North Africa

armies swept westwards, settling in the conquered territories and bringing with them their weaving skills. Today, pile rugs are made throughout Asia and North Africa.

Parallel traditions

The earliest rugs in existence – e.g. the Pazyryk carpet and Paracas cameloid tapestries (found in Peru) – were probably woven during the first millennium BC and a number of other items have been found (mainly in the Middle East and Peru) that date from between the 2nd and 10th centuries AD. Most are the products of highly organized civilizations, but a number are more likely to be of nomadic origin. We know from Chinese and Arab chroniclers that both tribal and more sophisticated court flatweaves and pile rugs were being produced during the Sassanian Empire in Persia (c. 224–c. 641). In all probability this parallel tradition between tribal weavers, who continued to produce essentially functional rugs for personal use, and their court counterparts (who may have been imported tribal weavers, or originally learned their skills from tribal weavers) producing much more elaborate, sophisticated and prestigious items had already been established in Asia and North Africa as early as the 1st millennium BC. However, it was not until the 15th and 16th centuries that a more detailed picture of these two parallel traditions emerged.

In the Americas rugs have been produced by both tribal and urban cultures for over two millennia, but, prior to the arrival of the Europeans, it is uncertain whether a clear divergence of traditions took place. In the USA and Canada there has never been an Amerindian workshop tradition, and in Central and South America more commercial workshop/regional rug-making is essentially a post-European cottage industry.

The tribal tradition Has remained relatively faithful to the earliest known examples of Central Asian and other nomadic weavings, and is typified by the use of relatively bold, angular designs, with strong colours, and an emphasis on overall character and functionality, rather than technical or visual sophistication. The Venetian explorer, Marco Polo (c. 1254–1324), in an account of his travels through Turkestan, described a tribal rug that could be like any number of Turkoman or Turkic rugs produced today. Similarly, it is clear from surviving tribal items – as well as those featured in the backgrounds of paintings by Fra Angelico (c. 1387–1455), Carlo Crivelli (c. 1430–93), Holbein (c. 1497–c. 1543), and a number of other, mainly Italian and Flemish, artists of the period – that tribal weaving throughout the oriental rug weaving region

has changed very little, in essence, since the 14th and 15th centuries. Several traditional tribal groups have subsequently merged into the general population and their rugs have gradually evolved into a more collective regional style. But others still retain their tribal independence and produce items that largely conform to the traditional criteria of character, appearance and design.

Workshop or court tradition Probably has its origins in one of the civilizations that flourished during the 1st millennium BC, but in Asia and North Africa does not become clearly evident as a separate entity until the 13th century onwards. When the Safavid Shahs (in Persia), the Ottomans (in Anatolia), the Mamelukes (in Egypt), Kublai Khan (in China) and the Moghuls (in India) all established court workshops that were geared to produce extremely lavish, intricate and sophisticated items that would echo the wealth and splendour of their reign. Many were later imported into Europe, stimulating the creation of a European carpet weaving industry that flourished between the 16th and 19th centuries in France (e.g. Aubusson and Savonnerie), Britain, Ireland, Italy, Poland, Spain, Romania and other parts of Europe. They also provided the commercial and stylistic foundation for the massive workshop rug weaving industry that is now a vital element in the economies of India, Pakistan, Iran, Turkey, China and other parts of Asia and North Africa.

Regional tradition Essentially a fusion of tribal and workshop traditions that gradually took place as different tribal groups began to settle in the same area, or become assimilated into the general urban population. This resulted in a number of weaving groups (usually based in villages or small towns), whose inhabitants can no longer be considered to be tribal, but who produce rugs that are distinctly tribal in character and appearance. Regional groups can be found through the entire oriental rug weaving area and in Central and South America.

Top North America: major Amerindian ethno-linguistic tribal groups
Middle Central America: Pre-Colombian Amerindian civilizations
Bottom South America: contemporary weaving centres and Pre-Colombian Amerindian civilizations

CHAPTER TWO

How tribal rugs are made

Tribal rugs are either knotted or flatwoven, or a combination of both, although a small number of weaving groups also produce items (e.g. *namads* or felt rugs), using non-weaving techniques, that are sometimes classified under the general heading of tribal rugs. Knotted rugs are usually referred to as pile rugs (or simply rugs) and are all made by the same basic weaving technique. Flatwoven rugs may use a variety of weaving techniques and may be known by different names, usually reflecting the weaving technique (e.g. *soumak, jajim*), or the purpose for which it was made (e.g. *dastarkan, purdah*), or collectively as flatweaves or kilims. Items that employ areas of pile and kilim are called semi-pile or combination rugs.

The basics of weaving

Tribal rugs are made to varying degrees of technical excellence, using a variety of weaving techniques and materials, but they all conform to the same basic weaving principles.

Warps and wefts

Warps and wefts are the basic constituents of all textiles. In pile rugs, they provide the structural foundation of the rug, allowing the design to be articulated by the insertion (or knotting) of the pile material. In flatweaves, the warp and weft make up both the physical structure and the underlying design, which may then be further enhanced with supplementary material, depending on the specific weaving technique employed. The same material is often used for both warps and wefts (especially in flatweaves), but pile rugs often use different materials (e.g. cotton warps and woollen wefts).

Warps are the strands of yarn that are secured to the loom and run lengthways, culminating in the fringes at the top and bottom. They are generally used solely to help secure the physical structure, but, in some flatweaving techniques, they also articulate the design.

Wefts are the strands of yarn that run widthways, culminating in the selvedges at the sides. In pile rugs, wefts are used to secure each row of pile yarns. In flatweaves, they are normally the main influence on the design, as well as helping to secure the physical structure. Also, supplementary wefts (without a structural function) are used in some weaving techniques to enhance the design.

Selvedges and fringes

Selvedges are the sides (or outer edges) of a rug – formed by wrapping the weft strands around the last few warp strands, which bind the rug securely across its width. They are frequently reinforced by stitching and are more or less the same on both flatweaves and pile rugs, although some weaving groups use goat hair (which is believed to act as a barrier to snakes) or some other additional material.

Fringes are the ends of a rug that are formed from the warp strands, which extend lengthways beyond the main body of a rug and secure it across its length. They are essentially the same on both flatweaves and pile rugs, but may be formed in a variety of ways – often adding a final decorative flourish to the completed rug. Some weaving groups nearly always employ the same basic method of forming fringes, which can aid identification, but others may use a variety of methods.

Tied (or knotted) fringes Formed by pressing two or more warps against the final weft, tying them into a knot and then repeating the process across the width of the rug. This is the most common method of producing fringes.

Net fringes Basically tied fringes that have been extended into an interlocking net formation to add an extra touch of artistry to the finished item. Especially common on flatweaves.

Kilim fringes Formed by interweaving the warps and wefts, usually in plainweave, beyond the main body of the rug. Usually only found on pile rugs and plainwoven kilims.

Loop (or chain) fringes Produced by looping one warp over and under two adjacent warps

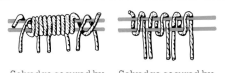

Selvedge secured by parallel wrapping   Selvedge secured by ground weft

and then taking them back in the opposite direction to create a continuous chain.

Plaited fringes Formed by taking three groups of three or four warps and interweaving them in the same way that women plait their hair.

Diagonally plaited fringes Produced by interweaving one warp diagonally, through five or six adjacent warps, back to the final weft.

Warp-loop fringes Made at the beginning of the weaving process by passing the warp strands over a bar at one end of the loom and then running them back to form a continuous loop. On completion, the bar is removed, leaving the warp strands uncut and secured against the last weft. Loop fringes can only be formed at one end of a rug, the opposite end must be secured by another method. They are very common on Hamadan rugs.

Weaving techniques

Weaving techniques and designs

One of the main differences between pile rugs and flatwoven rugs, in addition to their basic physical structure, is the way in which specific weaving techniques can determine the range and nature of achievable designs.

Pile rug designs Created by the juxtaposition of different-coloured strands of the pile material, which can be arranged vertically, horizontally, diagonally, or in a variety of curvilinear forms. The physical structure of the rug is determined solely by the integrity of the interwoven warps and wefts. Consequently, the only restriction on the type or intricacy of pile rug designs is imposed by the fineness of the knotting, which depends more on the weaver's skill than the weaving technique.

Flatwoven designs Created by the specific method of interweaving the warps and wefts, which also form the physical structure of the rug. Consequently, the design and structure of all flatwoven rugs are interrelated, and some designs can only be achieved when specific techniques are employed.

Monochrome and speckled designs are most conducive to plainweaving.

Striped and banded designs (pls 5, 20) can be created by warp- or weft-faced paterning, interlock or by stitching together sections woven in other techniques.

Vertical or diagonal designs (pls 23, 32) run contrary to the natural interlocking of the warps and wefts, and each design segment would therefore separate unless held in place using a weaving technique known as warp-sharing (e.g. slitweaving, single-interlock).

Curvilinear designs (pl 47) require the insertion of supplementary warps or wefts solely to articulate the design.

Flatweaving techniques

Plainweaving Simplest and most common technique, which requires individual wefts to be interwoven, from side to side, over and under adjacent warps, in successive rows up the length of the item.

Balanced plainweave uses warps and wefts of the same thickness, which show equally on

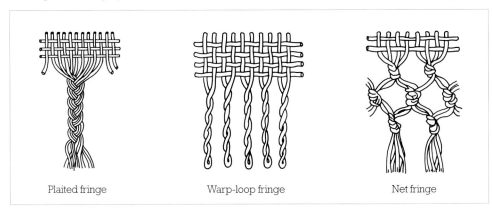

Plaited fringe   Warp-loop fringe   Net fringe

both sides, and is only suitable for monochrome or – if different-coloured yarns are used – speckled designs. It does not combine well with supplementary techniques and is normally employed for the reverse side of bags, undecorated sections and end panels.

Weft-faced plainweave uses more wefts than warps, so the warps are hidden from view, limiting designs to those that can be created by the wefts alone. It is normally used for rectangular monochrome sections or banded designs and can be employed in conjunction with some supplementary weaving techniques. Common in North Africa, Afghanistan and parts of Central Asia, for both conventional flatweaves and combination items that alternate horizontal strips of kilim and pile.

Warp-faced plainweave works on the same principle as weft-faced plainweave, but employs more warps than wefts. It shares similar design features, but because the design is dictated by the warps, vertical stripes (rather than horizontal bands) can be woven.

Twill involves interweaving two (or more) wefts over two (or more) warps in staggered, horizontal rows. This produces a zigzag or herring-bone effect, and may be either warp- or weft-faced. Normally only used on bags, tent bands and end panels.

Stripweaving General term for flatweaves produced by sewing together several strips (or segments) woven by various techniques. Called *ghudjeri* in Afghanistan (and parts of Central Asia) and *jajim* in Iran.

Slitweaving The most common warp- sharing technique, which was often taken as the defining criterion for kilims, as opposed to flatweaves, until the last few decades of the 20th century. It involves locating a common warp strand at the junction between two adjacent segments of the design, wrapping the two adjacent wefts around it and then interweaving them back (through the interweaving warps). This process is then repeated up the length of the kilim, using successive rows of the same coloured wefts, until an entire block of colour (which corresponds to a particular segment of the design) has been produced. Eventually, each design segment will be held firmly in place by the counter-tension of a successive row of wefts interlocking over a number of common warps. There are always some unsecured vertical sections (resulting in the small slits from which the technique gets its name), but a sufficient number of common warps are shared to ensure the kilim's structural integrity. Slitweaving is ideal for articulating stepped, diagonal motifs (e.g. angular medallions, diamonds), but is incapable of reproducing curvilinear forms. It is employed by almost every weaving group throughout Asia and North Africa, with the exception of the Berbers.

Single-interlock or dovetailing Almost identical to slitweaving, except that all the end wefts share a common warp, which eliminates the unsecured slits and enables extended vertical patterns to be produced, although there is often some blurring at the junction between separate design segments. Commonly used throughout Asia, except Turkey.

Double-interlock Employs the same basic technique as single-interlock, but the two different-coloured wefts are interlocked around each other, rather than a common warp, forming a type of counter-tension knot. This allows vertical patterns, which have a clear delineation between adjacent design segments, to be produced without undermining the rug's structural integrity. Commonly found on Luri, Bakhtiari and Turkoman kilims.

Weft- or warp-faced patterning Hides the wefts or warps by floating them along the back of the kilim so that they only show on the front when they are required to delineate the design. Weft-faced patterning is ideal for producing narrow, intricately patterned, horizontal bands, and is used extensively by the Belouch and to a lesser extent other weaving groups in Afghanistan, north-east Iran, Central Asia and North Africa. Warp-faced patterning is usually confined to the production of tent bands and binding strips, or the narrow decorative segments that are stitched together to form a stripweave, because the warp strands lose their counter-tension once anything wider than two or three inches has been woven.

Supplementary weft wrapping and weft insertion Involve adding extra wefts to items woven in plainweave, slitweave, and weft- or warp-faced patterning to enhance the variety of achievable designs. Supplementary wefts may be of any colour or length, and are introduced during the basic weaving process; often producing a slightly sculptured or incised effect on the front of the kilim, as well as leaving strands of weft material hanging from the back.

Compound weft wrapping interweaves two separate wefts around the same warp – one of which acts as a ground weft, binding the structure, while the other provides the colour for the

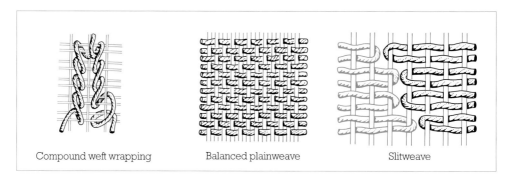

Compound weft wrapping   Balanced plainweave   Slitweave

design and can be wrapped horizontally, vertically, diagonally, or sinuously.

Simple weft wrapping does not use an additional design weft, but achieves similar results by wrapping a single weft over and under the warps, in a ratio of 2:1, and securing the structural integrity through warp sharing.

Plain weft inserts are often used either to re-shape a lop-sided design or to rectify any loss in the symmetry of the weave by inserting additional wefts into the lower side of the kilim until the weft is at right angles to the warp.

Curved weft inserts employ the same basic principle, but are often used to create curvilinear designs by deliberately inserting additional wefts until a curve is created in the line of wefts forming individual motifs, thus enabling more flowing, naturalistic forms to be produced. Especially common in Iran, the Caucasus and parts of Turkey.

Twining and tablet weaving The former involves twisting (or twining) two pairs of different-coloured wefts around a single warp (either clockwise or anti-clockwise) to create a barber-pole or herring-bone effect. The latter uses a similar principle, but requires a piece of stiff card (or leather) to interweave the wefts and warps, and produces bands or strips that have reverse patterns on the front and back. Both techniques were used, mainly for bags, by North American Indian weaving groups.

Braiding Manual weaving technique, similar to plaiting rope or hair, used by a number of North American Indian weavers.

Brocading General term applied to any supplementary wrapping or insertion technique.

Cicim Sometimes used as a generic name for items woven in this technique. It is related to weft insertion and wrapping, and incorporates small, decorative elements into the basic design by continuously wrapping extra wefts around a number of warps. This creates a distinctive pattern – usually in the form of narrow, semi-linear contours – on the face of the flatweave. *Cicim* is closely associated with Turkish kilims, but is also fairly common in items from Iran and Afghanistan.

Jajims and ghudjeri (pl 16) Alternative names for stripwoven items that are used for a variety of purposes. Items woven in Iran (e.g. Luri, Qashga'i) are usually referred to as *jajims,* and those produced in Central Asia as *ghudjeri.*

Soumak (pl 19) Sophisticated weft-wrapping technique, believed to have derived its name from the old Caucasian town of Shemakha, that produces extremely durable and often intricately patterned flatweaves. *Soumaks* are closely associated with the Caucasian weaving groups, but the term is often used generically to describe any item woven in this technique.

Wadding Semi-weaving technique involving the insertion of narrow rolls (or wads) of unspun cotton between the warps and wefts, creating flexible, lightweight items that look like roller blinds. Used extensively by the weavers of San Pedro de Cajas, in Peru, to produce their distinctive wall-hangings.

Zilli Often used as a generic term – mainly in Turkey – for items using weft wrapping, which have a distinctive cording (or contoured) effect on the front, running parallel with the warps.

Pile rug weaving

The technique is basically the same on all pile rugs and involves tying (or knotting) a short length of coloured yarn around two, or more, adjacent warps so that both ends protrude through the foundation (i.e. the warp and weft) to form a pile surface on the front of the rug. This process is referred to as knotting because a securely tied knot is formed once the wefts have been beaten together to hold the pile yarn firmly in place. Each knot creates two individual strands of pile – creating the design by the juxtaposition of different-coloured yarns. There are two main types of knot – the Senneh and the Ghiordes – in common usage, but they both do essentially the same job and neither is fundamentally superior to the other. However, knowing which type of knot has been used may help in determining exact attribution.

Senneh or Persian knot Takes its name from the Iranian town of Senneh (now called Sanandaj), which ironically is noted for rugs woven with the Ghiordes knot, and is formed by looping a single strand of the pile yarn through two adjacent warps and then drawing it back through one warp so that both ends flank a single common warp. It is sometimes called the asymmetrical knot because the pile yarn may be drawn back to either the right or left of the warps. Some experts argue that it is more conducive to producing intricate, curvilinear designs. It is widely used throughout Iran, Afghanistan and Pakistan, but may also be found in items produced elsewhere.

Ghiordes or Turkish knot Named after the Turkish town of Ghiordes. It is formed by looping a single strand of pile yarn through two adjacent warps so that both ends of pile yarn are compressed between the same two adjacent warps. It is sometimes referred to as the symmetrical knot, and some experts argue that it is better for weaving extremely compact rugs. It is used extensively in Turkey and the Caucasus, and is also used by several weaving groups in Iran, Central Asia and elsewhere.

The fineness of the knotting Refers to the number of individual knots that have been tied on any given surface area of the rug. It is usually measured in either knots per square inch (in²), or square metre (m²) and is determined by measuring the number of knots per linear inch, or linear metre, along both the vertical and horizontal axes of any part of the rug, and then multiplying the two linear measurements together. For example, if a rug has 10 knots per linear inch along its vertical axis and 15 knots per linear inch along its horizontal axis, the two linear measurements multiplied together would result in 150 knots (or 300 individual strands of pile) per square inch.

Some dealers use the fineness of the knotting as the main criterion for assessing the quality of pile rugs (i.e. the more knots per square inch, the better the quality of the rug). However, in tribal items the fineness of the knotting is only important in judging whether it is fine enough to articulate the design.

Semi-pile (or combination) weaving (pl 38) General term for items that employ both flatweaving and pile weaving techniques. These usually take the form of either alternating bands of kilim and pile running throughout the entire length of the rug, or segments of pile introduced to a basic flatweave in order to highlight parts of the design or introduce figurative or pictorial elements. Especially common on Berber, Belouch and Aimaq items, but may also be used by other weaving groups.

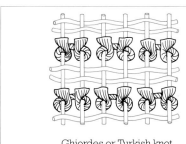
Ghiordes or Turkish knot

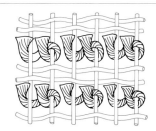
Senneh or Persian knot

Tools

The beating comb Used to press (or beat) successive wefts together, ensuring the finished item's compactness. They are basically larger, tougher versions of hair combs, and may be metal or wood, or a combination of both.

The knife (or scissors) Needed to cut and trim the warp, weft and pile yarn. Knives often have a slightly curved blade, which helps to pull the pile yarn through the warps, or (in flatweaves) unpick any imperfectly woven strands.

The shears Used on pile rugs to clip the pile to an even plane once the weaving has been completed. Manual shears are popular with nomads and semi-nomads, but electric shears may be used by some settled and most regional weaving groups.

The shuttle Basically a stick that has notches cut into the ends to hold each individual weft in place, so that passing it over and under the warps interweaves the warp and weft. In practice, weavers often prefer to interweave the wefts by hand, using the shuttle only in exceptional circumstances or on areas of a flatweave where shuttle weaving is quicker and easier.

Looms

The type of loom limits the size, shape and, to a lesser degree, sophistication of the rugs that can be woven, but they all fulfil the same basic function of providing a secure frame on which to tie the warps. Looms are usually made of wood – although they are occasionally made of metal, or a combination of both – and may be of fixed dimensions or have one or more sides (usually the vertical axis) adjustable so that the inner dimensions can be altered. In practice, however, the main types of loom that are used by tribal weaving groups are:

Horizontal (or nomadic) looms Used primarily by nomadic and semi-nomadic weaving groups. They vary considerably in size and sophistication – from little more than four stripped branches, arranged in a rectangle and then tied to pegs which are driven into the ground, to more sophisticated, purpose-built structures. In essence, however, they have hardly changed since their inception several millennia ago and are still the most compatible with the nomadic way of life. This is because of the ease with which they can be erected, dismantled (with unfinished items left attached to the vertical beams, rolled into bundles, strapped onto the back of a horse or camel), and transported between encampments where the loom can be reassembled quickly. However, they place some constraints on the size, shape and, to a much lesser degree, the sophistication of the rugs that can be produced because the weaving process is undertaken on a horizontal plane (sometimes only a few inches above the ground). This prevents the weaver from reaching more than 2' or 3' (0.5 m) across a rug, from any side, before losing her balance. Consequently, most nomadic rugs are usually fairly small or long and narrow. It is also not uncommon to find occasional lapses in their overall compositional symmetry, or strangely discordant motifs appearing (or being omitted altogether) in otherwise perfectly articulated designs. However, serious flaws in nomadic designs are remarkably rare, and minor ones invariably add to the rug's character and nomadic charm.

Vertical (or village) looms Permanent structures of varying sizes and degrees of sophistication (with fixed inner dimensions) used mainly by settled tribal weavers, and, to a much lesser degree, by semi-nomads during their sedentary periods. Vertical looms allow the weaver unrestricted access across the entire width of the rug, enabling her to view her work from a constant position during the entire weaving process and facilitate the production of items whose size is restricted only by the inner dimensions of the loom.

Semi-portable vertical looms Used occasionally by nomads, especially during periods of extended encampment, but most rely exclusively on traditional horizontal looms.

Adjustable vertical looms Usually of fixed dimensions across their width (i.e. the vertical axis), but have been adapted so that one of the two beams restricting the length of the rug (i.e. on the horizontal axis) can be adjusted, allowing items that are considerably longer than the height of the loom to be woven. There are a number of different types in current usage, but most settled tribal weavers still rely mainly on traditional, non-adjustable village looms.

Backstrap loom, taken from a 16th-century Spanish drawing

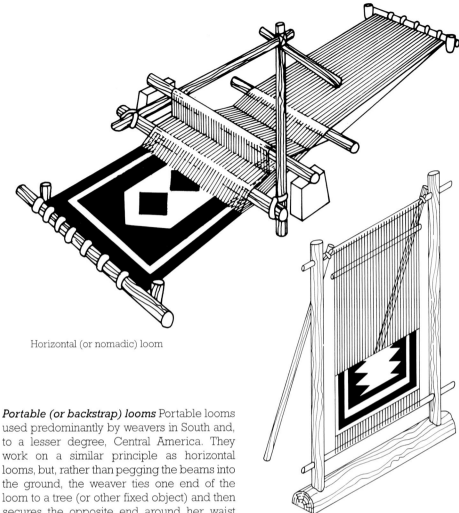

Horizontal (or nomadic) loom

Vertical (or village) loom

Portable (or backstrap) looms Portable looms used predominantly by weavers in South and, to a lesser degree, Central America. They work on a similar principle as horizontal looms, but, rather than pegging the beams into the ground, the weaver ties one end of the loom to a tree (or other fixed object) and then secures the opposite end around her waist with a belt or strap. They are traditionally used by women to produce relatively small, intricately decorated items.

Treadle looms An adjustable loom that was developed in Europe (to produce cloth) and introduced into Central and South America in the 16th century. It is now widely employed in the region, usually by men, to weave rugs and wall-hangings (as well as cloth).

Materials

Tribal rugs normally use only natural fibres. However, a number of nomadic groups, in particular, often decorate their rugs with strands of brightly coloured synthetic fibres, glass beads, coins, shells, pieces of gold or silver foil and an assortment of other found materials.

Wool

The best and most popular rug-making material, wool is durable, supple, easy to work and combines tactile comfort with a reasonable degree of tensile strength. It also contains lanolin and other natural oils that resist dirt and moisture, making woollen rugs relatively easy to clean. Wool may be used for warps, wefts, or as pile material. It is usually the only material employed in flatweaves, and forms the pile in the overwhelming majority of pile rugs.

The wool used for rug making needs to combine suppleness with durability, and tensile strength with the capacity to be spun easily into yarns, and is derived from several varieties of both wild and domesticated sheep. The two original breeds of wild sheep – the Mouflon (which looks like a small antelope), and the Urial (from which most domesticated varieties have descended) – are still found in their natural state in a few areas, but the majority of rug-making wool is derived from domesticated varieties of sheep. Fat-tailed sheep are endemic to Central Asia, the Middle East and North Africa, and are fairly common throughout northern Afghanistan, Iran and Turkey. Fat-rumped sheep, which flourish in harsh conditions, and are favoured by several North African, Central Asian and Turkoman weaving groups; and long-tailed sheep are found in eastern Afghanistan and also North Africa, parts of Arabia and the Persian Gulf. However, the quality of the wool is largely determined by local grazing and climatic conditions, and, as a general rule, the best rug-making wool is obtained from sheep inhabiting the colder upland regions. Wool from European and Antipodean breeds of sheep is used extensively in the Americas, and, to a lesser extent, Asia and North Africa. Generally the wool used in tribal rugs is of excellent quality.

Alpaca, llama and vicuna Cameloids (i.e. animals related to camels), native to the Andean region of South America, that provided the main source of textile material prior to the introduction of sheep into the continent during the 16th and 17th centuries by the Spanish. A number of items are still woven with wool from domesticated alpacas – composed of long, relatively scale-free fibres that can easily be spun into yarn – which produces rugs that have a soft, luxurious pile and an extremely lustrous (almost iridescent) patina. Vicuna wool has similar qualities, but is rarely used because very few animals have been domesticated. Llama wool is not unlike sheep's wool.

Cotton

Used mainly for warps on flatweaves, and warps and wefts on pile rugs, but may occasionally be employed as pile material (*see* art silk) or to produce pure cotton flatweaves (e.g. *sutrangis*). Cotton is a less suitable, and less versatile, rug-making material than wool. It is susceptible to mildew – rugs containing cotton should never be placed on the floor near potted houseplants – but it is more vermin resistant, capable of being spun into thinner yarns, stronger and better at retaining its shape. It grows wild in many parts of the rug-weaving areas, and is often available to tribal weavers.

Mercerized cotton Known in the trade as 'art' silk (or artificial silk), and is used occasionally, mainly for design highlights.

Silk

Obtained from a species of moth (*bombix mori*) commonly known as the silkworm, which is native to Iran, China and other parts of the weaving region. Silk is capable of being spun into the very thin strands needed for exceptionally fine weaving, as well as possessing a natural iridescence, and is also extremely strong and durable. It is believed to be able to repel (or even reflect back) malevolent psychic forces. However, it scuffs easily, retains creases (silk items should always be rolled, never folded), melts when it comes into contact with a flame or excessive heat, and is generally much more expensive than wool or cotton.

Raw silk Known as 'drawn' or 'reeled' silk because it is drawn or reeled directly from the cocoon. Very expensive and rarely used in tribal weaving.

Waste silk Obtained from damaged cocoons and has to be carded and spun like wool or cotton. It is much cheaper and is the type most often found in tribal rugs.

'Art' silk see Mercerized cotton

Other weaving materials

Hair Obtained from several species of animals, including (in North America) an extinct breed of dog. It is sometimes used for warps and wefts, binding selvedges, or (normally in combination with wool) for the pile.

Goat hair has great tensile strength and possesses a silky sheen that can enhance the patina of the wool. It is often used by Belouch and some other nomadic weavers to bind the selvedges and fringes because snakes are reluctant to slide across goat hair.

Camel hair is strong and durable, as well as being a better insulator than wool, and may be used (with wool) to enhance a rug's durability, or to produce a natural 'camel-coloured' ground on a flatweave or pile rug.

Horse and donkey hair is normally taken from the mane and tail, and is generally used to add decoration to tassels and fringes.

Tree bark, jute and hemp The woven fibres of which were (and to some degree still are) used by a number of Amerindian weaving groups to produce a wide range of textiles. Cedar bark, in particular, was used by the Tlingit and Nootka to weave both ceremonial and functional rugs.

Found materials Include metallic threads (usually gold and silver), synthetic fibres (brightly coloured rayon, nylon, etc.), beads, shells, coins, pieces of coloured metal or tin foil, and almost any small, brightly coloured object. They are often used as supplementary decorations on nomadic and semi-nomadic items mainly from Afghanistan, eastern Iran, western Pakistan and North Africa.

Preparing materials

The preparation of fibrous rug-making materials is both simple and universal and is normally undertaken in five stages:

Shearing
Applies only to wool and fleece (e.g. sheep, alpaca) and is normally undertaken once, or sometimes twice, during spring and possibly the late summer or early autumn. After the sheep have been sheared, the wool is usually washed several times in clean water and carefully dried between each wash. Some weaving groups have their own jealously guarded pools or mountain streams, or employ their own distinctive methods of cleaning.

Carding
Teases the dry wool into the longer, straighter, untangled fibres – needed for spinning – by repeatedly drawing them over and through either a series of pins inserted into a block of wood or the carder's fingers.

Spinning
Stretches the carded fibres into a continuous strand that can then be intertwined with similar strands – usually by twisting them in opposite directions – to form a yarn capable of being woven. Both hand-spun and machine-spun yarn may also be used by tribal weavers.

Ply Term used to describe the number of individual strands that make up the yarn – i.e. yarn containing three strands is known as 3-ply – and, as a general rule, the more plies that go into the yarn, the thicker and stronger it will be.

Z and S twists Describe the direction in which the strands have been twisted – i.e. clockwise ('Z' twist) or anti-clockwise ('S' twist).

Dyeing
Normally takes place once the wool has been spun into yarn, which after rinsing – either in clean water or a weak solution of soda and soap – is then soaked in either a dye or mordant bath. A few items are dyed after weaving.

Mordants Help bond the dye to the yarn and usually consist of weak solutions of alum, copper sulphate, chrome, copperas (ferrous sulphate), tin or uric acid (urine). Mordanting normally takes place prior to dyeing, but it is sometimes done afterwards or the mordant is added directly to the dye.

Dye bath Used to soak the yarn in an appropriately coloured dye which is then left out to dry. Most tribal weaving groups can only dye the yarn in relatively small batches, making it extremely difficult to reproduce the exact shade over several batches (*see* abrash). Dyeing is very much a male preserve, and the dyer is often treated as a wise man whose counsel may be sought on a wide variety of matters. It is also regarded as a science, whose secrets are jealously guarded and handed down from generation to generation.

Abrash (pls 21, 28) Term used to describe any sudden change in the tone or intensity of an individual colour that does not correspond to a new element in the design. It is normally the result of the weaver changing to a separately dyed batch of yarn and often takes the form of a dramatic lightening or darkening of a specific colour in a continuous monochrome area or a similar variation in the tone of the same colour used in different parts of the rug. Minor abrashes are common and are perfectly acceptable in all but the most sophisticated tribal rugs, and may even imbue them with an extra degree of individuality and charm.

Fugitive Term used to describe dyes (pigments) that change their colour.

Washing
The final process that removes surface dirt and excess dye, and also gives the rug its characteristic finish. Some items are simply washed in soap and water, but others may be soaked (or washed) in a chemical solution, which usually includes some form of moth-proofing.

Chemical washes Often used to mellow, or tone down, the rug's colours artificially; often reproducing the effects of age and sometimes adding a surface gloss to the rug's patina. It is now fairly common for tribal rugs to be chemically washed by western importers.

Patina Term used to describe the surface appearance of the rug (e.g. a glossy or dull patina), which is influenced by the quality of the wool and the type of wash.

Dyes and colours

Natural (or vegetable) dyes

Derived from several (often indigenous) vegetable, animal and mineral sources. A number of natural pigments are intrinsically fugitive, and some colours (e.g. green, purple) have few suitable natural sources, and the dyer needs usually to combine two or more pigments in order to produce the required colour or tone (which he cannot always repeat successfully). Some natural dyes are also expensive, or difficult to obtain, and even those that are cheap and plentiful (such as indigo) may not always produce the exact same shade or intensity of colour, due to the differing amounts of pigment in each plant. However, many natural dyes create a subtlety of tone that is unsurpassed by the finest synthetic equivalents, and many collectors cherish slight variations in tone as an essential ingredient to the overall charm, uniqueness and ethnic authenticity of tribal rugs. Natural dyes are still used by most tribal weaving groups (especially for basic colours such as red and blue).

Blue Obtained from plants of the ubiquitous *Indigofera* and *Isatis tinctoria* (woad) genera, generally referred to collectively as indigo, which in addition to producing a wide variety of attractive and stable shades, is also one of the very few pigments that is colourfast without the addition of a mordant.

Red Derived from the indigenous madder plant (*Rubia tinctorum*), or, to a lesser degree, poppy and tulip petals, rhubarb, rose roots, cherry skins, jujube bark and other plants sources. Cochineal and carmine are obtained from the crushed bodies of the female cochineal (*Dactylopius coccus*), or kermes (*Chermes abietis*) and lac (*Laccifer lacca*) insects.

Yellow Found in several plant species that contain the pigments quercetin, apigenin, fisetin, crocin or datiscetin. These include St John's wort, onion, spurge, buckthorn, dyer's camomile (*Anthemis tinctoria*) and tanners' sumach (*Rhus coriaria*), which all produce a basic yellow or yellowish brown. Camomile, wild camomile (*Anthemis chia*) and dyer's weed (*Reseda luteola*) give a brighter yellow. Bastard hemp (*Datisca cannabina*) produces a brilliant yellow. Dyer's sumach (*Cotinus coggygria*) and the saffron crocus produce an orange-yellow. In addition, centaury, turmeric, artemisia, vine leaves, rhubarb, *Sophora*

japonica, *Gardenia jasminoides* and varieties of the reseda plant may also be used.

Orange Usually derived from a mixture of red and yellow pigments, but henna, grass roots, plum bark, dyer's sumach and the saffron crocus are occasionally used.

Black Obtained from plants with a high tannin content (e.g. pomegranate peel, oak apples and tanners' sumach) which may be mixed with iron rust or filings that eventually corrode (or disintegrate) the yarn. This is a common feature of Traditional Caucasian rugs.

Tan and brown May be obtained from acorn cups and walnut husks, but natural brown wool is frequently preferred, and often found on rugs from a number of Iranian tribal groups.

Purple and violet Usually the result of mixing red and blue, but grape skins or reddish blue pigments (e.g. cochineal) are also used.

Synthetic dyes

Increasingly used by a number of tribal weaving groups, especially for colours that are difficult to achieve using natural dyes. The first synthetic, or aniline, dye (a violet colorant called fuchsine) was derived from benzene by an English chemist, and, three years later, a similar dye (mauveine) was developed in France. A wide range of additional colorants followed over the next two decades – revolutionizing the commercial production of textiles in the west by providing an almost in exhaustive supply of cheap and easily manufactured dyes – and, by the end of the 19th century, were available to rug weavers throughout most of North Africa and Asia. However, several of the early aniline dyes proved to be both fugitive and unattractive, and were eventually banned in a number of rug-producing countries – especially in Iran, where a dyer found using aniline dyes could be sentenced to have his right arm amputated and his dye-house burnt to the ground.

The development of far more stable and attractive chrome dyes (during the 1920s and 1930s) revolutionized the attitude towards synthetic dyes, and they are now used extensively by a number of tribal weaving groups. Nearly all modern synthetic dyes are of excellent quality, and, although they may lack the subtlety of some alternative natural pigments, they are generally attractive, stable and used increasingly by tribal weaving groups.

Mellowness

Term often used to describe the natural process of fading that takes place as a result of exposing pigments, over an extended period of time, to any light source. It usually takes several years for colours to lose their initial intensity and soften to an optimum tonal mellowness. Tribal rugs sometimes deliberately have bright (or even garish) colours, which allow for the mellowing effect of sunlight, and reach their optimum tonality ten or twenty years after the rug has been taken off the loom. Today, this tonal mellowness is often precipitated by the use of chemical washes.

The relationship between colour and age There is a general assumption that because colours fade in direct proportion to their exposure to light, the greater the degree of fading on a rug, the older the rug must be. This is simply not true. The degree of fading is also determined by the strength of the light source and chemical washes also reproduce the effects of ageing. It is therefore unwise to assume automatically that a rug must be old because its colours have begun to mellow or fade.

The meaning of individual colours Varies between different cultures, and generally has less symbolic importance in the predominately Islamic rug-producing regions of North Africa and West Central Asia than it has in the mainly Buddhist/Taoist countries of the Far East.

Green (the colour of Mohammed's coat) is considered sacred in most Islamic countries and is rarely used (except in Turkey) as a main colour. Red signifies wealth, prosperity and rejoicing in most Islamic cultures, but is associated more closely with power and the lifeforce in the Americas. Orange is connected with the sun, and in Buddhist/Taoist cultures, in particular, is often synonymous with piety and devotion. Blue generally symbolizes the sky and heaven (and consequently peace and serenity in Iran), but is also associated with power and authority by some of the Mongol/Turkic tribesmen of Central Asia. White is synonymous with grief in Iran, India and China. Yellow is a sacred colour in most Buddhist cultures because evolved souls are believed to develop yellow auras as they get closer to reaching the state of nirvana.

Special rugs, bags and artefacts

A wide range of artefacts, bags and animal trappings – as well as rugs made for special purposes – are generally included under the broad umbrella of tribal rugs and may be marketed under their western names (e.g. tent partitions, kit bags, eating·cloths) or under a variety of local names that describe their function (e.g. *purdah*, *torbah*, *soufreh*). However, trying to establish the exact usage of some special rugs, bags or artefacts is extremely difficult because a number of tribal groups produce items that are very similar in structure and appearance, and chemical analysis is frequently required before a dealer can be sure that a particular rectangular bag of uncertain provenance was used, for example, to store grain, clothes or wool. Western dealers often apply a specific local, or functional, name to similar items (e.g. small bags may be referred to collectively as *torbahs*), regardless of their exact origins or usage – although dealers in the same vicinity may opt for alternative names.

Rugs for special purposes

Tribal rugs are commonly made with versatility in mind, but the following have very specific functions:

Soufreh or soufrai (pl 38) Farsi (Persian) word for cloth, which is used either as a prefix to describe a specific function – e.g. *soufreh-i-ghamir* (flour cloth) and *soufreh-i-nan* (baking cloth) – or as a general term for any item connected with the preparation and consumption of food (often known collectively as 'eating cloths'). *Soufrehs* vary considerably in size and shape and are normally either flatwoven, or a combination of kilim and pile. They are produced by several (predominantly nomadic) tribal weaving groups, particularly in Iran, Afghanistan, Pakistan and Central Asia.

Dasterkan or dashterkhan Alternative name for *soufrehs*. Commonly applied to items produced by Belouch, Aimaq and some other weaving groups, mainly in Afghanistan, eastern Iran, Pakistan and parts of Central Asia.

Rukorssi Abbreviated term for a *soufreh-i-rukorssi* (cloth for covering an oven), which is sometimes used as an extra blanket in the winter. They are similar to *dasterkans* in structure, appearance and origin, but are normally around 4' sq (0.3 m²).

Prayer mats (pls 14, 37) Made specifically for kneeling on during prayer. They are usually relatively small (about 5' x 3' or 13 cm x 8 cm), but can vary in design from basic monochrome fields to elaborate *mihrab* and tree-of-life compositions. They are known commonly as *namazlyks* throughout Central Asia and should not be confused with more general purpose items which employ prayer-rug designs – although, in practice, the difference is often purely one of usage.

Saphs Sometimes called family prayer rugs because their composition is based on repeating *mihrabs*, but they are usually general purpose items, rather than functional prayer mats.

Special items Include *Ayatlyk*: Turkoman funerary rug. *Dezlik*: Turkoman small tent-door rug, also used as a collar for the lead camel in a wedding procession. *Enssi*: common term for a tent-door flap, which also gives its name to a specific design. *Purdah*: used to separate male and female living quarters, often produced in *enssi* designs.

Shapes and sizes

Tribal rugs are often produced in a number of relatively standard shapes and sizes that correspond to their specific function or location in the traditional floor arrangement (*see* p. 34), many of which have specific names.

Ceyrik: Turkish name for rugs about 4' 6" x 2' 9" (1.37 x 0.84 m). *Dozar* (pls 8, 9): Persian word meaning two *zars* (a *zar* being a unit of measurement, about 4' 2" or 1.28 m) that is applied to rugs around 8' x 5–6' (2.44 x 1.52–1.83 m). *Kellegi*: derived from the Persian word for 'head' (*kelley*), applied to the head or top rug in the traditional floor arrangement, which can measure anything from 12'–24' long and 6'–8' wide (3.66–7.32 x 1.83–2.44 m). *Kenareh* (pls 23, 25): derived from the Persian word for side (*kenar*), and applied to rugs used at the sides, in the traditional floor arrangement, which are slightly smaller and narrower than *kellegis*. *Khali* or *qali* (pls 13, 17, 18): respective Turkoman and Persian names – literally meaning carpet – which can be applied to any large, room-sized items of 10' x 6' (3.05 x 1.83 m) or more. *Pushti (or yastik)*: respective Persian and Turkish names for small rugs of about 3' x 2' (0.91 x 0.61 m). *Yastik* also means cushion. *Seccade* (pls 1, 6): Turkish name for rugs around 6' 6" x 3' 9" (1.98 x 1.14 m). *Zaronim* (pls 12, 24): Persian name, meaning a *zar* and a half (*see dozar*), used for rugs of around 6' x 4' (1.83 x 1.22 m) or 5' x 3' 6" (1.52 x 1.07 m).

Bags

A huge variety of bags of different shapes and sizes, fulfilling numerous separate functions, are produced by most nomadic, semi-nomadic, and, to a lesser degree, settled tribal weavers throughout the entire weaving region. Many will have been woven for personal (or collective) use, and then sold, or bartered, after replacements have been woven, but their increasing popularity may result in a greater number being made specifically for sale. They may be sold under western names (e.g. saddle-bags), or local equivalents (e.g. *khurgins*).

Personal bags (pls 32, 33) Small bags used for carrying coins, tobacco, jewelry, combs, mirrors and other personal items. They vary in size and shape, and may be either single bags (with or without compartments), or wallet-type double bags, but are normally sufficiently small to fit either into a pocket or to be carried using handles or a shoulder-strap. *Chanteh*, *canta*, *chanta* and *kap* are common names for general purpose bags. *Chinakap*, *igsalik* and *aina khalta* are Turkoman names for bowl cases, spindle bags and mirror bags respectively. *Kese* is Turkish for a wallet or money-bag, and *namakdan* is a general name applied to the salt bags, which have distinctive bottle-shaped necks that are used by herdsmen.

Tent bags Larger bags used for storing a variety of items. They vary in size and shape and often double up as kit bags or cushions. *Chuval*, *juval*, *bashtyk* and *napramach* are all common names.

Mafrashes (pls 19, 34) Common name for bedding bags, often woven by young women as part of their dowry, which are used to store bedding, clothes and other personal belongings. They are similar to the large holdalls used in the west, and often have woven or leather handles.

Jallars Large, horizontal bag with a distinctive long fringe on the bottom, which is normally suspended from a pole inside the tent and used for general storage.

Kit bags Fairly small, normally around 1' 6" sq (45 cm sq) and are generally used for carrying tools, food, etc. They also double up as tent bags, and may be sold as *torbahs*, *chavans*, *karshins* and *shabadans*.

Cushions Bags of various sizes that serve as cushions (or other items of tent furniture), which can also be used for transporting items between encampments. *Balisht*, *yastik*, *tatrayin* and *usada* are all common names.

Saddle-bags Produced by most nomads and semi-nomads in a variety of sizes, designed to fit the backs of horses, donkeys and camels. They are used to transport goods between encampments and may also serve as tent bags. Saddle-bags frequently suffer wear and tear, prior to reaching the west, and it fairly common for only one half of the original double-bag to be left intact. *Khordin, khurgin, hurgin, heybe* and *keite* are common local names.

Artefacts

A variety of other woven artefacts are also produced by many weaving groups, which may be either primarily decorative or functional or a combination of both.

Tent bands Woven strips, usually between 2" (5 cm) and 12" (30 cm) wide, which are used as tent decorations and a variety of practical functions (e.g. tying baggage, lashing roofing poles and acting as tent securing ropes). *Iolem* and *kapunuk* are Turkoman names for tent bands and door surrounds respectively.

Tent-pole covers Long cylindrical bags used to house tent poles during transportation that are often sold as *kola-i-chergh* (tent-pole bags) or *uuk bash* and *uuk kap* (strut-pole bags).

Animal trappings (pl 15) A huge variety of bridles, head-dresses, harnesses, blankets and other functional and decorative trappings are produced to fit horses, camels, donkeys, and, in South America, llamas and alpacas. They may be simple and functional, or highly elaborate and ceremonial. They are often decorated with beads, bells, coins, shells, etc., and may be sold under their collective western descriptions (e.g. donkey bridals) or under a variety of local names. For example, *deve baslik* (Turkish for a camel's head-dress); *asmalyk* (Turkoman name for the twin-flanked trapping used primarily on wedding camels); and *eyerlik* (Turkoman for a saddle-cloth).

Miscellaneous weavings

A number of items woven by tribal weavers do not fall into any precise definition of tribal rugs, but nevertheless have close associations due to their origin, function or allied symbolism.

Chumpis and wampums Functional and ceremonial belts woven by Amerindians in South and North America, respectively, that often contain detailed ideogrammatic messages or ceremonial, commercial and historical data.

Gebbehs (pl 2) Generic term (meaning long hair) used for deep pile, heavy duty rugs that were originally made by Lurs and other tribesmen of southern Iran. They featured primitive, minimalistic pictorial and geographic motifs, often using mainly natural undyed wool. They are now made more specifically for export in a wider range of designs (sometimes western) by a variety of weaving groups and usually fall into the medium price bracket.

Ikats Flatweaves that are waxed on the surface, and normally used as either wall-hangings or as clothes-making material. They are most closely associated with Uzbek and other Central Asian weaving groups.

Moj Farsi for 'wave' that is used to describe a particular style of stripwoven blankets, bedcovers and similar items produced, mainly by settled Qashga'i and Luri weavers, in Iran.

Namads General term for 'felt' rugs, bags, etc., which are produced by soaking wool and then pressing it until the fibres compact and bind.

Serapes and ponchos (pl 46) Alternative names for a type of blanket/garment, common to the Americas, that has a slit in the centre so that it can be worn over the shoulders.

Silehs Name given to a specific range of old Caucasian rugs, woven in a variation of the *soumak* technique, which feature large s-shaped motifs, usually interpreted as mythological dragons. They are now extremely collectable and expensive.

Sutrangis Cotton flatweaves, originally woven by the inmates of Maimana prison in Afghanistan, that are usually composed of simple triangles and diamonds, mainly in pastel colours, and range in size from small mats to huge carpets (e.g. 200 sq ft or 18 sq m). They are the Afghan equivalent of Indian *dhurries.*

Vernehs (pl 23) Originally the name give to a range of old Caucasian flatweaves, woven in either *soumak* or embroidery techniques, that are believed to have been made (probably in Azerbaijan) until the early or mid-19th century, primarily for export. They usually feature geometric shapes – often decorated internally with stylized birds – in relatively sombre colours. Some contemporary tribal groups (especially the Shahsavan) make items in similar (usually simplified) designs and techniques, which are frequently sold as *vernehs*, although they should not be confused with the originals, which are extremely expensive.

CHAPTER THREE

Buying a tribal rug

Before buying a tribal rug you should think about why you want it and how much you can afford to pay because, regardless of how attractive or inexpensive a rug may be, it must fit the space allocated, match its surroundings and serve the purpose for which it was bought.

Some tribal rugs, for example, may be excellent value as functional floor coverings, but unreliable as long-term financial investments; whereas others, which have a higher investment potential, may be less suitable for your decorative and functional requirements.

Making the right choice

A few tribal rugs are bought primarily as investments, but the overwhelming majority are purchased by people who simply want something that will both serve a practical function and add to the decorative impact of their home. Consequently, before considering price or general value for money, you need to ask yourself is it the right type of rug for its proposed function and location, will its colours and design be compatible with its surroundings, will it fit into the space allocated and how can I be sure of its quality?

Pile rugs and flatweaves are both generally excellent value for money, as well as being one of the few remaining examples of affordable authentic tribal art on the market today. They are normally cheaper than workshop items of comparable quality, and usually retain their resale value to a much higher degree. They are also often less expensive and far more versatile than decent quality western machine-made alternatives, and can be moved around easily to avoid localized wear and tear, or transferred to different rooms (modifying their decorative atmosphere without redecoration).

Flatweaves Generally more versatile than pile rugs – functioning equally well as floor coverings, wall-hangings, furniture covers or peripheral decorations. They are also lighter, more manoeuvrable and, with a few notable exceptions (e.g. Navajo rugs), slightly cheaper.

Pile rugs Normally a little more expensive than flatweaves, but usually more durable and made in a wider range of colours and designs.

Colour considerations

A rug's colour scheme, rather than its design, usually has the most critical influence on the decorative tone of a room, and, providing that the colours complement the surrounding decor, there is normally a reasonable degree of flexibility in the choice of design.

Most tribal rugs employ a palette of either predominantly dark and sombre, or bright and vibrant, colours and tones, which may appear at first to be intrinsically incompatible with western decorative tastes. These colour schemes can, however, be surprisingly effective in enhancing even the most conventional western decor, and an increasing number of items are now being produced in pastel or muted colours. Prospective buyers should therefore have little difficulty in obtaining a suitable rug provided they are prepared to shop around, and, if in doubt, it is always advisable to take advantage of the home trial arrangements offered by several retail outlets.

A harmonious effect Most easily achieved by selecting a rug whose colour scheme reflects the overall tonality of the room (pastel, sombre). However, a brightly coloured rug in a pastel room can also create a harmonious effect, provided that at least one colour is present in both the rug and the room. Optimum results are often achieved by choosing a colour that is dominant in the rug and subsidiary in the room (or vice versa), rather than trying to match two equally dominant tones.

A contrasting effect Normally created by choosing a rug whose colours provide a strong counterpoint to the colours in the room, and often works best in a tonally neutral environment (e.g. a room with white or monochrome pastel walls) that allows the rug's stronger colours to dominate the overall tonality. Care should be taken to ensure that the two sets of colours do not clash or nullify each other, which can be reduced if a common colour is present in both the rug and room.

Dark or sombre shades (pls 20, 21) Dark reds, blues, browns, and deep yellow and orange ochres are often found on some tribal rugs, particularly Belouch, Aimaq and Kurdish items. They are perhaps most suited to slightly austere farmhouse or country cottage settings, but can be equally at home in any room that has a predominance of natural wood and a neutral or autumnal decor (e.g. studies).

Bright or vibrant colours (pls 23, 42) Primary shades of red, blue, orange, yellow and occasionally green (often highlighted with pale ochres and white) are used by a number of weaving groups throughout Iran, the Caucasus, Turkey, North Africa and the Americas. These can complement and enliven almost any decor, provided there are some colours present in both the rug and the room, and that the rug does not overpower the room.

Rich colours (pls 11, 13) Deeper, more subdued shades of red, blue, orange, yellow and, to a lesser extent, green, are found in the rugs produced by several weaving groups, especially in Central Asia, Iran and the Caucasus. Rich shades are perhaps most compatible with classic furnishings (e.g. upholstered furniture, velvet or chenille curtains, or drapes, and richly pattern fabrics), but can also work well in simpler, more frugal surroundings by giving an opulent focal point to the room.

Pastel colours (pls 27, 38) Pale or muted reds, blues, oranges, yellows, greens, browns and ochres are generally less common in tribal rugs than in more commercial regional and workshop items. However, modern washing techniques allow western importers to chemically tone primary colours. In addition, an increasing number of items produced by weaving groups that were traditionally associated with rich or vibrant colour schemes (e.g. Luri) are now appearing on western markets in muted, slightly pastel, colour schemes. Also, some tribal weaving groups (e.g. Shahsavan) have traditionally produced a number of items that are dominated by white, cream and ochres, and the primary colours on many older items have now mellowed to softer, more muted shades. Pastel or muted colours are generally well suited to most western decorative environments (especially in bedrooms), and rarely present problems of tonal compatibility, although careful thought should be given

to placing in areas of heavy traffic because they show dirt and marks more easily than rugs with brighter, richer or darker colours.

Design considerations

Design is usually less critical than colour in the placement of a tribal rug – as a general rule, almost any design can fit successfully into a room, provided the colours are compatible. Designs, however, not only add to the intrinsic attractiveness of a rug, but they can also make the vital difference between merely supporting and positively enhancing the decorative impact of a room.

Geometric designs (pls 5, 30) Used by almost every tribal group throughout the entire weaving region, in both pile rugs and flatweaves, and can be employed successfully with most types of decor. However, they are perhaps best suited to more sparsely decorated rooms that have plain, or simply patterned, furnishings and angular, Scandinavian-style furniture.

Curvilinear designs (pls 12, 13) Usually found only on pile rugs and flatweaves that employ sophisticated supplementary weaving techniques (e.g. *soumaks*). Their most successful expression is often seen in classically furnished surroundings, although they may add a touch of opulence to simply furnished rooms.

Repeating designs (pls 18, 29) Employ a single motif, or group of motifs, which is repeated throughout the rug, so that the design is basically the same when viewed from any angle, which is crucial in the successful placement of runners and room-sized items. Repeating designs appear on both pile rugs and flatweaves, and are used by numerous weaving groups mainly in Asia.

Centralized designs (pls 8, 28) Based on a single central motif, or group of motifs (generally a medallion). They are found on items from a wide range of tribal weaving groups, primarily in Iran, the Caucasus and Turkey. Centralized designs can be difficult to place because the essential symmetry of the scheme can be disrupted if one side of the rug is disproportionately close to a wall, or large piece of furniture. This is especially important with room-sized items, which should either be in the centre of the room – with the furniture evenly distributed on all four sides – or with one side a few feet from the wall and the opposite side roughly the same distance from a large piece of furniture. Small rugs with centralized designs make excellent wall-hangings.

Vertical and horizontal designs (pls 2, 14) Run in one direction along the length or breath of a rug, and therefore can only be viewed effectively from one of the rug's four sides. Prayer and pictorial rugs are common examples of these designs, and need to be located where the design can only be seen from the optimum direction (e.g. on the floor with the top of the design close to a wall, or as a wall-hanging).

Size and shape

Choosing a tribal rug of the right size and shape is not simply a matter of ensuring that it fits the available space. Every rug needs a degree of breathing space, and the more powerful the colours and design, the greater the space required. Therefore careful thought should always be given to the relative strengths of the colours and forms present in both the room and the rug, and the way they might interact when placed in close proximity, especially when trying to locate room-sized items. It is also necessary to make allowances for doors opening across a rug (especially one with a thick pile); and remember that fringes are not normally included in the measurements, so that a 12' x 3' (3.7 x 0.9 m) runner, for example, could in fact be almost a foot longer.

Traditional rug sizes Governed by local needs and conventions – a number of which are incompatible with western furnishing requirements – but are nevertheless sufficiently varied so as to provide western buyers, who are prepared to be flexible in their selection and placement, with a wide choice. However, tribal weavings are generally longer and narrower than western or workshop equivalents, and very few large room-sized items are produced, although some weaving groups now make some items specifically in western sizes.

Location and function

Some rugs are more suited to certain locations and functions than others. A lightweight, pastel-coloured kilim, for example, may be ideal for a bedroom, or lounge, but is unlikely to resist the wear and tear of heavy traffic in a hallway as effectively as a more sombre-coloured pile rug. Consequently, it is always advisable to choose runners or rugs for use in busy rooms or near doors that are especially durable.

Hanging rugs Often provide a room with a dramatic focal point, and are a perfect way of protecting old or worn items and placing prayer rugs, pictorial rugs and other items with unidirectional designs. However, hanging is only suitable for items that are not too large or heavy (e.g. small pile rugs and medium-sized flatweaves), and that are also relatively even in shape. They can be hung directly against a damp-free wall, suspended in front of alcoves, doorways or wardrobes, or used as a room divider, with one of the following methods:

Carpet grips (i.e. narrow strips of wood or metal, with small pins protruding from one side) are ideal for lightweight items. Simply cut a strip, approximately one inch shorter than the width of the rug, and attach it to the wall (level with the top of the rug) with the pins pointing outwards and upwards, and then press the rug against the pins.

The rod and sleeve method is based on inserting a rod through a cotton sleeve sewn along the top, reverse side of the rug, and then suspending the rod from hooks or brackets. Similarly, curtain tape and hooks can be used, exactly as you would for hanging curtains or drapes, and then attached to a pole or runner. Wooden beading can also be tacked or stapled along the top, reverse side of the rug, and then attached to a length of wire or string. All of these methods are useful for suspending items from ceilings or alcoves.

Perspex or glass frames are suitable for mounting small rugs, or fragments, either by fitting them into a ready-made clip frame, or sandwiching them between two sheets of perspex or glass. They can then be hung on the wall as they are, or fitted with a surround frame.

Bags (pls 32–34) Produced in a variety of shapes and sizes that can be easily adapted to serve a number of practical purposes. Small bags are suitable for use as purses, vanity bags and handbags. If the original shoulder straps or handles are missing, appropriately

Traditional floor arrangement

coloured cord, webbing or other strong fabric, can be sewn on to the sides. Larger bags are perfect for storing clothes, children's toys or other household items, and can be attached to a wall or the inside of a wardrobe by means of a length of cord (which can double up as a shoulder strap). Saddle-bags can serve as double-sided storage bags by simply draping them over a rail or bannister (smaller ones make ideal magazine racks), and, if both compartments are filled with cushions you can create an extremely comfortable seat.

Cushions can be made from all but the smallest bags by simply filling them with pillows or pieces of foam, and securing the open end by means of a zip, toggles, hooks and eyes, velcro or some other form of fastener. This range of fasteners can also be used on bags that have been adapted for personal use.

Artefacts, animal trappings and special items (pls 15, 38) Depending on their size and shape, they can function as wall-hangings, or be attached along the edges of furniture (e.g. chairs, mirrors) as highly decorative protective trims, or used for the purpose for which they were produced (e.g. eating cloth).

Miscellaneous usage Most flatweaves can be used as tablecloths, bedspreads and furniture covers and badly worn or damaged rugs can be cut and used to make cushions, bags and seat covers, etc. Small, narrow runners can also be sewn together to make bolster cushions.

Assessing quality

The quality of a tribal rug is determined by a combination of the materials used in its manufacture, how it was made, and its overall character and appearance. Assessing quality therefore requires both subjective and objective judgments, based on careful observation, coupled with a little basic knowledge and experience. (*See* Chapter II)

Subjective criteria Essentially, whether you find the rug attractive, combined with its functional and decorative suitability. However, if you wish to re-sell a rug, it is important that your personal tastes are tempered by more generally held ideas of what constitutes an attractive and functional tribal item.

Objective criteria Used to assess the texture and durability of the materials, the clarity and permanence of the dyes, the fineness and integrity of the weave, and whether the rug lies flat on the floor. However, a rug's overall quality is often greater, or less, than the sum of its parts.

Materials can be gauged to a certain degree by a simple combination of look and feel. If the wool appears dull, lifeless and brittle, it is likely that it is either poor quality or has lost its natural oils due to careless washing or neglect. This can be further determined by running your fingers across the surface and then pinching sections together; good wool is supple and springs back into shape easily after being creased and should leave a light residue of grease on your finger, showing the presence of natural lanolin (and other oils) that keep the wool supple and prevent dirt from adhering to the pile. Tugging the rug, both lengthways and widthways, is a useful way of checking the tensile strength of the warp and weft. However, the wool and other materials used in tribal rugs are generally of excellent quality and the vast majority of items on the market today will last for many years, provided they are treated with a modicum of care.

The integrity of the weave is influenced by the specific weaving technique and, to a certain degree, by the demands of the design. Pile rugs all employ the same basic knotting technique, but the successful articulation of intricate, curvilinear designs requires much finer knotting than is necessary for simple, geometric compositions. Viewing the rug from the back will enable you to gauge the fineness and regularity of the knotting, and a well-made rug (even one that is not especially finely knotted) should show a relatively even grid pattern, created by the warps and weft, running at right angles to one another. Flatweaves, in contrast, need to be assessed according to the relative strengths and weaknesses of each specific weaving technique – some of which result in finer, tighter or more compact physical structures than others – but a general test is to hold a section up to a light and then pull gently in opposite directions, noting the space between the weave. A tight, compact weave will show very little space between the warps and wefts, whereas a loose weave will show sizable gaps, creating the impression of looking through a net curtain. Tightly woven flatweaves are generally more durable, but the relative quality of an individual flatweave can only be assessed against items that employ the same weaving technique. (*See* Chapter II)

The clarity and permanence of the dyes can only be properly ascertained by laboratory analysis, but this is usually only warranted for dating or establishing the provenance of rare and valuable old or antique items. However, modern dyes (whether natural or synthetic) are normally both attractive and permanent, and, apart from a degree of natural mellowing, should retain their colours throughout the life of the rug. Consequently, if the colours look good at the outset, they are unlikely to deteriorate, but if they are garish or lacklustre, they will not improve. Colour irregularities (abrashes) are common in tribal items, and, provided they are not too severe, rarely detract from a rug's value. (*See* Chapter II)

Whether a rug lies flat on the floor can be easily established by placing it on a flat, even surface, and then walking around and across it from every direction. It is also useful to look across it from a few inches above the floor (because some ridges and troughs may not be visible from above) and then run your hands over the surface to discover any bumps or unevenness. Some unevenness is acceptable in most tribal rugs, and rarely detracts from its value, but extremely misshapen or uneven items are more difficult to locate and are generally less desirable to collectors.

Assessing investment potential

The investment potential of attractive rugs in good condition is normally much greater than that of unattractive items that show considerable amounts of wear and tear. A rug's collectability is also influenced by its age and provenance, and a relatively mediocre item in moderate condition can therefore prove to be a better investment than an more aesthetically pleasing item in a better state of repair, depending on their respective ages and origins. However, determining exactly when, where and by whom a particular rug was produced is almost impossible unless there is an unbroken record of its provenance stretching back to its manufacture, which is rare.

Attribution Term for an informed opinion of a rug's origin, which should never be taken as an indisputable fact. For example, a rug described as being attributed to Bidjar is of less certain origin than one that is labelled simple as a Bidjar. However, it is not unknown for experts to disagree so it is advisable to seek opinions from two or three independent sources, especially for old or exceptional items because attributed rugs are usually slightly more expensive that unattributed ones.

Provenance Simply means origin, but is often used to describe the recorded history of an individual rug (e.g. records of sales and ownership), and items with a provenance often attract higher prices – especially if they were owned by famous individuals, or were featured in books or exhibitions – than items with less precise histories.

Age and dating A consensus of opinion is common in placing a rug's date of manufacture within three or four decades, but obtaining a more precise attribution can be extremely problematic. Chemical analysis of the materials and dyes may help, but it is advisable to treat all dating with a degree of scepticism.

Rugs containing dates and signatures Despite being woven into the fabric of the rug, these should never be taken as conclusive proof of when or by whom it was made. Deliberate forgery is extremely rare, but it is common practice for illiterate weavers to copy older items and simply reproduce the original date or signature as part of the design. Mistakes in the articulation of letters and numbers, or the treatment of them as motifs that can be modified to enhance the design, are quite common.

Reading dates and signatures Usually fairly straightforward because they are normally written in Roman, Cyrillic (Russian) or, more frequently, Arabic or Farsi (Persian). The dates usually conform to the Muslim, Gregorian or Julian calendar systems.

Roman and Cyrillic are written from left to right and are used almost exclusively by Amerindian, Armenian and other Caucasian weaving groups, who employ the Gregorian (or Western) calendar. However, a number of older Caucasian items were dated according to the almost identical Julian calendar, which was used throughout the Russian sphere of influence until it was superseded by the Gregorian system in 1918.

Arabic and Farsi are both written from right to left, and, although their lettering systems are slightly different, their numbers are almost identical. They are used throughout Asia and North Africa, and adhere to the Muslim calendar, which begins on 16 July 622 (the date of Mohammed's flight from Mecca to Medina).

Converting dates from the Muslim calendar First, divide the date on the rug by 33 – because the Muslim year is approximately $\frac{1}{33}$ (or 11 days) shorter than the western year – subtract the result from the original date, and then add this figure to 622. This gives you the Gregorian (or western) year. For example, a rug dated 960 would be calculated as follows: 960 ÷ 33 = 29; 960 − 29 = 931; 931 + 622 = 1553.

Age classification Differs slightly from country to country, but generally, anything made in the last 20 to 30 years is viewed as being contemporary; earlier this century old; and during or before the 19th century, antique.

The relationship between colours and age The degree to which the colours have faded can be an indication of approximately when a rug was made, but it is extremely unwise to assume that a rug must be old because its colours have faded. It could also be caused by a number of other factors. (*See* Chapter II)

What to pay

The amount you are prepared to spend on a tribal rug should be determined primarily by what you can afford, and secondly by the current market rate. This may appear to be obvious, but it is not uncommon for people to be swayed by the salesman's patter, or swept along by the momentum of an auction, only to realize later that they have paid more than they could reasonably afford, or purchased an old, highly collectable and relatively expensive item when a cheaper, more functional alternative would be better suited to their needs.

Shopping around The price of almost identical items can vary considerably between retail outlets in the same town or even the same street. Never allow yourself to be pressed into making a hasty decision, keep a note of the prices being asked for items of the same origin, quality and size in different outlets, and do not be afraid of mentioning that you are considering buying from another shop, as the possibility of losing a sale to a rival can have a favourable impact on the asking price.

Home trials Available at some retail outlets, they give you the opportunity of viewing the rug in context, which is always advisable, especially if it is needed for a specific purpose or location. Home trials usually take the form of either a fixed loan period (two to three weeks) or as a basic purchase with a money-back guarantee if returned within a specified time.

Factors affecting rug prices

The retail prices of tribal rugs are determined by a combination of the individual retail outlet's variable internal operational costs (e.g. profit margins, high or low sales turnover), and the relatively fixed wholesale costs.

Wholesale prices Usually dictated by the purchase price in the country of origin, the costs of shipping, washing, storage and transportation, and the respective import tariffs, exchange rates and tax levies of the importing and exporting countries involved. Wholesale costs can vary quite considerably, depending on the specific producing and importing (western) countries involved, and consequently there is always likely to be some discrepancy in the relative prices of items of comparable quality, or even from the same weaving group, depending on where they were made and where they are sold.

Worldwide fluctuations in wholesale price Caused by increases or decreases in either the costs of production or the number of rugs being exported, which normally affect all the importing countries equally. Fluctuations in the prices of rugs from individual producing countries are frequently the result of the start or cessation of war, revolution, political or economic instability, a natural disaster, or a reversal of domestic policies (e.g. the Ayatollah Khomeini, in Iran, reversed his decision to suppress rug making, which he said 'pandered to Western decadence', after he realized, during the Iran–Iraq War, that rugs earn foreign currency, and foreign currency bought guns). Price changes affecting all producing countries are normally caused by increases in the cost of, or shortages of, raw materials (e.g. wool).

National fluctuations in retail price Influenced by the relative standards of living and tax levels in each importing (western) country, as well as local variations in the popularity of tribal rugs in general. Prices are also affected by variations in the wholesale cost of rugs due to the respective exchange rates, import tariffs and the political relationships between the individual producing and importing nations. For example, the USA impose a wide range of import tariffs (from 0% to 40%), depending on their support for the political regime in the producing country, and any change in the nature of a regime (e.g. if it moves from communism to democracy), or a modification in US foreign policy (e.g. stemming from a desire to increase trade or the election of a new administration) can herald a change in these tariff levels.

Local retail variations in price Largely determined by the differing overheads, profit margins and sales policies of rival retail outlets. However, it is common practice for most retail outlets to sell selected items as loss leaders, and, if these coincide with your requirements, you can obtain a tribal rug for a bargain price. Similarly, individual outlets sometimes acquire a consignment of rugs for an exceptionally low wholesale cost or have items in stock that were purchased when tribal rugs were generally cheaper. In contrast, some outlets may have acquired a batch of rugs prior to a reduction in wholesale costs, and are therefore faced with the choice of either reducing their profit margins and selling them at the current market price, or endeavouring to sell them for as near as possible to their original retail price before releasing their newer, cheaper stock. Consequently, retail prices in the same town, or even the same street, for almost identical items can vary significantly.

Flexible pricing and bargaining Normal practice in most retail outlets, with the possible exception of some department stores, but there is almost always a lower limit below which the dealer is not prepared to go. Your bargaining position will stronger if you have done your homework (by shopping around) and know the prices being asked in other retail outlets for similar items. Some dealers tend to start high and give large discounts – in the belief that this gives the customer the feeling of having secured a real bargain – whereas others opt for a much lower starting price, hoping to engage the prospective buyer's interest at the outset, and then give a smaller discount as a gesture of goodwill. However, regardless of the dealer's approach, the only price that really matters is the final selling price, and skilful haggling often results in similar selling prices being agreed across a range of outlets whose starting prices were extremely diverse.

Price and service Often closely connected as retail outlets tend to operate on the basis of either high turnover, low profit margin and minimal service, or low turnover, high profit margins and more comprehensive service.

Price and quality Not necessarily connected, so never assume that something is better simply because it is more expensive. The respective purchase and export costs in different countries can lead to good quality rugs from one country being cheaper than inferior items from another. In addition, the prices of tribal rugs are normally dictated more by their general collectability and availability than their individual technical merits. For example, Navajo rugs have become highly collectable in recent years, and are therefore generally much more expensive than flatweaves of equal aesthetic and technical merit from Asia and North Africa. However, there is some truth in the maxim that 'you get what you pay for', and exceptional items are normally more expensive than more ordinary examples from the same or similar weaving groups.

Price and size Related in so much as larger rugs normally cost more than smaller ones of similar origins, but, unlike commercially produced workshop rugs (which are often sold by the m² or ft²), tribal rugs are generally sold as individual pieces and priced according to their specific merits, rather than their size.

The price of old and antique items Normally dictated by a combination of rarity, collectability and physical condition.

Comparing prices

Comparing the prices of tribal rugs in terms of cash amounts is impossible because they would soon be out of date due to changes in local retail overheads and global wholesale costs. However, allowing for the possibility of exceptional circumstances (e.g. war, natural disaster) arising in specific regions, the average price of the rugs produced by one weaving group can be fixed, with a reasonable degree of accuracy, in relation to those of other weaving groups – i.e. Belouch and Qashga'i rugs are all roughly similar in price, but generally cheaper than Shahsavans. However, these price differentials are only applicable to average quality rugs of approximately the same size and they do not allow for local price variations based on popularity or short-term supply.

Choosing a yardstick Necessary to create a simple and effective system of comparison. A rug from almost any weaving group could be used, but, in order to provide a viable yardstick, it needs to be both widely available and sufficiently distinctive to enable easy comparison with other items. Therefore, by choosing a standard Afghan Belouch it is possible to provide an indication of the price of rugs from other weaving groups by marking them plus or minus x per cent of the yardstick. For example, a rug retailing at roughly the same price as an Afghan Belouch would be marked '0%'; one costing about 30% more would be '+ 30%'; and one costing 20% less would be '- 20%'. Some weaving groups produce rugs of a rea-

Approximate price comparisons

Afshar		+10/40%	Kurd		0/+60%
Aimaq	(e.g. Taimani)	-30/+10%	Luri		-10/+40%
Armenian		+40/100%	Navajo		+50/200%
Ayuchucho	(Peru)	-40/+10%	Qashga'i		0/+50%
Azerbaijan	(Province, Iran)	+10/50%	Quchan	(Kurdish)	+30/60%
Azerbaijan	(Republic)	+40/100%	Senneh	(Kurdish)	+20/70%
Bakhtiari		0/+40%	Shahsavan		+20/60%
Belouch	(Meshed)	0/+30%	Turkoman	(Tekke or Yomut)	+20/60%
Belouch	(war rugs)	+20/60%	Van	(Kurdish)	+20/60%
Berber		-40/+10%	Yuruk		+20/50%
Bidjar		+30/100%	Zaiane	(Berber)	10/0%
Khorassan	(Kurdish)	0/+40%	Zemmour	(Berber)	-60/-20%

sonably consistent standard, and consequently their cost parameters will normally vary very little in relation to the yardstick figure. However, a number of weaving groups produce items of widely varying standards, which oscillate in price between 10% and 50% (or even more) of the yardstick, and will therefore be marked as '+10/50%' or '- 20/40%'.

Old, antique and exceptional rugs Priced according to their collectability, and therefore fall outside the yardstick price comparisons.

Comparison between rugs from transnational weaving groups Can distort relative prices because of the disparity in purchasing costs, exchange rates and import tariffs between the various combinations of importing and exporting countries. For example, a rug woven by the Herki (Kurdish) tribe – who straddle the Turkish, Iraq and Iranian borders – may vary in price depending on where it was initially purchased (i.e. Turkey, Iraq or Iran) and that country's relationship with the individual importing (western) nation. However, the approximate price comparisons still provide a useful indication of the relative prices.

Price categories

Generally, the rugs from most tribal weaving groups fall into the same, broadly defined price bracket, but those from some weaving groups may straddle two categories, and exceptional or inferior rugs from the same group may be found in separate categories.

Low category Cost roughly the same or less than the yardstick and include most average quality: Aimaq, Bakhtiari, Belouch, Berber, Hamadan, Khamseh, Kutchi, Luri, Qashga'i, Shiraz, and most modern Central and South American items.

Medium category Costing up to 50% more than the yardstick and include most Afshar, Belouch War Rugs, Bidjar, Kolyai, Kurdish regional, Nishapur, Quchan, Shahsavan, Turkoman, Uzbek, Van, Yalameh and Yuruk, as well as better quality low-priced items.

High category Rugs which normally cost over 50% more than the yardstick, which include: Armenian, Azerbaijani (Republic), Traditional Caucasian, Navajo, and better quality Turkoman and other items from the medium price category, and most old and antique rugs.

Where and when to buy

Most countries in Europe, North America, Australasia and the Far East have several different types of retail outlet, ranging from specialist shops to market stalls, each offering a slightly different set of advantages and disadvantages to the prospective buyer. Some dealers may try to persuade you that their type of outlet is intrinsically better than others, but this simply is not true. It is possible to find genuine bargains across the entire range of retail outlets, especially if you shop around.

It is important to remember that the rug trade is no different from other areas of commerce in that the levels of knowledge, helpfulness and integrity, displayed by individual members of staff in every type of outlet, may vary considerably, and it is a mistake to assume that the people employed by one type of outlet are automatically more knowledgable or trustworthy than those employed by another. **Confirming attributions** Deliberate deception in attributing rugs to wrong (usually more expensive) weaving groups is extremely rare, but if this does occur, there are laws in every country pertaining to trading standards, which normally apply to the sale of rugs. However, mistakes in the attribution of tribal items are not uncommon because (unlike commercially produced workshop rugs) they may be purchased by the retailer in circumstances where their exact origins are extremely difficult to confirm (e.g. from a souk in Algiers, Morocco, or an itinerant dealer in Peshawar, Pakistan). Also dealers in the producing countries are generally more concerned with the rug's quality, rather than by whom it was made, and are often either oblivious to their western counterparts' desire for exact attributions or cynical enough to tell them whatever they think they want to hear. In addition, some shop assistants may make a wrong attribution due to their ignorance of the subject, or faulty labelling, or confusing similar names (e.g. Bidjar/Beshir). Therefore, unless you are collecting specific items, it is advisable to choose a rug on its individual merits, rather than its possible origins.
Specialist shops Normally stock a wide selection of rugs from a variety of weaving groups. They usually allow you to examine individual items at your leisure, and sometimes include home trials as part of their sales service. The staff are often fairly knowledgable (although this may be limited to the more commercial aspects of the business) and you can usually contact them if you have problems or require further advice. Their main disadvantage is that because they are often situated in prestigious locations, carry large stocks and employ several staff, they have relatively high overheads, which are generally passed on to the customer.
Department stores Fall into two categories: the first operates on a franchise basis – whereby the oriental rug department is run by the franchisee totally independently of the store – and is more or less the same as a specialist shop. The second category includes all the department stores that own and control their own oriental rug department, but needs to be divided into those selling a few tribal rugs in with their machine-made carpets, and those operating a specialist oriental rug department. The former usually carry a very small stock of items from a few weaving groups, the prices are fixed and the staff have a very limited knowledge of the subject. They can still be a useful source of reasonably priced, popular items. Department stores that run a specialist oriental rug department normally have the same advantages and disadvantages as specialist shops, often with the added bonus of credit facilities.
Auctions An unpredictable and often exciting way to buy; excellent bargains are possible, but, unless you are familiar with the subject, you can just as easily pay too much or walk away with something that is totally unsuited to your needs. It is therefore important to do your homework – decide on the type, style and size of rug you wish to buy; check the prices of similar items in a range of retail outlets; and finally set yourself an upper limit on the amount you are willing to pay. Also, if possible, attend one or two auctions (not necessarily ones selling rugs) in order to familiarize yourself with the procedure and atmosphere; and ask the auctioneer to explain the sales conditions before the auction starts. You especially need to know how the bidding is to be regulated, whether there are reserves (a price below which an item will not be sold) on any items, and what, if any, additional charges will be added to the hammer (selling) price. It is common practice for tax and, sometimes, a buyer's premium (usually 10–15%) to be added to the successful bid. Remember that regardless of the reason for the auction, the basic dynamics are the same (i.e. the auctioneer will endeavour to obtain the highest price he can for the vendors, and the audience will try to secure the rug they want for as little as possible). Consequently, your chances of getting a bargain will be determined on the night, partly by how much rival bidders are willing to pay for each item, and partly by the auctioneer's (or vendor's) willingness to set reasonable reserves. Never take auctioneers' claims of having no reserves on any of the rugs too seriously – this may be true for average items, but auctioneers have a responsibility to the vendors and are therefore

usually unwilling to sell valuable items for a fraction of their normal retail price. Nevertheless, auctions are governed by fairly strict rules of procedure and advertising – as well as general trading regulations – and, although these may vary from country to country, the buyer will normally be protected by law if they purchase a rug that proves to be damaged or otherwise sold under a false description. Auctioneers usually point out any flaws in a rug before starting the bidding, and, although mistakes in attribution or cataloguing sometimes occur, very few auction houses would risk their reputations with such blatant deceptions.

Auctions are sometimes the only means of buying locally for people living outside the major conurbations and can also provide a valuable, additional source of tribal rugs for people in cities and larger towns. Their main disadvantages are that you have to make an instant decision on what to buy, pay in full at the end of the auction, and forego the opportunity of a home trial or the choice of returning a rug if it proves to be unsuitable for your needs.

Ethnic shops Normally carry a wide range of ethnic artefacts (masks, clothes, jewelry, etc.) in addition to tribal rugs, and can be broadly divided into those selling a few rugs as part of their general stock (which can be a useful source of the cheaper, more widely available items) and those that carry a substantial collection of tribal rugs. The latter sometimes have a better selection of interesting and reasonably priced items from certain regions than specialist oriental rug shops. The owners frequently have a genuine interest in the subject and sometimes visit the producing countries and select the rugs individually, rather than buying through a wholesaler. These ethnic shops offer many of the same advantages as specialist shops, but are often in less prestigious locations, and have lower overheads.

Exhibitions Usually arranged by dealers who do not have a retail outlet, or retailers who want a short-term outlet in another location, and are organized along the same lines as commercial painting exhibitions – i.e. a selection of rugs are displayed for a limited period in a gallery (or other suitable location) and the public can look around and purchase anything on display. Exhibitions have similar advantages and disadvantages to auctions – but give a much longer time to make a decision – and provide a useful method of buying for people living outside the larger conurbations.

Private sales Buying from private individuals normally falls outside the laws governing commercial sales, and, although the exact legal position varies from country to country, the buyer generally has limited statutory protection. However, private sales should not be discounted because most people are fairly honest and bargains can be found. Obtaining a professional valuation, especially for expensive items, is a useful precaution against deception and also provides a reasonable starting price for negotiations.

Private dealers People who earn their living by selling rugs are governed by normal trading regulations, and you may be required to pay tax on top of the sale price. Private dealers can offer a more personalized (and possibly less expensive) service than specialist shops while retaining many of their advantages, including home trials, and may also prove especially helpful in locating specific items. However, unless you know them personally or by reputation, there is always the risk that they may prove hard to find if problems arise.

Catalogues and mail order Useful for people who are unable to visit a retail outlet in person, but you cannot assess the quality of a rug from a photograph, so make sure that there is a money-back guarantee.

Markets and antique shops An unreliable but occasionally valuable source of tribal rugs, as long as you remember that most non-specialist traders know very little about the subject and are just as likely to overcharge as undercharge.

Buying in countries of origin Not always the cheapest place to buy (especially after the addition of import tariffs and shipping costs), and, unless you carry it with you, there is always the risk that your rug will not arrive, or that you'll receive an inferior one in its place. However, genuine bargains can be found and there is often a particular satisfaction in bringing back a memento of your visit. Buying in most producing countries is fairly straightforward, but remember that most retail outlets are geared to tourism and charge tourist prices, although skilful bargaining, or visiting places off the main tourist routes, may increase your chances of buying something for considerably less. Also, some countries, most notably Turkey, have strict rules regarding the export of national treasures, which may include some old or exceptional tribal rugs.

Buying rugs in other countries in the west Can be worthwhile because, even allowing for the extra cost of shipping and import tariffs, some tribal rugs may still be cheaper than at home. Remember that some countries levy their import tariffs depending on where an item was bought, and others on where it was made: for example, importing an Afghan Belouch from Germany into the USA would attract an Afghan import tariff, rather than the one applied to German goods. So always check with your own customs how import tariffs are applied before making a purchase.

Choosing the best time to buy If possible, buy when supply is outstripping demand, which is often indicated by a plethora of sales, auctions and special offers. Also, at any given time, rugs from some countries may be disproportion-

ately cheaper than those from others (due to a variety of localized economic and political factors). In addition, some retail outlets may be using the type of rug you want as loss leader, or have recently obtained an unusually inexpensive consignment of items.

Insuring tribal rugs Always recommended; cheaper rugs can be included on a general household policy, but separate cover should be sought for more expensive items. Retain photographs and descriptions of all your rugs, and obtain a valuation when you buy, or (for a small fee) from an accredited valuer at a later date. Remember that the insurance valuation is not the price you paid for your rug, but the cost of buying a replacement, which may be more.

Where and when to sell

It is just as important to do your homework when trying to sell a rug, as when buying, and a similar range of factors should be borne in mind if you wish to obtain the optimum price.

Resale value

Influenced by a combination of a rug's physical condition, appearance and origin, as well as the general state of the market and current popularity of items from each weaving group. Most retail outlets, with the possible exception of department stores, may be interested in buying or re-selling on your behalf, provided that it falls within their remit or specialization.

Physical condition A major influence on where to sell because most retail outlets will usually only be interested in items in good condition – unless they are exceptionally rare or collectable. As a general rule, you can expect more for rugs in good condition than for similar items that show wear and tear. However, severely worn rugs may be of interest to dealers or retail outlets that specialize in making bags and cushions out of damaged items.

Origin Influences both the selling price and the optimum retail outlet because rugs from some weaving groups, or areas, may be more popular, at any given time, than comparable items from elsewhere. Also most retail outlets specialize to some degree, and a shop that concentrates on Afghan rugs is unlikely to consider items from North Africa or the Americas.

Collectability Difficult to define or predict – and frequently has little connection with the respective qualities of rugs from different weaving groups – you simply have to accept

that, at any given time, some rugs are likely to be more popular (and consequently more expensive) than others. Therefore, if possible, try to sell a rug when similar items are in vogue. Old or unusual items are often sought by specialist collectors – it is therefore advisable to approach a retail outlet that has a track record of selling similar items, or try to locate individual collectors by advertising in a specialist magazine.

Prevailing market conditions Influence the selling price of rugs generally, and, if possible, wait until the demand for tribal rugs is outstripping the supply (which is usually indicated by rising prices). However, old and unusual items are often unaffected by general trends.

Outlets for sales

Specialist shops Simplest source for a potential sale, but accept that you will be paid considerably less than the rug's anticipated retail price. Some specialist shops may be willing to sell on your behalf at a fixed percentage – you stand to obtain more this way, but will have to wait for your money until the rug is actually sold. Old and exceptional rugs should be sold through specialist shops that have contacts with established collectors of similar items.

Auctions Always an element of risk, which can be considerably reduced by fixing a reasonable reserve (minimum selling price), but has the potential for realizing a higher return. Some auction houses charge the vendor a flat fee, or a percentage of the hammer (selling) price, whereas others obtain their fee solely from the buyer's premium, so it is essential to establish the conditions prior to entering into any agreement. Most contemporary items can be sold through any general auctioneer (i.e. those dealing with items other than rugs), but old, unusual or exceptional items should, if possible, always be sold via specialist auction houses; preferably those with a proven track record of selling similar items.

Private sales Useful option for most contemporary items, but, unless you have an independent valuation, it is not advisable for the sale of old, unusual or exceptional items.

Care and repair

Tribal rugs are generally exceptionally durable, but their continued life, attractiveness and resale potential will be greatly enhanced if they are given proper care and attention. In addition to normal wear and tear, exposure to central heating, air conditioning, insects, and a range of household chemicals can undermine most rug-making materials; and there is always the risk of accidental damage, especially if there are children or animals in the house. However, adherence to a few simple precautions will maximize the life of your rug.

Correct underlay Needed to protect a rug from the damaging effects of continually compressing the rug's fibres between the soles of your shoes and the floor. Therefore, always place a rug on a carpeted floor or use an underlay made from solid sponge rubber or jute and animal hair (which is normally coated with rubber on both sides). Foam or ripple rubber underlays are less suitable.

Cleaning Essential on a regular basis in order to minimize insect damage. Always work slowly, and begin by removing the surface dust – with a carpet sweeper or vacuum cleaner (preferably one without beater bars, which could damage the fibres) – and then dislodge the more ingrained dirt by shaking the rug gently. However, professional cleaning is recommended for valuable or damaged items.

Shampooing Replaces the fibres' essential moisture and also removes more entrenched areas of grit and dirt. Begin once the rug has been cleaned, using any good quality wool detergent (most of which are also compatible with cotton and silk), possibly adding a cup of diluted vinegar, and then dab (never rub) the solution evenly and gently over the surface of the rug. The rug should then be dried carefully and systematically (preferably by leaving it out in the sun) and then checked for pockets of dampness, which can be removed by using a hand-held hair dryer. Old, expensive and delicate items should always be cleaned by specialist oriental rug cleaners; not general carpet cleaning companies that normally use chemicals which can damage the rug's fibres.

Removing stains Should always be done by dabbing the affected area (never rub because this can cause the colours to run), using a cleaning solution that is both compatible with the material (e.g. wool) and also suitable for removing the specific stain (e.g. coffee). After removing as much of the stain as possible, dry the area carefully. There are several books that provide information on the different cleaning agents best suited to removing specific stains, and most manufacturers will give advice on removing stains caused by their products. However, if the stain persists, or is on an old or valuable item, a specialist cleaner should be consulted.

Moth proofing Vital, especially if rugs are kept in storage for any period of time. It is often part of the original washing process, but this does not last forever, and some items are sold unwashed. Using a suitable moth-proofing solution is therefore advisable.

Repairs Large holes, tears or other serious damage (especially on old or expensive items) should always be repaired by professionals, but minor repairs to the fringes, selvedges or damage to the body of the rug can be undertaken at home by sewing the affected area using matching coloured wool or other compatible material.

Additional maintenance measures Localized fading and uneven wear and tear can be minimized by moving the rug around so that different parts of the surface are exposed to sunlight or heavy traffic. Periodic storage can also enhance the life of a rug (especially during the summer if fading is a problem), and should preferably be undertaken – after it has been cleaned, shampooed and moth proofed – by covering both sides with polythene and then rolling it into a tight cylindrical form. Also, never place houseplants directly on the floor near a rug because cotton is highly susceptible to mildew (a type of fungus).

CHAPTER FOUR

The cultural context

Tribal societies are not the socially immutable, territorially parochial entities that they are often portrayed to be in the west. They have been at the forefront of numerous invasions, occupations, religious conversions, migrations, and forced expulsions and resettlements throughout different periods during the last three millennia. Some tribes have been wholly assimilated into other tribes or absorbed into the general national population, and at the same time, a number of new, socially autonomous tribal confederacies have evolved – or been formed for political or commercial reasons – from diverse groups of ethnically unrelated people. A degree of familiarity with the ethnic, religious, social and cultural backgrounds of the weavers, as well as their movements throughout the rug producing regions, is therefore necessary in order to gain an insight into the factors that have formed, and continue to form, the character, appearance and attribution of tribal rugs.

The major ethnic groups

Most tribal rug producing regions are occupied by people who are racially and culturally diverse – some are indigenous to the area (e.g. Persians), others arrived by way of conquest or migration over the last 2,000 years (e.g. Arabs) – which results in varied and often confusing patterns of cohabitation and weaving traditions between essentially tribal and non-tribal ethnic groups. The general trend in Iran, for example, has been for traditional tribal people (e.g. Kurds) to adopt the more urbanized lifestyle and culture of the ethnic Persians. However, small pockets of Persians have either retained a tribal lifestyle, or have been assimilated into a number of tribal confederacies.

In some areas, a single ethnic, tribal or cultural group dominates the weaving traditions of all the other inhabitants of the region (e.g. Turkomen in Turkmenistan). In other areas (e.g. Iran), a number of different tribal, ethnic or cultural groups continue to maintain their unique weaving traditions, and their rugs are often closer in character and appearance to those woven by their kinsmen in other regions and countries than they are to items woven in the next village by people of different ethnic or tribal origins.

Note To avoid unnecessary repetition, the tribes that form cohesive weaving groups will be covered in Chapter VII and information on general regional or national production can be found in Chapter VI.

Asia and North Africa

Afghans Relatively fair-skinned people (also known as Pathans, Pashtuns or Pushtoons), who form the largest and the politically dominant ethnic group in Afghanistan; they are also widespread throughout Pakistan and northern India. Afghans are traditionally divided into a number of nomadic, semi-nomadic and settled tribal groups – which include Mohmands, Mangals and Wiziris (who claim descent from one of the lost tribes of Israel). However, despite their frequent adherence to a tribal lifestyle, the absence of a unifying style in the rugs they produce means that there are no universally recognized Afghan tribal weaving groups. The term Afghan is also used as a general description of any inhabitant of Afghanistan, regardless of their ethnic origin.

Aryans Collective term that is often used to define northern Europeans (proto-Aryans), but should be applied more correctly to all Indo-European people, including Berbers, Kurds, Persians, Afghans and most people in the Middle East, Asia Minor, Central Asia and northern India prior to the Turko-Mongol invasions. (*See* Aryan migrations)

Bedouins Arabic word, meaning desert dweller, used to describe the nomadic herdsmen – living mainly in the desert regions of North Africa and the Middle East – who operate a strict caste system based on noble tribes, who can trace their ancestral origins either to Qaysi (northern Arabia) or Yamani (southern

Arabia), and 'ancestorless' vassal tribes living under their protection. Authentic Bedouin rugs sometimes appear on the market, but dealers often use the term to describe any Arab or Berber item of tribal appearance.

Georgians Indigenous Indo-European people, who live mainly in the Georgian Republic and, to a much lesser extent, the other former Soviet Caucasian Republics. They are found in some tribal confederacies. (*See* Chapter VI: Georgia and Chapter VII: Shahsavan and Traditional Caucasian weaving groups)

Medes Ancient Indo-European inhabitants of north central Iran who founded an empire, under King Deices (*c.* 708–655 BC), based around Ecbatana (Hamadan). (*See* Persians)

Mongoloids Anthropological racial division, which encompasses the indigenous people of eastern Siberia, China, South-East Asia and the Americas. Not to be confused with Mongols, who are a distinctive ethnic and cultural group.

Mongols Indigenous inhabitants of Mongolia, northern China and south-east Siberia, who are closely related to the Tibetans. They were traditionally nomadic herdsmen, whose social structure was based on allegiance to specific tribes (or clans), each under the authority of an individual tribal leader (or Khan), and it was only after Genghis Khan or 'Great Leader' (1162–1227) united all the disparate tribes that a Mongolian nation could be said to exist. Today, the majority of ethnic Mongols – many of whom still adhere to a semi-nomadic lifestyle – live in the Mongolian Republic (Outer Mongolia). However, the successive Turko-Mongol invasions have resulted in isolated pockets of ethnic Mongols (e.g. Borchalu) or people of Mongol descent (e.g. Kazakhs) living in Iran, Afghanistan, the former Soviet Central Asian Republics and other countries along their invasion routes. Mongolian rugs are still made by semi-nomadic and settled tribesmen throughout Mongolia. They are similar to both Tibetan and eastern Chinese (e.g. Sinkiang) items, but are often slightly more sombre in colouring and feature variations of the *ay-gul* and geometric Buddhist/Hindu motifs (e.g. *frets*, swastikas, *wans*). A large number of animal trappings, bags and artefacts are made, although very few ever find their way to the west. (*See* Tamerlane and the Turko-Mongol Empire)

Oghuz or Ghuzz Turks One of the largest and most influential Turkic tribes. (*See* Turkic tribes, Seljuk Turk and Ottoman Empires)

Persians Early Indo-European inhabitants of south and central Iran, who were established in southern Iran during the 7th century BC. Most historians believe they migrated through the Caucasus to the Iranian plateau around the turn of the 2nd millennium BC, although some suggest that they may be of Mediterranean racial stock. The Persians, under Cyrus (Kouresh) the Great (*c.* 559–529 BC), conquered and rapidly assimilated the Medes, and founded the Persian Empire. Today, ethnic Persians (who are an amalgamation of Medes and Persians) constitute approximately two-thirds of the Iranian population, and are the dominant political and cultural group. (*See* Persian, Parthian, Sassanian Empires and Persian Safavid, Qajar and Pahlavi Dynasties) *Note* To avoid confusion, the term 'Persian' will be used when discussing ethnic Persians and 'Iranian' when referring to inhabitants of Iran.

Tajiks (or Tadjiks) Tribesmen believed to be descended from a mixture of Persian, Arab and Turkic people, who live mainly in the Tajikistan Republic. Some authentic Tajik tribal rugs are made, although very few ever reach the west. Tajik weavers form part of the Shahsavan and other weaving groups.

Tartars (or Tatars) Turkic-speaking tribesmen who are generally thought to be descended from indigenous Kipchak Turkic tribes, Mongols and Bulgars. Their name is now a byword for intractability and ferocity, and the culinary dish Steak Tartar was inspired by their habit of eating raw meat that had been tenderized by riding with it under their saddles. Tartars once ruled a vast region that stretched from the Crimean peninsula, through the middle Volga valley to southern Siberia and northern Mongolia, but today the majority live in the Tartar ASSR and the Uzbekistan Republic. In common with the Kirghiz, Yakut and other more Mongoloid Turkic tribes, they are sometimes known collectively as Turanian Turks. A few rugs are made by Tartar weavers, which are generally similar to other Central Asian items, but they rarely reach the west; and the rugs marketed as Tartari are generally made by Uzbeks. (*See* Chapter VII: Tartari)

Tibetans Mongoloid people who have close ethnic, cultural and religious links to the Mongols. The vast majority of ethnic Tibetans lived in Tibet prior to its annexation by China (1950–51) when thousands were forced to flee to Nepal, India and Bhutan in order to escape Chinese persecution, which has included a systematic suppression of all aspects of Tibetan culture. The vast majority of Tibetan rugs are now produced by refugees in Nepal and India, but a gradual relaxation in China's policy of cultural genocide, during the 1980s, has seen a slight re-emergence of weaving in Tibet – especially by semi-nomadic and isolated village communities. Tibetan rugs share a number of common features with Mongolian and eastern Chinese items, but are produced using a unique weaving method (employing a weaving stick to thread the knots) which results in horizontal ridges, running along each row of knots, on the back of the rug. Most Tibetan designs feature either mythological animals (e.g. dragons, tigers, snow leopards), symbolic vegetal forms or amulet/medallions, and normally employ a mixed palette of warm, slightly pastel reds, oranges, browns and blues, contrasted with very dark blues, browns or black. Tibetan rugs are generally very similar, regardless of whether they are produced by villagers or semi-nomads in Tibet, or by refugees in the more commercial workshops of Nepal and India, but only the former can be legitimately described as tribal, although they rarely appear on western markets.

Timurids Collective term for the followers and descendants of Tamerlane, which should not be confused with the Timuri weaving group.

Turkic tribes Collective term for an ethnically diverse people who are unified by a close affinity of culture, language and history. Their exact origins are unclear, but are generally traced to early nomads – inhabiting territories south of Lake Baikal, in south-eastern Siberia, towards the northern border of Mongolia – who, according to legend, were descended from a union between a boy and a she-wolf. After the boy was killed by enemy soldiers, the she-wolf escaped to the mountains, near Turpan, and bore ten sons; one of whom married a human female and fathered the Turkic tribes. The Chinese referred to them as Tu'kiu (or T'uchueh), and in the 6th century they founded an empire that stretched from Mongolia, through Siberia and Central Asia to the Black Sea. However, by the end of the 7th century, the empire had begun to fragment into semi-independent territories or khanates – under the control of individual tribal groups – which by the 8th century could be broadly split into (West) Turkestan and East Turkestan. During this period they became known as the Turks (Turkomen or Turkic tribes), and these

names were applied indiscriminately to almost any ethnic group who subsequently came under their influence or were involved in one of the Turkic or Turko-Mongol conquests that swept through Asia and eastern Europe from the 11th century onwards.

Today the various Turkic-speaking tribes are generally divided into the western branch (who are dispersed throughout eastern Europe, Turkey, north-west Iran and western Asia), and the eastern branch (who are concentrated in the former Soviet Central Asian Republics, Afghanistan and the Sinkiang Province of Eastern China). Both branches are composed of people from a broad spectrum of racial types, but eastern Turks are predominantly dark-skinned, whereas many of the western Turks are as fair-skinned as Europeans. (*See* Tajiks, Tartars, Tamerlane and the Turko-Mongol Empire, Seljuk Turk and Ottoman Empires; and also Chapter VII: Afshar, Azerbaijani, Karakalpaks, Kazakhs, Kirghiz, Qashga'i, Uighurs, Uzbeks) *Note* Only the Turkic tribes that have a direct bearing on tribal rug weaving are considered in this book.

Turko-Mongol Collective term for people of mixed (or indeterminate) ethnic origins who now form cohesive ethno-cultural groups.

Turks Sometimes employed as a collective name for Turkic tribes, or Turkomen, but is generally used more specifically to describe the descendants of the Seljuk and Ottoman tribes, who now live in Turkey and, to a lesser degree, the Balkans and Caucasian Republics. It is also used to describe any inhabitant of Turkey, regardless of their ethnic origin.

The Americas

Algonquin Major Amerindian linguistic/cultural group that encompasses a number of tribes in eastern Canada and the Atlantic coast of the USA (e.g. Cree, Mohicans), the northern border states (e.g. Cree, Blackfoot), and parts of the Great Plains (e.g. Cheyenne, Arapahoe) of central and southern USA.

Amerindians Collective term for the indigenous, pre-European inhabitants of the Americas, who (according to popular belief) were called Indians by Christopher Columbus because he was convinced that the first land he encountered on his westward circumnavigation of the world would be India and the native inhabitants would therefore be Indians.

Amuzgo Amerindian tribe, inhabiting the Oaxaca and Guerrero provinces of southern

Mexico, who are fine weavers, although most of their output is confined to clothes.

Apachenean Collective term for the Apache, Navajo and other Athapascan-speaking tribes of the south-western USA.

Athapascan The most widely dispersed of the major Amerindian linguistic/cultural groups found mainly in western Canada (e.g. Dogrib) and the north-western USA, but also include the Apacheneans and other splinter groups in the south-west and northern Mexico.

Ayamara One of the largest Amerindian linguistic/cultural groups in South America, who now inhabit Bolivia, Peru and northern Chile. They speak their own unwritten language, and, prior to Inca domination of the region, established a highly organized urban and agricultural society, centred around the city of Tihuancaca on Lake Titicaca in southern Peru. They are excellent weavers – who refined their skills, during the Inca Empire, as vassal-weavers in the Inca workshops – and are now responsible for many of the rugs and woven artefacts produced in Peru and Bolivia, which are usually marketed under the name of the town or regional centre, rather than the tribe. As a general rule, women weave more authentically tribal items on horizontal or backstrap looms, and men produce more commercial items (often based on tribal designs) using treadle looms. (*See* Chapter VII: Ayuchucho, Cuzco and San Pedro de Cajas)

Huichol Agricultural Amerindian tribe – inhabiting the Sierra Madre region of Mexico – who weave bags and other artefacts (mainly featuring stylized animals and geometric, vegetal forms) on backstrap looms.

Iroquois Amerindian linguistic/cultural group (also known as the 'Real Adders' or long-house people) that included the Susquehannock and the Hurons, who inhabited the Great Lakes region of North America. An Iroquois confederation (called 'The Five Nations', i.e., Cayuga, Mohawks, Oneidas, Onondago, Seneca) was founded (according to tradition) in 1570 by Hiawatha, a priestly title (Hia-wen-Wat-ha) that means 'he who seeks the wampum'.

Koluschan Amerindian linguistic/cultural group (said to include the Tlingit) that inhabited north-west Canada. A number of their mythological beliefs, dances and medicine ceremonies echoed, almost exactly, those of certain Asiatic tribes (especially the Ostiak).

Mapuche Amerindian tribe in southern Chile, who were finally defeated by European settlers, in 1882, and either escaped across the Andes into Argentina, or became absorbed into Chile's Mestizo population, or were forcibly resettled onto tribal reservations. These reservations were abolished during the 1960s and so the Mapuche became small, landowning subsistence farmers, who supplemented their income by selling ponchos, belts and shawls, mainly in the town of Temuco.

Maya Amerindian tribe – inhabiting the Yucatan peninsula in south-east Mexico – who are presumed to be direct descendants of the ancient Mayan civilization that flourished in the region from *c*. 2,600 BC. However, the ancient Mayans were a confederation of tribes, rather than a single ethnic-cultural group, and the tribes that are now considered to be part of the Maya family include the Mayos, Chontals, Huastecs, Lacadons, Tojolabals, Tzotzils and Tzetals. The most important weavers of the Maya family are the Tzotzils and the Tzetals.

Mestizo Spanish term used, in Central and South America, to describe people of mixed Amerindian and European descent.

Mixtec Amerindian linguistic/cultural group (which also includes the Tacuate), inhabiting the southern Mexican provinces of Oaxaca, Guerrero and Pueblo (known as la Mixteca). They are descendants of the Mixtec civilization that flourished in the region before the European conquest and practise a number of crafts, including weaving.

Nahua Mexico's largest Amerindian linguistic/cultural group, who inhabit a broad area, extending from Mexico City, encompassing the southern central region of the country. They speak the ancient Aztec language (Nahuatl), and continue to produce a number of traditional crafts, including weaving.

Nez Perce Amerindian tribe, who inhabited the inland plateau region off the US–Canadian Pacific coast, and made twined blankets and other weavings that are similar to Salish items.

Nootka Amerindian tribe, inhabiting Vancouver Island and the adjacent mainland of Canada, who were primarily village-based fishermen, responsible for producing numerous visually powerful twined cedar-bark blankets and other weavings. Nootka items are usually associated with those of the other tribes in the adjacent Salish coastal region, but they are generally closer in appearance to items made by the more northern coastal tribes (e.g. Kwakiute, Bella Coola) and their figurative items resemble slightly less overtly heraldic and totemic versions of Tlingit weavings, especially Chilkat blankets.

Otavalos Amerindian tribe, descendants of the pre-Colombian Cara Indians, who are believed to have emigrated from Colombia, during the 10th century AD, and settled in and around what is now the town of Otavalo in northern Ecuador. The Otavalos speak Quechua (the Inca language) and are one of the very few Amerindian tribes to have combined material success with the preservation of their native traditions. They are accomplished weavers and traders, who sell their products (and those of the neighbouring Salasca Indians), not only in the town of Otavalo, but also in Ecuador, Colombia, Venezuela, the USA and, to a lesser degree, Europe. Otavalo weavings are generally marketed simply as Ecuadorian rugs, and are usually bolder, both in colour and design, than those made in Mexico and Peru, and often feature either mythological figures or animals.

Otomi Amerindian linguistic/cultural group (which includes the Mazahua), found primarily in the state of Mexico and Hildalgo Province (in southern central Mexico), who weave a number of ponchos, sashes and bags, which often employ traditional pictographic motifs.

Perpechua (or Tarascan) Amerindian linguistic/cultural group, living in the Michoacán Province of south-western and central Mexico, who produce weavings and other crafts.

Pueblo Generic term (meaning village in Spanish) applied to a number of tribes – belonging to the Uto-Aztecan, Tano-Kiowa, Zuni and Keresan language groups – who lived in sophisticated village societies throughout the south-western states of America. Their cultural (if not ethnic) origins can be traced to the Hohokam people, who flourished from c. 300 BC and appear either to have been colonists from Mexico, or to have had close ties with contemporary Mexican civilizations (possibly Olmec or Mayan). The Hohokam were superseded by the Anasazi and Mogollon cultures, whose influence extended as far north as Utah and the Yuman tribes of the Colorado River. However, Pueblo culture (within the generally accepted meaning of the term) is largely confined to the Zuni, Hopi, Pima and other tribes of Arizona, New Mexico and California, who constructed sophisticated (sometimes multistorey) adobe buildings, irrigation canals, and townships. They were also accomplished weavers, who produced attractive cotton flatweaves and passed on their skills to the nomadic Navajos. (*See* Chapter VII: Navajo)

Quechua Amerindian linguistic/cultural group, who speak the unwritten Inca language (Quechua) and are believed to be direct descendants of the Incas. According to one legend, they were originally a small tribe, living around Lake Titicaca (in southern Peru), who gradually expanded the Inca Empire northwards through Cuzco and the Sacred Valley of the Incas to Quito (in Ecuador), and southwards to Santiago (in southern Chile). However, alternative legends suggest that the Incas originated from the north or west, conquering the Lake Titicaca region and forcing some of the local tribes to speak Quechua (which then became a generic term for tribes that spoke the Inca language). Today, the Quechua are mainly concentrated in the Andean highlands of Peru and, to a lesser extent, Bolivia and Ecuador. They are one of the major weaving tribes in South America, but their items are usually sold under the names of the regional weaving centres. (*See* Chapter VII: Ayuchucho, Cuzco and San Pedro de Cajas)

Salish Amerindian tribe, possibly related to the Algonquins, who occupied the Pacific coastal region of southern Canada and the northern USA. They produced a number of weavings – using plant fibres, goat wool and hair from a (now extinct) breed of dog – usually featuring a variety of diamond, zig-zag and other geometric forms – that were generally closer in character and appearance to Nez Perce, Pueblo and Navajo weavings than to the items woven by their coastal neighbours (e.g. Tlingit, Nootka). Salish is also used as a generic term for both the region and the local tribes that share similar cultural and artistic links.

Shoshonian North American Amerindian linguistic/cultural group (meaning snake people) which includes Shoshones and Hopis believed to be related to the Aztecs. (*See* Pueblo)

Tlingit Amerindian tribe inhabiting the Pacific coastal region of Canada, responsible for producing numerous twined cedar-bark blankets – usually featuring either intricate geometric patterns or remarkably powerful totemic figures and images – that were first collected by Captain Cook in 1778. The Tlingit, in common with the Haida and a few other tribes in the region, are the only North American Amerindians to employ specialist 'artists' (who were supported by the tribe) to produce totemic and ceremonial carvings, paintings and weavings, which have close thematic similarities to Innuit artefacts. It is generally believed that the Tlingit inherited their weaving skills from their southern neighbours, the Tsimshan, and later became closely associated with the remarkable Chilkat blankets – convex-edged weavings, usually in cedar bark and wool, that take their name from a closely related tribe (*see* p. 108). Tlingit, Tsimshan and Chilkat weaving declined rapidly early in the 20th century, but a small-scale revival began during the 1970s and '80s, although as yet few items are available on the market.

Wayuu The only 'desert' nomadic (and semi-nomadic) tribe in South America. They are an Arawak-speaking people, who inhabit the La Guajira peninsula in northern Colombia and Venezuela. The women weave vivaciously coloured, elaborately decorated hammocks (using geometric and naturalistic forms) on vertical looms.

Zapotec Amerindian linguistic/cultural group – inhabiting the Oaxaca Province of southern Mexico – who are sub-divided into nine distinctive dialect groups. Their ancestors built the ancient city of Monte Alban (some time between *c.* 1000 and *c.* 500 BC). Prior to the arrival of the Europeans, they were skilled builders, potters and craftsmen. Today, they are noted for a wide range of textiles, especially serapes and wall-hangings, woven on treadle looms, which often feature copies of paintings by Matisse, Miro, Escher and other European painters, as well as more Pre-Colombian Amerindian subjects.

Invasions, migrations and empires

Asia and North Africa

Early civilizations It is believed that a number of Indo-European civilizations existed in Mesopotamia at the beginning of the 7th millennium BC, but our knowledge of the region really dates from *c.* 4,000 BC with the arrival of the Sumerians. They were probably of Semitic origin, worshipped anthropomorphic gods, carried out sacrifices, wrote epic poetry and applied geometric and algebraic problem-solving methods to urban construction. They were followed during the next 3,000 years by the Amorites, Akkadians, Babylonians, Hittites, Kassites, Mitannis and Phoenicians – who had a profound influence on succeeding cultures.

In India, during the 3rd millennium BC, an urban civilization – centred on geometrically designed cities with underground sewers – was established, probably by the ancestors of the Dravidians (e.g. Tamils, Kanares).

In China, the Chou Dynasty (*c.* 1122–*c.* 221 BC) – founded by a former subject tribe of unknown, although probably Mongoloid, origin – exercised only token control over a number of semi-autonomous rival tribes or states; and Mongolia, Tibet and eastern Siberia were largely controlled by Turko-Mongol tribes. During this period most of Central Asia, the Middle East and North Africa was inhabited by mainly Indo-European tribal peoples – e.g. Scythians (north of the Black Sea), Lydians (Anatolia) and Bactrians (Afghanistan).

The Silk Route Common name for the overland trade route, connecting China to Europe, that crossed the ancient territories of Turkestan, Ariana, Bactria, Persia and Anatolia on its westward journey to the Maghrib and Thrace, with subsidiary routes branching off into India, Arabia and Europe. The origins of the Silk Route are unknown, but a combination of archaeological evidence and historical records point to its existence during the latter half of the 1st millennium BC, and it is quite possible that trade links between east and west were established at a much earlier date. Excavations, between 1900 and 1915, by the Hungarian-born archaeologist, Sir Aurel Stein, in the Takla Makan Desert and Tarim Basin (East Turkestan) uncovered physical evidence of trade links with Mesopotamia. The discovery of jade cylinder-seals in archaeological sites in ancient Babylonia also supports the existence of a trade route because East Turkestan (especially the Altai Mountains which literally mean 'Mountains of Gold') are the nearest source of jade to the Middle East. Further confirmation is found in the records of Marco Polo (the Venetian explorer who traversed the Silk Route, in the late 13th century, and served as an adviser at the Court of Kubla Khan, in China) and other historical documents.

The great conquests and migrations that swept across Asia in both directions during the last 2,000 years – as well as the numerous smaller incursions – have also generally followed the established and reasonably familiar territory of the Silk Route, rather than fighting their way across thousands of miles of unknown terrain, dispersing tribal weaving traditions. The influence of the Silk Route waned rapidly after the Portuguese navigator and explorer, Vasco da Gama (*c.* 1460–*c.* 1524), discovered an eastern sea-route from Europe to India, via the Cape of Good Hope, in *c.* 1487.

Aryan migrations Began during the 2nd millennium BC, when successive waves of Indo-European tribesmen migrated from the Eurasian Steppes to the Indus and Nile valleys. The latter founded the Hyksos Empire in Egypt and Syria (*c.* 1720–1520 BC), but most settled in northern India, dominating the existing culture and eventually inter-marrying with the indigenous Dravidians. They belonged to several independent tribes or clans and their ensuing battles for supremacy – as well as their religious beliefs – are the inspiration for the Rig-Vedas (the earliest Hindu scriptures); their language is also the basis for all the Indo-European languages.

Hun invasions Nomadic Mongol (or Turko-Mongol) tribesmen who raided China (across the Great Wall) during the 2nd century BC; and in the 5th century, under the leadership of Atilla, swept through Central Asia and the Caucasus, attacked the Byzantine Empire, invaded Gaul (France) and threatened to march into Rome. After Atilla's death, in *c.* 453, the empire collapsed, leaving its legacy of ethnic Huns in Hungary and other parts of the invasion route. The name 'Hun' (or Hungarian) is believed to stem from the Turkic word 'on ogur' (meaning ten arrows) and is possibly the origin of the English word 'ogre'.

The Persian Empire Founded by Cyrus (Kouresh) the Great, in 559 BC, who – after uniting the Medes and the Persians – conquered much of Asia Minor and overthrew the Babylonian Empire. His grandson Darius (*c.* 522–486) consolidated and extended the empire northwards into Central Asia and eastwards as far as the Indus valley.

Alexander the Great Inherited the Macedonian throne, in 336 BC, and, within thirteen years, transformed a small Hellenistic kingdom into an empire that extended through Egypt, Babylonia and Persia, and northern India. It was divided after his death, in 323 BC, into the Macedonian (Greek), Ptolemaic (Egyptian) and Seleucid (Persian) Empires.

The Parthian Empire (*c.* 250 BC–AD 229) Founded in Persia by native Parthians and immigrant Scythian tribes, who overthrew the Seleucid Empire.

The Roman Empire (*c.* 238 BC–AD 500) At its territorial peak (2nd century AD) it extended from western Europe into North Africa, Palestine, Turkey, western Mesopotamia, and the Caucasus. It was divided, for administrative convenience, by the Emperor Dioclecian (r.*c.* 284–305) into western and eastern sections, which, after his abdication, devolved into the Holy Roman and Byzantine Empires.

The Sassanian Empire (*c.* 229–651) Resulted from an uprising by a powerful Persian family against the Parthians, and, despite constant threats to its borders, re-established Persia as a major political and cultural force in the region.

The Byzantine Empire (*c.* 330–1453) The exact date when the eastern Roman Empire changed into the Byzantine Empire is usually taken from the founding of Constantinople (*c.* 330), on the site of ancient Byzantium, by the first Christian Emperor, Constantine. It lasted, in some form, for over 1,000 years until Constantinople was captured, in 1453, by the Ottoman Turks, leaving a profound religious, cultural and artistic legacy that has shaped the evolution of Russia, the Balkans, and much of eastern Europe. It also acted as a Christian buffer against the spread of Islam.

White Huns (or Ephthalites) Eastern tribesmen, believed to be related to the Huns, who raided Persia, Afghanistan and northern India, during the 5th and 6th centuries.

The Caliphates and the Arab Empire (*c.* 632–*c.* 1492) Spread Islam and Arab culture and settlement throughout the Middle East, the Caucasus, North Africa and parts of southern and eastern Europe. It can be traced to the election of Mohammed's successor that resulted in Abu Bakr (*c.* 573–*c.* 634) being installed as the new Islamic spiritual and political leader (or Caliph) in Mohammed's stronghold of Medina (Saudi Arabia). The next thirty years saw the Four Great Caliphs (Abu Bakr, Umar, Uthman and Ali) extend both Caliphate rule (based on locally elected Caliphs) and the influence of Islam into Syria, Mesopotamia, Persia and Egypt. However, the rise to power of Mu'awiyah, in 661, heralded a change to more centralized control – with each region governed through a general, a judge and a vizier (administrator) – and, after moving his capital from Medina to Damascus, he made the position of Caliph hereditary, rather than elective, thus paving the way for family dynastic rule.

Mu'awiyah's own family, the Umayyids, ruled the centralized Caliphate territories until

747, when a rebellion by the Abbasid family led to the foundation of their own independent (Abbasid) Caliphate in the newly built city in Baghdad, Syria. A succession of similar provincial rebellions followed and by the mid-10th century, the central authority of the original Medina Caliphate had been replaced by a loose confederation of independent states (or family empires), unified by Islam and their adherence to Arab culture. During the succeeding centuries, Arab political, cultural, artistic and religious influence spread rapidly throughout North Africa, the Middle East, western Asia and southern Europe, bringing with it remarkable advancements in art, literature, science, mathematics and astronomy, as well as converting most of its subject people to Islam. However, from the 11th century, a combination of Mongol, Seljuk and Ottoman invasions from the east, coupled with an ongoing conflict with the Crusaders in the west, gradually eroded Arab territory and influence, which effectively ended in the 15th century when their eastern territories became part of the Ottoman Empire and the Moors were expelled from Spain.

The Seljuk Turk Empire (c. 1055–c. 1258) Clan or sub-tribe of the Oghuz (or Ghuzz) branch of Turkic tribesmen – named after their former leader (Seljuk), who conquered Baghdad, in 1055, and swept through Persia, Iraq and most of Asia Minor. During the 12th century, their empire split into several independent states – the most influential of which were the Kurdish Ayyubid Dynasty, founded by Saladin (Sala-ud-din) in Egypt and Syria, and the later Mameluke Empire, which was established, in Egypt, by former Seljuk soldiers and mercenaries. The Seljuk were Muslim converts who consolidated the influence of Islam, settled in large numbers in their conquered territories (especially Turkey and the Caucasus) and introduced their weaving skills to the region.

Genghis Khan and the Mongol Empire (c. 1279–c. 1368) Timujin (c. 1162–c. 1227) united the warring Mongol tribes in c. 1206 and was given the title Genghis Khan (Great Leader). Within a few years, he had assembled the most efficient fighting force (based around highly mobile cavalry) since the Roman Empire and, by c. 1220, having already subjugated much of China, the Golden Horde (as his army became known) swept westwards through northern India, Persia and most of Central Asia. The Mongol conquest was continued after his death by his son, Chagatai – who extended Mongol rule over an area that stretched from China to the Danube, and from the Siberian steppes to the Arabian Sea – and was later consolidated by his two grandsons. Kubla Khan who founded the Yuan (or Mongol) dynasty in China (c. 1279–1368) and Hulagu who ruled over the western sector. Hulagu's followers converted to Islam and assimilated into the host cultures, which quickly reverted to their former individual states.

The Ottoman Empire (c. 1290–c. 1923) Clan or sub-tribe of the Oghuz (or Ghuzz) branch of Turkic tribesmen named after their leader Osman or Uthman (r. c. 1290–c. 1326) who founded an empire that stretched from the Zagros Mountains (in western Iran) through Turkey, the southern Caucasus, most of the Balkans, parts of south-east Europe, as far as Hungary, to Palestine and North Africa. The Ottomans were Muslim converts and their empire was governed in accordance with Islamic law. Non-Muslims were allowed to practise their religions, but were segregated, banned from carrying arms, required to pay extra taxes and denied the privileges of full citizenship; there was also an annual levy of Christian youths who were forcibly converted to Islam and conscripted into the army. The Ottoman Empire reached its political, territorial, cultural and artistic zenith during the 16th century under Suileman the Magnificent (c. 1520–c. 1566), who ruled from Constantinople. He relaxed religious discrimination by employing highly skilled Albanian, Italian, Greek and other Christian slaves in government positions, as well as absorbing European ideas and inventions. However, subsequent rulers rejected anything western and employed only Islamic Turks in positions of authority. The Ottoman Empire formally ceased to exist in 1923, shortly after the massacre and forcible expulsion of millions of non-Muslims (mainly Armenians) and its territory devolved into modern Turkey. However, the enforced expulsions of indigenous peoples (e.g. Armenians, Kurds), coupled with the mass settlement of ethnic Turks throughout the conquered territories, dramatically altered the dispersal of tribal weaving groups.

Tamerlane and the Turko-Mongol Empire (c. 1336–c. 1405) Genghis Khan's Mongol dominance was revived briefly during the late 14th century by one of Genghis Khan's descendants, Timur Lenk, or Timur-the-Lame (anglicized to Tamerlane), who united Mongol and Turkic tribesmen and established an empire that stretched from his capital, Samarkand (in Uzbekistan), through Persia, Iraq, Syria and Egypt. He then turned eastwards towards China, but, he died on route, which effectively ended four centuries of Mongol influence throughout Asia and parts of eastern Europe. Many descendants of his followers, who settled in the conquered territories (especially Central Asia) now form a number of tribal weaving groups.

The Persian Safavid Dynasty (*c.* 1502–*c.* 1736) Founded by Ismail (r. *c.* 1500–24) and named after his descendant Safi-al-Din. The dynasty made Shi'ite the state religion – bringing Persia into conflict with the Sunni Muslim Ottoman Empire – and advanced art and culture to the point where Persia acquired its reputation as the spiritual home of the oriental carpet. Shah Abbas (*c.* 1587–*c.* 1629), in particular, was responsible for the forced relocation of several tribal groups, as well as forming others into multi-ethnic tribal confederacies.

The Moghul Empire (*c.* 1526–*c.* 1857) Derives its name from a corruption of Mongol and was founded by Babur (*c.* 1483–1530), the Mongol King of Afghanistan, who is believed to have been a descendant of Tamerlane. Much of northern India had been under Turkic Muslim control since the 12th century, and Babur extended Islamic influence throughout Afghanistan, Pakistan and northern and central India. Hindu art and architecture was destroyed and the subject Hindus were forced to convert to Islam. This led to conflict between Hindus and Muslims and inspired the Hindu reformer, Nanak (*c.* 1469–*c.* 1538), to advocate Sikhism as a bridge between the two religions. Subsequent Moghul rulers incorporated Persian (and Arabic) arts, crafts and architecture (including weaving) into traditional Indian artistic expression, leading to the fusion of styles known as the 'golden age' of Indian art. The arrival of the British, in the 18th century, heralded the decline of Moghul rule.

The Romanov Russian Empire (*c.* 1613–1917) Ivan the Great (*c.* 1440–*c.* 1505) rebelled against Tartar domination, in 1440, and claimed the title of Tsar, but the first person to be officially crowned as the Tsar of all the Russias, in 1544, was Ivan the Terrible (*c.* 1530–84). He conquered the Tartars' capital, Kazan, in 1552 and established an Asian Russian Empire that was consolidated and expanded until the last of the Romanovs – Nicholas II (1868–1918) abdicated, in 1917, leaving most of Central Asia, Siberia and the Caucasus under Russian control.

The Persian Qajar Dynasty (*c.* 1794–*c.* 1906) Usually traced to Nadir Kuli (r. *c.* 1736–*c.* 1747), who reclaimed Persian territory from Ottoman and Afghan rule and opened the way for a leading Persian family, the Qajars, to establish a native dynasty. The Qajars largely maintained Persia's independence and territorial integrity and also instigated tribal relocations and the formation of tribal confederacies. Some dealers consider the rugs produced during this era to be the last examples still to contain the true spirit of Persian weaving.

The Persian Pahlavi Dynasty (*c.* 1924–*c.* 1979) Founded – after a brief period of rule by civil assembly – by Reza Shah Pahlavi who took his name from an ancient Persian language and attempted both to modernize the country (renaming it Iran in 1936) and also to restore the 'golden age' of Persian culture (achieved under the Safavids). He sponsored the production of exceptionally sophisticated workshop rugs, but was largely unsympathetic to tribal weaving and instigated various programmes aimed at converting them to a settled lifestyle.

Stalin and the Soviet Union In 1927 – after the death of Lenin and the ideological defeat of Trotsky – power in the new Soviet Union effectively devolved to Joseph Vissarionovich Dzugashvili (*c.* 1879–1953), the son of a Georgian shoemaker, who adopted the name Stalin (which means steel in Russian) and set out to establish himself as the absolute ruler of a new, territorially expanded Soviet Empire. He pursued a series of 'five-year plans', aimed at 'collectivizing' industry and agriculture, and ruthlessly eliminated any opposition (real or imagined), culminating in the 'Great Purges', between 1934 and 1939, in which over ten million people were either executed or sent to labour camps. He also pursued a policy of enforced resettlement to stifle the possibility of insurrection by the non-communist ethnic and tribal peoples under Soviet control. He established several quasi-independent republics (1920–36) in Central Asia and the Caucasus as homelands for the dominant ethnic group (e.g. Kazakhstan for the Kazakhs) and then relocated large concentrations of other (often traditionally hostile) ethnic groups in the same region (e.g. Christian Armenians in the Nagorny Karabagh region of Islamic

Azerbaijan). Further mass resettlements – mainly of Russians and Ukrainians in different parts of Central Asia were instigated, in the 1950s and 1960s, by Nikita Khrushchev (*c.* 1894–1971), as part of a policy to bring virgin agricultural land into use.

The Americas

Amerindian migrations from Asia It is generally accepted that the earliest inhabitants of the Americas were east Asian (Mongoloid) migrants, who first traversed the former land bridge between Siberia and Alaska (60,000–35,000 BC), and either populated an uninhabited continent, or were assimilated to varying degrees into an existing population about whom nothing is known. It is also highly probable that the migrations continued by sea after the land bridge disappeared, and that some Amerindian people (especially in the north) are relatively recent arrivals. The strong physical resemblance, coupled with several underlying cultural similarities, between the peoples living on both sides of the Bering Sea (which generally becomes less pronounced in the tribes living further south) support this theory. The wide variety of distinctive physical subtypes, lifestyles, cultures, spiritual beliefs and languages (estimated at 1,000 to 2,000) found throughout the continent are usually explained as adaptation to widely diverse environments, rather than a difference in ethnic origins. However, it is also possible that some of the physical, cultural and linguistic differences, present in the original bands of tribal migrants, have been retained. The total Amerindian population prior to European colonization is disputed, but a figure of around 50 million is accepted by most historians.

Amerindian civilizations Subsistence farming appears to have begun *c.* 7000 BC, but, as far as we know, Amerindian societies did not start to build cities until the 1st millennium BC, bronze did not appear until the 11th or 12th centuries AD, and iron was never developed. Amerindian societies did not invent the wheel, discover how to build arches, or develop their pictographic system of writing into phonetic written languages. However, some Amerindian cultures were far in advance of Old World cultures in many areas of mathematics, astronomy and calendars. For example, Mayan calendars were much more sophisticated and accurate than Greek or Roman equivalents, and they evolved the concept of negative numbers centuries before they were discovered by European mathematicians.

Early external contacts Evidence exists to suggest that a number of different societies had contacts with the Americas long before the official discovery of the Caribbean Islands, in 1492, by Christopher Columbus and, the mainland, in 1497, by Amerigo Vespucci (after whom the continent takes its name). We know that the Scandinavians, or Norsemen, colonized Greenland during the 10th to 14th centuries, and, according to Norse sagas, the actual discover of the Americas was Bjarni Herjulfsson, who (around the turn of the 10th century) accidentally landed on the New England coast (in the north-eastern USA) after his ship was caught in dense fog and heavy currents. On his return to Greenland he reported his discovery to Leif Ericsson, who immediately bought Herjulfsson's ship and embarked on a voyage of exploration of the north-east coast, from Rhode Island in the USA to Newfoundland in Canada. Further Norse explorations followed, *c.* 1002, under the leadership of Leif's brother, Thorwald and, in *c.* 1007, an attempt at colonization was repelled by the Skraelingrs (the Norse name for the natives). Evidence of Norse influence is found in Amerindian myths – e.g. Loki, or Lox, the mischievous spirit of Algonquin myth has the same basic function as the Norse god of the same name – and allusions to early contacts with Polynesians and other non-Amerindian people can be found in the myths and legends of several Central and South American Amerindian cultures.

European conquest of Central America Usually accredited to Hernado Cortes (*c.* 1485–1547), the Spanish conquistador, who entered Mexico, in *c.* 1518, with a contingent of around 500 to 600 men, and was at first received as a god by the Aztec Emperor Montezuma II before being expelled from the capital, Tenochtitlán (now Mexico City). He returned in *c.* 1519 and overthrew the Aztec Empire and rapidly extended Spanish dominance throughout most of Central America where it is still the major European influence.

European conquest of South America Normally attributed to Francisco Pizarro (*c.* 1475–1541), the Spanish conquistador, who, after exploring the north-west coast, moved eastwards into Peru, and, in 1531, with a contingent of less than 180 men, seized and murdered the Inca King, Atahualpa, and overthrew the Inca Empire. He founded the city of Lima, in 1535, which acted as the major administrative centre for subsequent Spanish dominance of South America where it is still the main European influence except in Brazil (which was colonized by the Portuguese).

European conquest of North America Can be traced to a number of perhaps equally valid events from Christopher Columbus's sighting of the Bahamas (*c.* 1492) to the landing of the Plymouth Pilgrims at Cape Cod (*c.* 1620). However, regardless of the exact starting point, the European conquest and colonization of North America was essentially different to that of the Spanish and Portuguese in the South. In New Mexico, California and Texas, the Spanish followed their familiar pattern of sending in soldiers and priests to conquer and convert before establishing colonies, but the British, French and, to a lesser extent, the Dutch, were initially more interested in trade and exploiting the continent's natural resources, than colonization or saving souls. It was only later that the New World was seen as a suitable place for depositing troublesome religious minorities (e.g. the Plymouth Brethren, Quakers, Amish), and then as a 'land of opportunity'. Over the next two hundred years millions of Europeans emigrated to North America in the hope of either founding their own religious communities or achieving a degree of material success that was denied to them at home, displacing the native Amerindians by a combination of military conquest and an enforced 'reservation' policy, which resulted in thousands being killed or dying of starvation.

Religious influences

Religious and spiritual beliefs vary to some degree throughout most weaving regions. However, as a general rule, Islam dominates Central Asia, the Middle East and North Africa, China, Mongolia and Tibet are predominantly Buddhist (with Taoist or Confucian elements) and the major religious influence in Central and South America is Catholicism, and in the USA and Canada a mixture of Catholicism and Protestantism. However, each of these orthodox religions has been modified, to varying degrees, either by earlier religious doctrines or, more commonly, by a variety of traditional animistic, totemic or shamanistic beliefs and customs. These diverse religious influences are clearly discernible in the motifs, symbols and compositional formats of tribal rugs.

Islam

Dominant religion throughout Central Asia, the Middle East, North Africa and the Caucasus (except Armenia). It was founded by Mohammed, a member of the Qureysh (Arabic) tribe, who was born in Mecca (*c.* 570) and died in Medina (*c.* 632) and, like all Meccans, traced his lineage through Ishmael to the prophet Abraham. He spent much of his adult life employed as a merchant (by a wealthy widow, Khadijah, whom he later married) before joining a group of religious agnostics (the Hanafa) who challenged the idolatry that dominated Arab culture and sought to return to the 'One God' doctrine of the prophet Abraham. Mohammed was around forty when – during his meditations, for Ramadan (the month of heat), in a cave near Mecca – he began to receive revelations from God.

The Koran The sacred book of Islam. It literally means 'the reading' and is composed of God's (Allah's) revelations to Mohammed while he was in a religious trance. It is divided into Surahs (or chapters), each of which conveys specific revelations (e.g. the Prostration, revealed at Mecca) that Muslims believe to be the literal words of God. The Koran states the existence of One God (Allah), and focuses on everyday behaviour and morality, making clear divisions between right and wrong.

The Hadith Sayings attributed to Mohammed when he was not in a trance, and, although influential, are open to different interpretations.

Islamic worship Based on five main duties: everyone, at least once in their life, must say with absolute conviction that 'There is no God but Allah and Mohammed is His Prophet'; pray, after ritually washing, facing in the direction of Mecca, five times a day – on rising, at noon, in mid-afternoon, after sunset and before retiring for the night; give alms generously and care for the sick and the poor; keep the fast of Ramadan (health permitting) by refraining from eating, drinking and indulging in worldly pleasures, between sunrise and sunset; make, if possible, the pilgrimage to Mecca.

Followers of Islam Usually called Muslims or Moslems, they consider Mohammed to be the last in a line of prophets from Abraham to Christ; often referring to him as the Prophet.

Sunnite (or Sunni) Muslims Known as 'Orthodox' Muslims, they are the largest and most widely dispersed Islamic sect, they dominate most of North Africa, Turkey, Afghanistan, Pakistan, Central Asia and the Caucasus.

Shi'ite (or Shia) Muslims Breakaway sect formed shortly Mohammed's death – after a dispute over his successor – who are dominant in Iran and parts of the Middle East.

Sufi Muslims Mystical sect, closely associated with the Dervishes (monks committed to a life of poverty, austerity and spiritual enlightenment). They are more pantheistic than other Islamic sects, and Sufi artists, writers and thinkers have been responsible for some of the most profound and influential Islamic output.

The spread of Islam Begun by Arabs in the 7th century, and continued, between the 11th and 15th centuries, by 'convert' Turkic and Turko-Mongol tribesmen. (*See* The Caliphates, The Seljuk Turk Empire, Genghis Khan and the Mongol Empire, Tamerlane and the Turko-Mongol Empire and The Ottoman Empire)

Christianity

The main religious influence in the Americas, where it has sometimes fused with native beliefs to produce a diversity of, usually short-lived, 'Christianized' pagan cults (e.g. the revived Sun Dance Cult) as well as more orthodox Christian sects that have been modified by native traditions (e.g. Indian Shaker Church). It is much less influential than Islam in Asia and North Africa, but it is the major religion in Armenia and pockets of Christianity still exist in Iran, Syria and other parts of the Middle East.

The Catholic Church Derives its name from the Greek word for 'universal', and is also known as the Roman Church because, in the 4th century, it became the official religion of the Roman Empire and its head, who is believed to draw his spiritual authority directly from Christ, via an unbroken lineage to the Apostle Peter, is still known as the Bishop of Rome or Pope (father). Catholicism combines mysticism and spirituality with secular and political authority, and has been adept at incorporating popular, often pagan, elements into its ceremonies, festivals and hierarchy of saints. It is the largest Christian Church in western Europe, and was spread throughout the Americas (especially Central and South America) by European colonization.

The Byzantine Church Challenged both Papal authority and a number of Catholic doctrines (e.g. the Trinity, Christology, Mariology and Holy Icons), as early as the 5th century, and, in *c.* AD 1054, finally severed its links with the See of Rome, establishing an Eastern Orthodox (or Byzantine) Church that incorporated the Patriarchates of Constantinople, Antioch, Alexandria and Jerusalem, as well as the national Churches of Greece, Russia, Romania, Bulgaria and Yugoslavia.

The Armenian (and Coptic) Churches Rejected the authority and some of the orthodoxy of the Byzantine Church – especially its doctrine on the divine and human dichotomy of Christ – and are still viewed as heretical sects by the Eastern Orthodox Church.

Nestorian Christianity Based on the doctrine of Nestorius, the 5th-century Patriarch of Constantinople, who argued that Mary was only the mother of the human, not the divine, aspect of Christ, which resulted in his excommunication and condemnation as a heretic by St Cyril (Patriarch of Alexandria), and the slaughter of many of his followers. However, a number survived in Syria and Iran or fled to India, Afghanistan and China, where they established Nestorian communities.

The Protestant Churches Collective term for several independent Churches that can trace their origins – either directly or indirectly – to the protestations in 1529 by German princes against the authority of the Roman Church, and the subsequent theological reforms espoused by Martin Luther, John Calvin, Huldreich Zwingli and other theologians. Individual Churches vary considerably in size, influence and approach to worship but most stress the authority of the Bible, salvation through actions and direct communion (through Christ) with God. Several early Churches (e.g. Methodists) were established by European immigrants in the Americas and 'new' ones (e.g. Shakers and Pentecostals) have subsequently evolved.

Other religious and spiritual influences

Buddhism Based on the teachings of Siddhartha Gautama – believed to be an Indian prince, living during the 5th or 6th centuries BC – which consist of the 'Four Noble Truths': existence is unhappiness; unhappiness is caused by selfish desires and cravings; desire can be destroyed; the way to destroy desire is to follow the 'Eight-fold Path' of 'right' thinking, speaking, conduct, occupation, effort, awareness, contemplation and meditation that leads to an 'enlightened state' (or Buddha nature); thereby achieving release (Nirvana) from the 'cycle of lives' (reincarnation). Buddhism is the dominant influence in China (where it has been modified by Taoism and Confucianism) and Mongolia and Tibet (where elements of earlier Shamanistic and Animistic beliefs have been incorporated).

Zoroastrianism Early religion – based on the teaching of Zarathustra or Zoroaster, who is believed to have lived during the 1st or 2nd millennium BC that has had a profound effect on the Judaic, Christian and Islamic doctrines on heaven and hell, the resurrection of the dead, the final judgment, and the concept of a 'saviour' or 'messiah'. It also influenced Gnosticism, Manicheism, Hinduism and Buddhism. The struggle between good and evil was anthropomorphized into the figures of Ahura Mazda (spirit of light) – who was represented by the flame – and Angra Mainyu or Ahriman (spirit of darkness). The dead were hung in the Daxma (or Tower of Silence) and left to be devoured by carrion-eaters so as not to defile the sacred elements of fire, earth, air and water. There was also an emphasis on the immortality of the soul and the necessity of supporting, by actions as well as words, the forces of good. Zoroastrianism emerged in Persia, some time before the 6th century BC, and remained the major religion in the region until the arrival of Islam after which most Zoroastrians either became Muslims or fled the country – mainly to India, where they are known as Parsees. Zoroastrian teachings also took root in Europe where Pope Innocent III condemned the Cathars (or Albigenses) as 'Zoroastrian heretics', leading to their total extermination in what was euphemistically known as the 'Albigensian Crusade' (1208–29).

Mithraism Focused on Mithras, a Hindu deity, who first appeared as a 'mediator' (or Lord of Contracts) and later as a 'saviour' of men, coming to Earth, via a miraculous birth, dying and then rising from the dead. It also recognized 25 December as the date of Mithra's birth; celebrated Easter; and set aside Sunday as a holy day. Mithraism flourished throughout the Roman Empire, between the 5th and 6th centuries, as a mystery cult that excluded women and involved the progression of its devotees through seven grades of initiation – Corvus (Raven), Nymphus (Bride), Miles (Soldier), Leo (Lion), Persis (Persian), Heliodromus (Runner of the Sun), and Pater (Father) – each of which was under the protection of the astrological influence of different planets. Ceremonies involved the sacrifice of a sacred Bull (whose blood brought life to the world) and normally took place in caves or temples built to resemble caves – believed to symbolize the 'Cosmic Cavern' or 'Primordial Womb'. Mithraism is echoed in a number of Western secret societies (e.g. Masons).

Animatism Belief that everything, whether animate or inanimate, possesses a unique spirit, personality or lifeforce, which, if harnessed correctly, can be transferred to an individual or tribe (e.g. because lions are the symbols and custodians of strength, anyone killing or wearing any part of a lion will automatically become strong). These 'essences' underpin the belief systems of many tribal cultures. They are known as 'manitou' by some North Amerindian tribes and 'soul substance' in China.

Animism Similar to animatism, but is based on the belief that objects, although not possessing a lifeforce of their own, can house gods, spiritual being or souls of the dead whose powers can then be harnessed and directed.

Shamanism Collective term for a belief system that employs a 'holy man' (called a Shaman by the Tungus tribesmen of Siberia) as a conduit between the physical and the spirit worlds – mediating with ancestral ghosts, environment spirits on behalf of an individual or the tribe. Shamanism underpins the belief systems of most Amerindian, Mongol, Turko-Mongol and Siberian tribal peoples.

Totemism Algonquin (Amerindian) word for the belief that specific objects or animals can act as tribal (or individual) guardians, teachers and kindred spirits. Some tribes take their name from the totem animal (e.g. Aztec means 'Crane People'), or, more commonly, employ it as a tribal emblem on their dress, weapons, standards, temples and homes, or on specific totem objects (e.g. totem poles). It also usually features prominently in their arts and crafts, including rugs. Totemism underpins the symbolism of most mainstream religious motifs (e.g. cross, Christianity), national emblems (e.g. Bald Eagle, USA), and heraldic coat-of-arms (e.g. Bear and Staff), but finds its most overt expression in Amerindian and other predominantly tribal cultures, where, in addition to its spiritual significance, it also often provides a safeguard against interbreeding by dividing the tribe into specific totem clans (e.g. Bear, Wolf, Hawk), with strict taboos against marrying into one's own clan.

1. **PESHAWAR (OR REFUGEE) BELOUCH** rug: animal design; settled Belouch weavers,
Pakistan/*Afghanistan*/*Iran*, contemporary

2. **GEBBEH** rug: animal design; nomadic/semi-nomadic/settled Luri/*Qashga'i*/*Khamseh* weavers, Iran, contemporary

3. **SHAHSAVAN OF MOGAN** rug: variant tree-of-life design; nomadic/semi-nomadic Shahsavan
weavers, Iran/*Azerbaijan*, c. 1950

4. **AZROU** flatweave: banded design with tassel inserts; semi-nomadic/settled (Middle Atlas)
Berber weavers, Morocco, contemporary

5. **BOUJAAD** rug: banded design; semi-nomadic/settled (Middle/High Atlas) Berber weavers, Morocco, contemporary

6. **SHIRKANI (HERAT) BELOUCH** rug: pictorial design; semi-nomadic Belouch/Alizai Pashtun
weavers, Afghanistan, contemporary

7. **HERAT BELOUCH** rug: Afghan War design; nomadic/semi-nomadic/settled Belouch/*Aimaq* weavers, Afghanistan, contemporary

8. **QASHGA'I** rug: amulet/medallion design; nomadic/semi-nomadic/settled Qashga'i weavers, Iran, contemporary

9. **AFSHAR** rug: amulet/medallion (animal-skin) design; nomadic/semi-nomadic/settled Afshar weavers, Iran, contemporary

10. **KHAMSEH** rug: pole-medallion design; nomadic/semi-nomadic Khamseh weavers, Iran, 1875–1900

11. **QASHGA'I** rug: amulet/medallion, nomadic/semi-nomadic Qashga'i weavers, Iran, 1875–1900

12. **HAMADAN** rug: *herati* medallion-and-corner design; semi-nomadic/settled Kurdish (or possibly Shahsavan) weavers, Iran, *c.* 1950

13. **AFSHAR BIDJAR** rug: floral medallion-and-corner design; semi-nomadic/settled Afshar weavers, Iran, *c.* 1930

14. **DAGHESTAN** rug: prayer-rug design; nomadic/semi-nomadic/settled Chechen weavers, Daghestan ASSR, late 19th century

15. **YOMUT** *asmalyk*: lattice design; nomadic/semi-nomadic Yomut Turkoman weavers, Turkmenistan, *c.* 1850

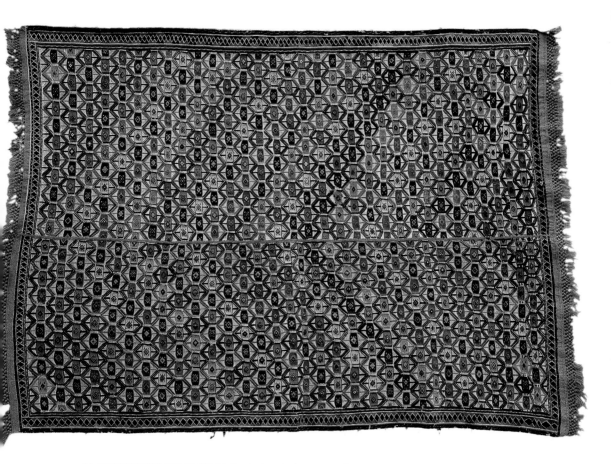

16. **SHAHSAVAN OF MOGAN** *jajim*: lattice design; nomadic/semi-nomadic Shahsavan weavers, Azerbaijan/*Armenia*/Iran, *c.* 1930

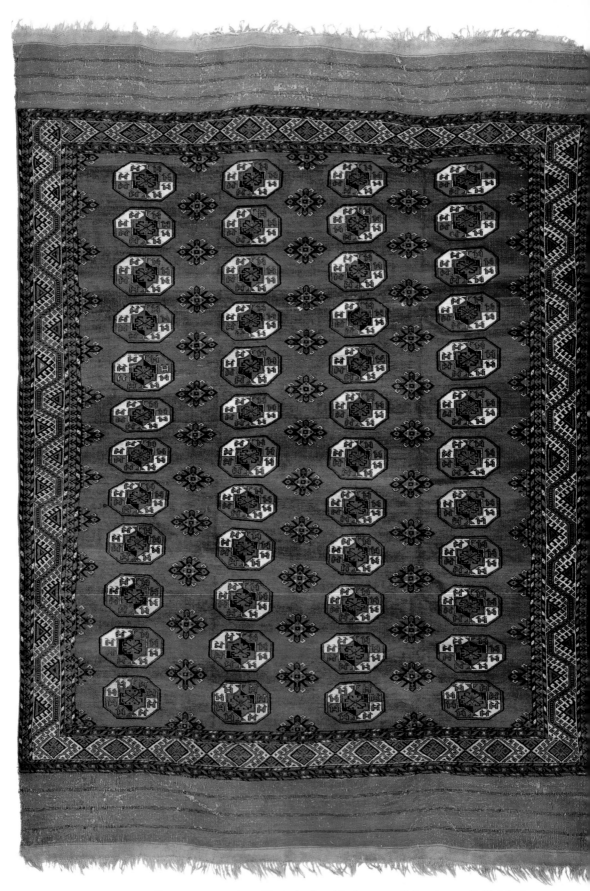

17. **KIZIL AYAK** main carpet: *tauk mushka* (animal) *gul* design; nomadic/semi-nomadic Kizil Ayak (Ersari) Turkoman weavers, Turkmenistan/*Afghanistan*, *c.* 1880

18. **YOMUT** main carpet: *dyrnyk gul* design; nomadic/semi-nomadic Yomut Turkoman weavers,
Turkmenistan/*Iran*/*Afghanistan*, c. 1900

19. **SHAHSAVAN OF MOGAN** *soumak*, *mafrash* panel: repeating hooked-diamond design; nomadic/semi-nomadic Shahsavan weavers, Iran/*Azerbaijan*, early 20th century

20. **VAN** rug: banded design; nomadic/semi-nomadic Kurdish (Herki, Hartushi, Goyan) weavers, Turkey/*Iraq*/*Iran*, contemporary

21. **ADRASKAND BELOUCH** rug: all-over hooked-diamond design; semi-nomadic/settled Alizai and Nurzai (Pashtun) weavers, Afghanistan, contemporary

22. **BORCHALU** runner: *herati* design; semi-nomadic/settled Borchalu (Mongol) weavers, Iran, contemporary

23. **ARMENIAN** *verneh* flatweave: all-over repeating diamond design; semi-nomadic/settled
Armenian weavers, Armenian Republic, *c.* 1940

24. **DERBEND** rug: amulet/medallion design; Soviet tribal/regional/workshop production, Daghestan/*Azerbaijan/Armenia, c.* 1940

25. **KURDS OF KHORASSAN** rug: *hawz* (water tank) design; nomadic/semi-nomadic/settled Kurdish weavers, Iran, contemporary

26. **KHORASSAN** rug: vase and tree-of-life design; nomadic/semi-nomadic/settled
Kurdish/Belouch weavers, Iran, contemporary

27. **KHOTAN (SINKIANG)** rug: pomegranate design; nomadic/semi-nomadic/settled Turkic/Turko-Mongol weavers, China (East Turkestan), *c.* 1880

28. **LURI** rug: Mazlaghan (lightning) design; nomadic/semi-nomadic/settled Luri weavers, Iran, contemporary

29. **QUCHAN** rug: panelled/repeating serrated diamond design; semi-nomadic/settled Kurdish
weavers, Iran, contemporary

30. **YALAMEH** rug: repeating diamond design; semi-nomadic Yalameh weavers, Iran, contemporary

31. **BAKHTIARI** rug: panelled design; semi-nomadic/settled Luri/Bakhtiari weavers, Iran, contemporary

32. BELOUCH OF BALUCHISTAN bag: striped design; nomadic/semi-nomadic Belouch weavers, Pakistan, contemporary

33. HERAT BELOUCH bag: banded design; nomadic/semi-nomadic Belouch weavers, Afghanistan, *c.* 1950

34. SHAHSAVAN OF MOGAN *mafrash*: repeating design; nomadic/semi-nomadic Shahsavan weavers, Iran/Azerbaijan, late 19th century

35. **NIRIZ** rug: tree-of-life design; settled Afshar weavers, Iran, *c.* 1900

36. **TAIMANI** rug: compartmented pictorial design; nomadic/semi-nomadic Taimani Aimaq
weavers, Afghanistan, contemporary

37. **MESHED BELOUCH** rug: prayer-rug design; nomadic/semi-nomadic/settled Belouch
weavers, Iran, contemporary

38. **KURDS OF KHORASSAN** semi-pile *soufreh*: animal design; nomadic/semi-nomadic weavers, Iran, *c.* 1950

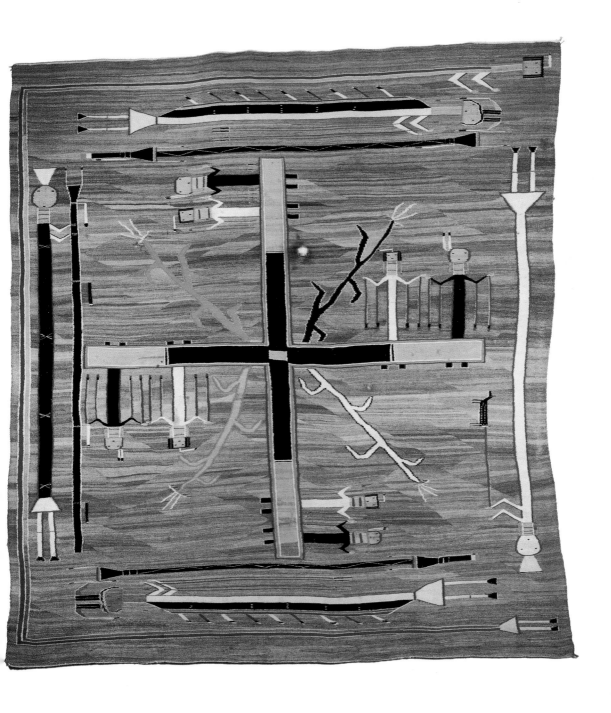

39. **NAVAJO** pictorial flatweave: the Whirling Log sand painting design; settled Navajo weavers, USA, 20th century

40. **AYUCHUCHO** flatweave: the flying man of the Paracas design; Peru, contemporary
41. **CUZCO** flatweave: repeating design; Quechua/Aymara weavers; Peru, c. 1950

42. **ECUADORIAN** pictorial flatweave: mythological figure, Ecuador, contemporary

43. **ECUADORIAN** flatwoven wall-hanging: repeating design; Ecuador, contemporary

44. **NAVAJO** Chief's Blanket: third phase pattern; settled Navajo weavers, USA, late classic period

45. **NAVAJO** flatweave: banded second phase chief's design; settled Navajo weavers, USA, 19th/20th century

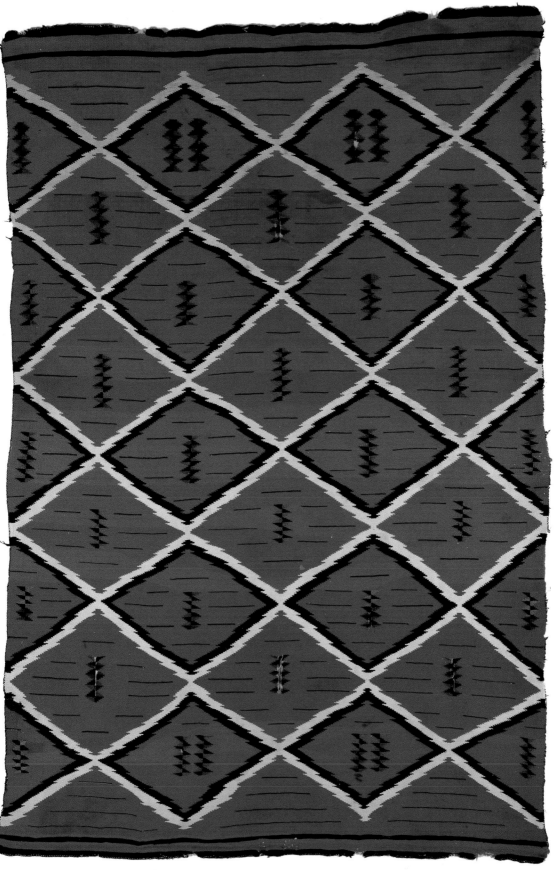

46. **NAVAJO** *serape*: lattice design; settled Navajo weavers, USA, late classic period

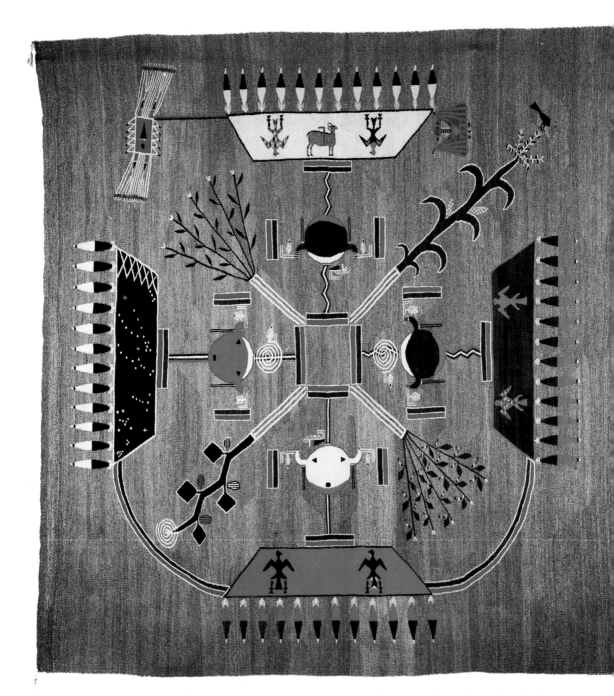

47. **NAVAJO** pictorial flatweave: Bat sand painting design from the *yei-be-chai* (nine-day chant) ceremony, attributed to the wife of Many Goats (Greasewood, Arizona), USA, *c.* 1950

CHAPTER FIVE

Designs

In tribal societies, the prime role of the artist/craftsman is to reproduce the objects and images that reflect the common heritage of the tribe, rather than (as in the west) strive for personal expression. Consequently, the vast majority of tribal rug designs have evolved over the centuries from a gradual fusion of each individual tribe's specific cultural, historical, religious, political, social, artistic and environmental heritage.

Named weavers The west's obsession with personal creativity has resulted in the elevation of a few individual weavers to the status of named artists/craftsmen, whose rugs are often more sought-after and expensive than those produced by anonymous members of the same weaving group. To date this has largely been confined to selected individuals from non-tribal workshop groups (mainly in Iran and Turkey). However, a small number of tribal weavers in the Americas have also been elevated to named status, and it is possible that this practice may eventually extend to selected tribal weavers elsewhere.

Tradition and innovation Coexist to varying degrees in the rugs produced by most weaving groups. The designs of some groups have hardly changed for centuries, whereas others have undergone considerable modification in response to changing social, cultural and environmental conditions. However, the vast majority of weaving groups employ designs that hover somewhere between these two extremes, usually with the emphasis more towards tradition.

Woven histories Clearly discernible in the rugs from some weaving groups, which, over a period of time, include (often subtle) additions, omissions and modifications to their traditional motifs and designs, in response to contemporaneous events; providing a codified history of the tribe. For example, the sudden appearance of Belouch and Aimaq rugs containing tanks and helicopters corresponded to the Soviet invasion of Afghanistan, reminding future generations of the conflict and providing a reference point for the earliest date (1979)

that any item containing these motifs could have possibly been made.

Ethnic, cultural and regional uniformity Exist to varying degrees across groups that have a general connection or association. For example, rugs made by the various Turkoman tribes (e.g. Yomut, Tekke) normally conform to design conventions that are common to Turkoman rugs as a whole. The same is true of the rugs produced by most ethnic tribes and tribal confederations, but is usually less pronounced in the rugs woven by different tribal groups who merely occupy the same region.

Sub-tribal or localized variations Usually stay within the overall design conventions of the general ethnic, cultural or regional weaving group (e.g. Belouch rugs, regardless of their sub-tribal variations, are usually instantly recognizable as such). However, this sub-tribal uniformity is less clear in the rugs produced by some of the larger ethnic tribes (e.g. Kurds).

Weaving techniques and designs Closely related in flatweaves because some designs can only be produced by specific flatweaving techniques. Pile rug designs are dictated solely by the skill of the individual weavers and the fineness of the knotting. (*See* Chapter II)

Identifying tribal rugs

Identification by colour and design Not always possible because several weaving groups produce very similar items. However, there are some clear thematic and stylistic divisions between many weaving groups and, armed with a modicum of knowledge and experience, it should be easy to distinguish between a Belouch and Navajo flatweave, or a Turkoman and Berber pile rug.

The first stage in identification is to eliminate the weaving groups and regions that do not produce items in the same (or similar) designs. For example, *gul* designs are almost exclusively found on Turkoman and other Turko-Mongol rugs from Central Asia, Afghanistan and also north-eastern Iran – thus eliminating Turkey, North Africa, the Americas, the Caucasus and southern and western Iran.

Next compare the specific design and colour scheme to those of a number of possible weaving groups. For example, we know that each Turkoman tribe employs its own distinctive *guls* and therefore arriving at a more precise attribution is a relatively simple matter of comparing the shape and size of the *gul* used in the rug with those employed by each of the specific tribe (e.g. Tekke, Yomut, Ersari).

Similarly, figurative designs are fairly common in Iran, Afghanistan and the Americas, but are rarely found on Turkish or Central Asian rugs. More precise identification is therefore a matter of examining the details of the figure or figures – especially who or what they are – and eliminating the weaving groups who do not use those particular forms. For example, mythological, quasi-human figures are common to Navajo and other Amerindian rugs but more intrinsically human forms are found on items from Asia and North Africa.

Colour is also an important indicator of origin because some weaving groups, who employ very similar designs, use totally different colour schemes. For example, banded designs are found on the rugs produced by a number of different weaving groups in Morocco, Iran, Afghanistan and the Caucasus, but the sombre colour schemes, usually dark reds and blues, employed by the Belouch (in Iran and Afghanistan) are easily distinguished from the brighter, primary shades common to Berber rugs from Morocco.

Angular and curvilinear designs Both are employed in tribal rugs and their predominance is largely determined by the specific design traditions of the individual weaving group. Curvilinear designs are fairly common in pile rugs, although there is usually a degree of angularity in the form of individual motifs. Angular designs generally dominate flatweaves – although curvilinear designs can be produced by *soumak* and other complex flatweaving techniques. (*See* Chapter II)

Figurative and non-figurative designs Both are found in the pile rugs and flatweaves of several weaving groups throughout the rug-producing world. However, figurative motifs are almost impossible to produce using some flatweaving techniques and are therefore extremely rare in items from the regions where these techniques predominate. Also, the different Islamic sects conform to conflicting interpretations of the *Hadith*. Sunnite Muslims – who are dominant in Turkey, North Africa, Afghanistan and Central Asia – generally forbid the depiction of human and animal forms, but Shi'ite Muslims, who form the majority in Iran, interpret the Prophet's words as a condemnation of idolatry – not the mere representation of human or animal forms. However, the presence of Shi'ite minorities in Turkey, North Africa and Afghanistan, as well as Sunnite minorities in Iran, ensures numerous exceptions to this rule. The complex mixture of animistic, shamanistic and Christian beliefs of the Amerindians do not impose any iconoclastic constraints.

The anatomy of a rug

Medallion (A) Any large central motif which acts as the focal point of the design.

Field (B) The main area of the rug.

Spandrels (or corners) (C) The four right-angled areas at the junction between the field and the inner border, which often contain distinctive design elements.

Borders (D) Clearly defined area/s around the inner perimeter of the rug, which can be single or multiple, plain or decorated.

Ground Sometimes used instead of a field, but more generally the term for the underlying, or background, colour employed in any part of the design (e.g. a blue ground border).

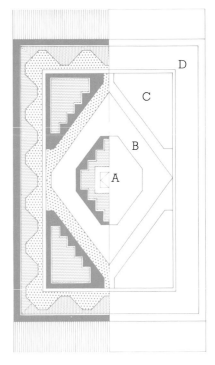

The anatomy of a rug

Motif Any form, or cohesive group of forms (e.g. a cluster of leaves), used in the design.

Open field An undecorated field or one with only a few, widely spaced motifs.

Variegated field Different-coloured grounds covered by the same repeating motif or all-over design.

Palette (or dyer's palette) Term for the overall tonality (e.g. a pastel palette).

Patina The sheen, or surface gloss, of the rug (e.g. a silky or dull patina).

All-over designs Cover the entire field, without leaving undecorated areas.

Repeating designs Employ a single motif (or group of motifs), which is repeated throughout the field.

Basic design formats

A number of basic compositions are commonly used throughout the entire weaving region and act as universal vehicles for a variety of different, localized expressions, rather than possessing a specific symbolic or cultural significance.

Banded designs (pls 4, 20, 44) Based on horizontal bands of motifs, or monochrome strips, running across the entire breadth of the rug, which may be broad or narrow, and either the same size throughout the rug or of alternating or varying dimensions. They are especially common in flatweaves – although they are sometimes found on pile rugs – and often feature on items produced using more than one weaving technique (e.g. alternating bands of kilim and pile). They are employed by several weaving groups, but are most closely associated with Berber, Kurdish, Shahsavan, Uzbek, Belouch, Aimaq and Caucasian (especially Shirvan and Kuba) flatweaves and semi-pile rugs.

Striped designs (pl 32) Similar to banded designs, except that the bands run vertically along the length of the rug, rather than from side to side. They are much less common and are found mainly on *jajims* produced by Qashga'i, Khamseh, Luri and Bakhtiari weavers from Iran, and on *ghudjeris* made by various Turkoman and Turko-Mongol tribes of Central Asia and Afghanistan. They sometimes feature on pile rugs from these same Iranian (and several Traditional Caucasian) weaving groups.

Diagonal striped designs Based on stripes (or bands) that run diagonally from left to right (or vice versa) across the entire field of the rug.

They vary in size – although they are usually fairly narrow – and may be undecorated or contain a variety of infill motifs. Diagonal designs can only be satisfactorily produced on pile rugs and kilims woven in the slitweave. They are most often found on Qashga'i, Luri, Khamseh, Gianja, a few other Iranian and Traditional Caucasian rugs.

Pictorial designs (pls 6, 36, 42) Feature clearly defined scenes drawn directly from nature, mythology or life, rather than designs that simply include incidental animal or human forms (pl 9) or that are based on general floral themes. The scene may be stylized or naturalistic, but must still be recognizable as a landscape, portrait or animal, or the depiction of a topical, historical or mythological event. Pictorial designs are fairly common on Qashga'i, Luri, Khamseh, Belouch and Aimaq rugs – as well as those woven by a number of other weaving groups in Iran, Afghanistan, Pakistan, Mongolia, Tibet, the Caucasus, China and the Americas – but are rarely found in rugs from Turkey, Central Asia and North Africa. The symbolic meaning of each pictorial design is dictated by its specific content.

Animal designs (pls 1, 2, 38) Any naturalistic representations of an animal, or group of animals, which form the main focal point of the design, as opposed to more general compositions that include some animals as subsidiary motifs (pl 36). Animal designs are fairly common on a number of Iranian (especially Qashga'i, Luri, Shahsavan), Amerindian, Tibetan and Mongolian rugs, and their symbolic meaning is dependent on the particular animal or animals involved.

European designs Do not feature in tribal rugs to the same degree as in workshop items, but the floral schemes – pioneered, during the 17th and 18th centuries, by the Aubusson and Savonnerie workshops in France – have had a direct influence on some Caucasian items (especially Karabagh) and a few Iranian rugs, mainly Afshar and Kurdish. European design influences are also found on several South and Central American items (e.g. San Pedro de Cajas).

Floral designs (pls 13–15, 27) Any compositions based on a predominance of leaf, frond or floral motifs arranged in either all-over or repeating formats. They are sometimes used in conjunction with non-floral motifs (e.g. *botehs*) or designs (e.g. medallion-and-corner) and there may be some confusion as to which is the dominant theme. Floral medallions (pl 13) are most frequently encountered in Kurdish, Afshar and Shahsavan rugs (from Iran) and in a number of Traditional Caucasian items. All-over and repeating floral formats (pl 14) are employed by those same weaving groups, and are also found (often in highly stylized variations) in Kirghiz, Kazakh, Uzbek, Belouch and Aimaq rugs (pl 15).

Panelled designs (pls 31, 40) Divide the field into distinctive geometrically defined segments, or panels, that usually contain either a variety of motifs or a series of undecorated, monochrome grounds (either in an alternating sequence of motifs or colours or separated by a clearly defined lattice). Panelled designs feature in items made by Khamseh, Kazakh, Kirghiz, Ayuchucho and other weaving groups throughout Iran, Central Asia and Peru. Those containing internal motifs are most closely associated with regional Bakhtiari rugs, and those with monochrome grounds are especially common in Qashga'i and Luri items.

Lattice designs (pls 15, 46) Variations of panelled designs, which separate repeating motifs across a uniformly coloured field. They are often found on Belouch, Aimaq, Turkoman, Turko-Mongol and some Caucasian items.

Designs, motifs and symbolism

The motifs and designs used in tribal rugs are drawn from a number of diverse environmental, religious, magical and cultural origins, and several common motifs, or design themes, appear in items produced by weaving groups as physically and culturally separate as the Navajo of North America and the Lurs of southern Iran. Sometimes they stem from the same environmental (e.g. mountains), religious (e.g. tree-of-life), magical (e.g. evil eye) or cultural (e.g. marriage emblem) source and possess the same, or a very similar, symbolism. However, identical motifs may also have totally different origins (e.g. zig zags normally represent mountains in Navajo rugs and rivers in Turkoman designs), or, even if drawn from the same source, possess widely differing cultural associations (e.g. a central cross on Armenian rugs is generally rooted in Christian imagery, but the same form on a Turkoman *enssi* is more likely to symbolize the four gardens at the heart of the Islamic afterworld). It is therefore important to modify the interpretation of a specific motif, or design, in light of the cultural, religious and environmental context of the weavers. Consequently, a medallion-and-corner design produced by Islamic weavers in Iran will have a totally different symbolic meaning to the same design found in a Navajo rug.

Also, some compositions and motifs can be traced to specific sources (e.g. sand paintings), but the exact origins of many of the most frequently encountered are open to debate. Consequently, the names and meanings attached to many common motif and designs (e.g. *botehs*, dragons) are at best probable associations and sometimes little more than vague guesses (often based on a superficial resemblance to a particular object) that have been adopted by the trade.

Names Vary considerably between different weaving groups, cultures and regions, as well as among individual dealers and historians in the west. Consequently, a star may be referred to by either its western name or by one of its numerous local names – e.g. *yildiz* in Turkey, *casca-lucero* in Peru or *setereh* in Iran. This is also true of many other common motifs and designs. The potential for confusion is often compounded by the practice (of some dealers) of ascribing the names common to their area of expertise to similar motifs and designs found in rugs from widely differing sources.

Religious origins Some motifs and designs have clearly evolved from a specific religion (e.g. Islamic prayer-rug designs) and can therefore be allocated the symbolic meaning implicit in that particular religious doctrine. However, a number of motifs (e.g. tree of life) are common to numerous religious and spiritual doctrines and, in some instances, could simply be secular renditions of natural forms.

Meaning and symbolism Designs and motifs that have specific meanings in the rugs made by one weaving group may possess different symbolic intents in items produced elsewhere. For example, the meaning of a swastika in a Navajo blanket will be significantly different from that applied to the same motif in a Berber rug. Similarly, some motifs could be included simply because they look good and conform to the overall requirements of the design.

Environmental origins Several motifs and designs have also been drawn directly from nature (e.g. plants, mountains), daily life (e.g. earrings, animal fetters), and important

Prayer rugs. *Left and centre* show triangular *mihrabs*; *right* head-and-shoulder *mihrab*

current or historical events (e.g. War Rugs) and provide useful indicators of each tribe's particular physical environment, lifestyle, social conventions and history. (*See* Chapter IV)

Mythological and magical origins Some motifs and designs are also clearly rooted in the mythology, folklore and legends of specific tribal groups (e.g. Navajo *yei'is*, or the Inca deity, Quetzalcoatl). However, a number of common mythological figures (e.g. dragons) are so universal as to negate any direct association with one specific tribal, ethnic, cultural or regional weaving group. Some magical and spiritual beliefs have been translated into specific motifs aimed at affording the tribe a degree of protection from hostile influences (e.g. the evil eye) or ensuring their continued survival and good fortune (e.g. fertility). These motifs may take the form of realistic or highly abstracted representations of the creatures or objects associated with specific supernatural powers (e.g. lions – strength or stylized scorpion/tarantula patterns – protection against poison). Alternatively, they may appear as totally abstract geometric patterns (e.g. swastikas), which may have been derived originally from either natural or purely philosophical sources.

Oriental and universal designs

Afghan War designs (pl 7) Generic term for a highly collectable group of pictorial rugs that provide a contemporary woven history of the Afghan–Soviet War. They feature tanks, helicopters, Kalashnikov assault rifles and a variety of other weapons, battle scenes and implements of war. They were woven by Belouch, Aimaq and other Afghan tribal weaving groups. The term should perhaps be confined to those items made during the conflict (*c*. 1979–89), but rugs containing war motifs are still being made – both in Afghanistan and by Afghan refugees in Pakistan.

Presentation (or ceremonial) designs General term for pictorial designs that feature scenes from a ceremonial occasion (e.g. weddings, visits from tribal dignitaries). They are a popular theme on Belouch and Aimaq rugs.

Prayer-rug designs (pls 14, 37) Echo the physical structure of the prayer area inside the mosque. The top represents the prayer arch (*mihrab*) – which houses the sacred stone (*qibla*) that is faced by the devotees during prayer – and the (usually rectangular) lower portion, known as the prayer field, symbolizes the clean spot on which Muslims have to kneel when praying. The shape of the prayer arch may vary and a wide range of objects associated with Islamic worship (e.g. washing vessels, minarets), or more purely decorative motifs, may be used as infill decorations. Prayer-rug designs are especially common in Belouch, Aimaq and some Traditional Caucasian items (e.g. Lesghi, Daghestan) and often incorporate tree-of-life designs.

Saph designs Often called multiple prayer rugs because they feature a number of adjacent prayer arches, usually running horizontally, across the entire field. Found occasionally on tribal rugs, mainly from Central Asia.

Hatchli (or enssi) designs Traditionally associated with the rugs that the Turkoman and other Turko-Mongol tribes use as door-flaps (*enssis*), or internal partitions (*purdahs*), for their tents (*yurts*). The design is based on a central cross – which divides the field into four quadrants – set within a complex series of intensely decorated borders, and normally features a plethora of tiny (usually geometric) infill motifs. Its precise origin and meaning is unclear, but the three most popular theories are: a husband and wife (or family) prayer rug; a representation of the security of the home, and the symbolic doorway to the Islamic heaven, with the four central, innermost gardens of Paradise.

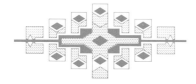

Gul designs. *From top to bottom* elephant-foot or *gulli-gul*; Yomut *kepse gul*; variant Tekke *gul*

Tree-of-life designs (pls 3, 35) One of the oldest and most universal of all religious or mythological symbols that is usually seen as representing the link between the world of men and the worlds above and below. Its articulation may vary from a fairly naturalistic depiction of an actual tree to highly stylized, sometimes purely geometric, forms, but it is always based on a central trunk extending upwards, with branches spreading out from either side. It may be used on its own (either as a single central form, or as small repeating motifs), or in combination with other (mainly prayer-rug) designs. It is especially common as a subsidiary design in Belouch and Aimaq prayer rugs, a repeating motif in Shahsavan items, and a central form in Niriz and Navajo weavings.

Pomegranate designs (pl 27) Variation of the tree-of-life motif – usually found only on East Turkestan rugs. Pomegranates are believed to be a symbol of fertility (due to their abundance of seeds) and first appeared in Chinese designs at the end of the 1st millennium BC.

Gul designs (pls 17, 18) Repeating, all-over formats based on the lozenge-shaped motifs (*guls*) that dominate the rugs of the various Turkoman and Turko-Mongol tribes of Central Asia (except Kazakhs). Each individual tribe has its own distinctive *gul* (or range of *guls*), which is repeated – normally in conjunction with a minor *gul* or other subsidiary motif – in off-set, horizontal rows across the entire field. The word *gul* means flower in Persian and some historians believe that the current motifs are simply highly stylized versions of natural floral forms; others trace its origins to an old Turkic word meaning clan and argue that *guls* have been used for centuries as identifying tribal emblems and that it was also common for tribes to incorporate the *gul* of a conquered (or assimilated) rival tribe into their future rug designs, usually as a subsidiary element.

Ay-gul designs Large medallion (or mandala-like *gul* variation) usually found on rugs from East Turkestan. Possibly a Buddhist/Taoist-influenced symbol of eternity or the moon.

Medallion-and-corner designs (pls 12, 13) Reflect a worm's-eye view of the dome of a mosque and take the form of a central medallion contained within surrounding corners that to varying degrees echo the medallion. The size, shape and internal decoration may vary considerably, but they always echo the dome's central boss and its surrounding perimeter (or spandrels). It is also known as the book-cover design because it was used to decorate the leather covers made to house the Koran. Medallion-and-corner designs are used by a wide variety of weaving groups – mainly in Iran, Turkey and the Caucasus – although it is often difficult to distinguish between Islamic medallion-and-corner designs, and some secular or totemic amulet/medallion designs.

Amulet/medallion designs (pls 8, 24) Based on an overtly heraldic, central motif that may or may not be echoed in the corners. They are most commonly found on Caucasian, Iranian, Turkish and Navajo rugs and are believed to have evolved from ancient tribal emblems, or identifying standards, rather than Islamic symbolism. Most were probably based originally on a specific animal, bird or plant that had a close environmental or spiritual affinity to the tribe, and which was later adopted as their totem or heraldic emblem, becoming increasingly abstracted over the centuries. Some amulet/medallions are still associated with specific sources and rugs employing these motifs may be referred to as, for example, cloudband or eagle Kazakhs – although these associations may be as tenuous as a superficial resemblance to cloud and eagles.

Pole medallions (pls 10, 11) Two or more amulet/medallions that are connected by a central stem. They are common to the same weaving regions as amulet/medallions, but may be favoured by different weaving groups.

Boteh designs Pear-shaped motif (or *boteh*), in a repeating format, commonly known in the west as the Paisley pattern after the Scottish town associated with producing textiles based on this design. The word *boteh* means cluster of flowers in Persian, but its origins have been traced to such diverse objects as a leaf, a pine cone, a foetus, a male sperm and the Zoroastrian flame. It was closely associated with Kashmiri shawls and the rugs made in the village of Mal-e-Mir (in the Serabend district of Iran) and is often referred to as the *Mir-i-Boteh*. The size, shape and internal decoration of individual *botehs* varies, but they are a major design format on several Iranian and Traditional Caucasian rugs, and may also be used as minor decorations on items from a wider range of weaving groups.

Herati designs (pls 12, 22) Repeating (usually all-over) formats based on the *herati* motif, which is composed of a central floral head, set inside a diamond-shaped framework, flanked by four outwardly curling crescent-shaped forms (or leaves). It is also known as the *mahi* or fish-in-the-pond design because some authorities believe that it represents the ancient Persian view of the world as a disc supported by four swimming fish. The name *herati* is derived from the town of Herat (now in Afghanistan), which was part of the Persian Empire when it became associated with rugs produced in this design. Today, it is closely linked with the Hamadan and to a lesser extent the Azerbaijan, Kurdistan and Khorassan regions of Iran.

Dragon designs Vary from the naturalist portrayals of dragons, found in Tibetan and Mongolian rugs, to highly abstracted forms (which may or may not be derived from actual dragon motifs) that are closely associated with 19th-century Caucasian kilims; either as large heraldic motifs called *vishapogorgs* or angular interpretations of the letter 'S'. Known as *silehs*, both now form specific, highly collectable sub-groups. (*See* Dragons)

Oriental and universal motifs

Washing vessel Used in Islam for self-purification before prayer – often found as a subsidiary motif on prayer rugs.

Hanging lamp Provide light and burn incense in mosques. Often used on prayer rugs.

Hand of Fatima Important Islamic motif – symbolizing the hand of Mohammed's daughter, Fatima – usually depicted as a splayed right hand (the 'hand of honour'), as opposed to the left hand ('hand of dishonour'). The thumb is believed to represent the Prophet Mohammed; the first finger, Fatima (who is also referred to as the 'Weaver'); the second finger, Fatima's husband, Ali; the third and fourth, their sons (Hasan and Hussain). It also mirrors the five pillars (or fundamental duties) of Islam. However, the 'open-hand' is also a universal symbol of power and protection against the evil eye and has been used for divination in Judaism, Christianity and other religious cultures.

Dragons Feature prominently in Chinese, Tibetan, Polynesian, Ancient Egyptian, Celtic, Aztec, Incan, and numerous other mythologies throughout the world. Different cultures have their own (or sometimes several) versions of the dragon, each with its own distinctive range of powers, attributes and associations. But they are all essentially a fusion between the snake-god and the bird-god (e.g. Quetzalcoatl, the 'Plumed Serpent' of Aztec and Toltec myth, or the *nagas* and *garudas* of Hindu/Buddhist mythology) that has been modified to suit local

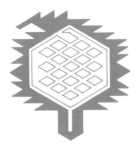

Boteh motifs

Herati motif

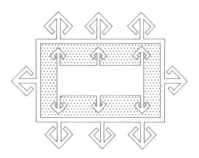

Kirghiz motif

conditions and survival demands without losing the essential qualities of a dragon. For example, the 'salmon/dragon' of Celtic and Icelandic legends, despite being adapted to the needs of a maritime race, still possessed many of the powers attributed to the more conventionally depicted dragons of China and Tibet. These included the ability to transform humans (e.g. the Celtic hero, Finn, became a seer after eating the 'Salmon of Knowledge'), act as 'were' animals for humans and gods (e.g. the Norse god, Loki, could change into a salmon), and cause earthquakes (e.g. when Loki twisted and turned, the earth would shake). Dragons are also seen as 'masters of wind and water', 'keepers of the tree-of-life', 'custodians of the secrets of the universe', symbols of fertility and general 'guardians' and 'protectors' (especially from the evil eye) by diverse cultures throughout the world and are found in various forms on rugs produced by numerous weaving groups in diverse parts of the weaving region, especially in Tibet, Mongolia, the Caucasus and South America.

Lions Universal symbols of strength and valour, traditionally used as guardians or protectors against both physical and supernatural threats. They are most closely associated with the Belouch, Qashga'i and Lurs, but may be used by other weaving groups, especially in Iran and Afghanistan.

Horses (pls 1, 2) Symbolic messengers in several religions (especially Buddhism), but, in rug designs, are probably used more for their social significance to the tribe – especially common on nomadic and semi-nomadic rugs.

Camels (pl 1) Feature on rugs from several weaving groups throughout Iran (e.g. Shahsavan, Kurds, Qashga'i), Afghanistan (e.g. Belouch) and to a lesser extent the Caucasus, Central Asia and North Africa. The Koran makes a number of references to a she-camel

being sent by Allah to Mohammed as a messenger (or as a test), but even in Islamic cultures, it is usually depicted simply as a familiar part of the local environment. (*See* Alpacas)

Birds (pl 1) Universal symbols of portents and messages, and, in many religions, the transporters of dead souls from the world of men to the worlds beyond. They feature, both realistic and stylized forms, in rugs from numerous weaving groups throughout the world.

Peacocks (pl 38) National bird of India and closely associated with ancient Persia (Iran), whose rulers sat upon the Peacock Throne. Peacocks feature strongly in Persian mythology, culture and art; and there are several references to them in the Hindu *Rig Vedas* (*c.* 1200 BC), as 'bringers of rain', 'killers of serpents' and 'steeds of the gods'. The Yezidis of northern Iraq refer to the devil as the Peacock Angel, and peacocks are variously associated with courage, pride, beauty and lamentation in diverse religious and mythological systems throughout Asia. There is also a widespread belief that peacock feathers afford protection from the evil eye (probably because their markings resemble dozens of eyes, reflecting back the malice), and also that different parts of the bird contain antidotes for poison, tuberculosis, paralysis, asthma, headaches, catarrh, impotence, barrenness, etc. They are common motifs on Shahsavan, Kurdish, Qashga'i, and Luri rugs and those of other weaving groups in Iran, Afghanistan and the Caucasus. They may be depicted either with one or two heads, although the latter is often referred to as the fabulous beast or bird. (*See* Birds)

Snakes Universal symbols – associated with sex, fertility and strength – which are considered to be either good or evil, depending largely on the attitude towards sex taken by each individual religion or culture. The snake's association with lust and temptation, which is so prominent in Christianity, is largely absent from Islamic, Buddhist and other religious mythologies. Consequently, snakes are generally viewed as powerful and benign talismen affording protection from evil influences, and ensuring individual and collective fecundity.

Stars (pls 6, 25) Symbolic associations vary between cultures, and, even in the same culture, a separate meaning is often attached to stars of different shapes. In most Islamic cultures, the number of points on a star alters its meaning (e.g. four-pointed stars symbolize stability, wholeness and the mysteries of nature; five-pointed stars – good luck, protection and power over matter; six-pointed stars – spiritual and corporeal happiness; seven-pointed stars – perfection; eight-pointed stars – wisdom; and nine-pointed stars – the spiritual exaltation of man and matter).

Crosses (pls 39, 43) One of the oldest and most universal symbols – predating Christianity by at least 3,000 years – found in slightly modified forms in cultures as far apart as the Middle Eastern Kassite kingdom, Celtic Britain and pre-Colombian America. Meanings vary (e.g. protection from evil, power over corporeal existence and a symbol of the Earth) and they are found in rugs from weaving groups throughout most parts of the world.

Swastikas (pl 24) Universal magical and religious symbol in both ancient and modern cultures throughout Asia, Europe and the Americas. It derives its name from a combination of the Sanskrit (Ancient Indian) words for 'well being' and 'good fortune', and has featured extensively in Hindu-Buddhist cultures throughout Asia, where it has been ascribed a number of meanings. These include happiness, the heart of Buddha and the number 10,000 in Buddhism; and *karma*, the 'male principles', the sun and the force for goodness and light, as manifest in the god Ganesh (lord of knowledge and learning) in Hinduism. The swastika may have originated among early Aryan civilizations in Europe, where it was a symbol of the Supreme God. It was adopted by the Jains (a religion arising out of Hinduism and Buddhism), and was later introduced into China where it symbolized the sun. The true swastika has its short arms facing to the right, signifying an anti-clockwise rotation, following the daily motion of the sun – from east to west – moving towards the light, and is found especially on Navajo, Caucasian and Mongolian items.

Sauvastikas (pl 24) Mirror image of the swastika – with the short arms facing to the left – representing a clockwise rotation, moving against the daily motion of the sun, away from the light. In Hinduism, it represents the 'female principles', the force for evil and darkness, as manifest in the goddess Kali (the devourer of the souls of the dead, and the guardian of dark and forbidden knowledge). It is found in the same range of rugs as the swastika.

Scorpions/tarantulas (pls 8, 19) Normally represented as several hooked legs extruding from a diamond-shaped body. They are especially common on Turkish, Caucasian, Iranian and Central Asian items and are generally believed to be a charm against venom or poison.

Evil-eye motifs (pls 20, 25) Take many different forms, and known by a variety of names (e.g. *nazarlyk*, *goz*), but are all founded in the widespread belief that a look can bring mischief and misfortune, and the logical way to combat (or protect yourself from) the evil eye is to confront it by a more powerful eye that will reflect back the malice. Consequently, most evil eye motifs are diamond- or lozenge-shaped, which echo the human eye, and feature in rugs from throughout the entire weaving region.

Hooks (pl 24) May be shown with the arms pointing either to the right ('s') or to the left ('z'), and are believed to afford protection

Xochiquetzal, Mayan goddess of weaving

against the evil eye. However, some authorities argue that 's-shaped' hooks are actually symbols of the dragon, whereas others suggest that the 's-' and 'z-shaped' hooks are simplified versions of the swastika and sauvastika, respectively. They are commonly found – in slightly different forms – in Navajo rugs and numerous items produced by weaving groups throughout Asia.

Elibelinde motifs Fertility symbols that usually take the form of a woman (or goddess) – who is often recognizably pregnant – and may be fairly realistic or highly stylized. They are also known as the hand-on-hips motif because they usually resemble the outline of someone standing front on, with their arms akimbo. They are found mainly on Turkish and Iranian rugs.

Ram's horn or perepedil motifs (pl 15) Closely associated with Kuba perepedil rugs, but are also often found on other Traditional Caucasian, Iranian and Turkish items. Sizes, shapes and meanings vary but they are generally believed to be symbols of power, virility and masculine virtues.

Wasms Literally means brands or distinguishing marks in Arabic. The nomadic and semi-nomadic tribes of North Africa have traditionally used their specific *wasm* as a means of identifying their possessions; include painting or tattooing the faces, necks, hands or feet of the women. In rug designs *wasms* are used as tribal emblems – in the same way that the Turkomen employ *guls* – and, although they are not always clearly discernible as individual motifs, they often provide the underlying theme for the design.

Fret, wan and lattice motifs Collective terms for a range of linear, inter-locking motifs that are often used as border decorations. The word 'fret' is derived from the Anglo-Saxon *fretan*, meaning to eat away, and all these motifs reflect a bird's-eye view of angular furrows, or mazes, that have been dug out or eaten away from the earth.

Meander motifs Collective term for a variety of sinuous, undulating linear motifs that are normally based on either the meandering course of a river or stream, or the labyrinthine growth pattern of tendrils or vines. A number of additional motifs (e.g. leaves, flower heads) are usually appended to the basic linear form and, depending on the region and additional motifs, are ascribed several names and meanings, e.g. *su yolu* (Turkish for running water) and *iashil su* (Turkoman for green water). They are generally believed to symbolize vitality and life. They are usually confined to weaving groups who employ curvilinear designs.

Environmental motifs Wide variety of motifs drawn directly from the weaver's physical environment that may be either naturalistic or stylized, and may possess a clear religious or magical significance, or merely reflect the natural world. They include *uriik gul* (apricot blossom), *ovadan* (floral form known as the flourishing or beautiful motif), *ay kochot* (moon motif), *gapyrga* (ribs motif), *buynuz* (horns), *it taman* (trace of the dog motif), *dyrnyk* (claws), *ok gozi* (arrow point), *chakmak* (lightning), *umurtka* (vertebrae motif).

Lifestyle motifs Similar to environmental motifs, but are based on people and personal possessions. These include *insan*, *zan* (human figures), *dast*, *gelim burmak* (hand), *tarak*, *shooneh* (comb), *kupe*, *sarkhalka* (earrings), *chemce* (spoon) and *sacbagi* (hairband).

Amerindian motifs and designs

Alpacas Found on South American rugs – either as purely environmental motifs, or (in common with llamas) symbolic companions for the dead.

Mountain deer (or tarukas) Carry treasures to the mountain gods, found on Andean items.

South American motifs. *From left to right* mountain deer; twin-headed snake; puma

Ducks (or nunuma) Symbol for the Mother of Water found in South American rugs.

Blackbird (or chiwaku) Fertility symbol in South American rugs.

Joined doves (jesa champi urpi) Stepped, two-headed birds in the Andean cultures, symbolizing marriage between both a man and a woman, and the tribe and the earth.

Fish (or pescado) Symbol of Viracocha, the god associated with creating and protecting fishes, found on South American rugs.

Twin-headed snake (or culebra de dos cabezas) Portrayed as a z-shaped hook, used to represent the deity Amaru or as a general fertility symbol in South American rugs.

Puma Common motif in South and Central American rugs, which has been attached several meanings, including, the god of the Aija (the high Andean plains), 'universal provider' and 'protector of the family's wealth'.

Venus (casca-lucero) Worshipped in South and Central American cultures, as both the morning and the evening star. Each phase of the planet has a specific meaning, including, princess, white and the sky clouding over.

Environmental pictographs Amerindian designs generally contain motifs that represent specific environmental features – e.g. the zigzags in Navajo rugs are normally stylized versions of mountains. However, the only authentic pictographic language, used in rug designs, is confined to the motifs based on the ancient pictographic languages of the pre-Colombian civilizations in South and Central America (e.g. Inca, Paracas, Aztec, Maya), which were used to record and convey information in exactly the same way as the alphabet-based languages. Contemporary pictographic writing undoubtedly contains some more recent additions, reflecting the weaver's changing lifestyle, environment and experiences. The ones most often found on contemporary rugs are: *kenko-maya* (meandering river, symbolizing anything that is 'holy' or 'forbidden', or alternatively 'precipitous' or 'dedicated' commitment to a task); *alpaka* (hybrid of the words for 'secret, hidden, mystery' and 'earth' or 'fertile field', which can be taken as symbolizing 'chewing cocoa leaves', 'ploughing', 'eagles', 'mushrooms' and the 'obligation to make sacrifices'); *kocha* (lake or pond, signifying 'purification'); *sojta suyu* (literally 'six lands', signifying land in common ownership); *kancha de papa con bandera* ('fenced lands reserved for planting the sacred

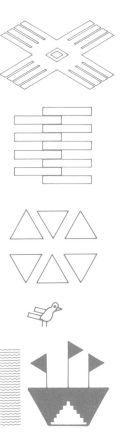

South American motifs and pictographs. *From top to bottom* Venus; mountains; communal land; pictographic calendar showing month of flowers

potato'); *orjos* (highest mountain peak housing the gods and spirits); and *cuenta de mesas* (literally 'counting the months', used to signify the month in which a rug was made and sometimes woven subtly into the border).

Pictographic calendar Based on the same origins as environmental pictographs, but used specifically as a symbolic reference to the agricultural and spiritual significance of each month of the year. They are perhaps most closely associated with the inhabitants of Taquile Island (in southern Peru), but are also used – in modified forms – by Ayamara, Quechua and other Amerindian weavers throughout South and Central America.

Mythological figures Common features on Central and South American rugs – either as a single supernatural being or deity (e.g. Quetzalcoatl) dominating the entire design, or as subsidiary elements in a more eclectic

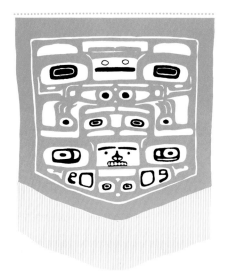

Spirit face motif of the Tlingit taken from the Chilkat blanket

composition – drawn from Inca, Aztec, Maya, Paracas and other pre-Colombian cultures.

Flying man of the Paracas (pl 40) Winged figure, who appears to be kneeling – discovered on Paracas textiles (*c.* 700 BC–AD 1100) – that often found on Ayuchucho rugs.

Sand (or dry) painting designs (pls 39, 47) Based on the Navajos' sacred sand paintings – created (using different-coloured sand, earth and organic materials) by the holy men (shamans or *brujos*) as part of their religious ceremonies, which have featured on a number of Navajo rugs since the turn of the 20th century. Each ceremony (e.g. Nightway

Chant) requires the creation of a specific sand painting (e.g. Whirling Log) to accompany prescribed incantations, dances and preparations, which must all focus on the same objective (e.g. curing 'ghost' sickness, bringing rain), and should not be used out of context. Consequently, when sand painting designs were first employed on rug designs, there was considerable outrage by numerous Navajo leaders and holy men, who felt that their use was an act of sacrilege, which would undermine both the spiritual integrity of the tribe and the power of the ceremonies. Sand paintings are used ceremonially in Tibetan and other Mongoloid cultures in Asia and Polynesia.

Yei'is Supernatural or mythological beings – normally represented as matchstick figures in short skirts – found on Navajo rugs.

Spirit faces Collective term for the totemic motifs and designs – found mainly on items from the Salishan region of south-west Canada (e.g. Tlingit, Nootka) – which are based on faces, often highly stylized.

Thunderbird Mythical deity that is usually represented as a single- or double-headed bird, shown front on with its wings outstretched. It was worshipped by the Dakota Indians as *waukheon* (the thunder bird) because its constant battle with *unktahe* (the water god) dictated the cycle of the seasons and sudden climatic changes. The thunder bird gradually replaced many similar tribal deities (e.g. the Cherokee thunder and lighting twins, Apocatequil and Piguerao) as the collective Amerindian thunder god in North America.

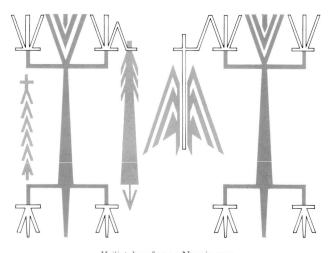

Yei'is taken from a Navajo rug

CHAPTER SIX

The weaving nations, territories and regions

Tribal weavers are generally influenced more by the cultural and social traditions of their tribe than they are by those of the country in which they live. However, it would be a mistake to ignore the importance of national boundaries because – in addition to the purely commercial considerations of price and availability, which are clearly affected by the social, economic and political situations in different countries – the host country can exert considerable influence on both the weaver's lifestyle and the character and appearance of their rugs.

Consequently, the rugs made by Kurdish tribes in Iran are slightly different to those produced by their kinsmen in Turkey and Iraq, and, although still essentially Kurdish, normally share common features with the items woven by the non-Kurdish Iranian tribes. Similar variations may also be found in the rugs made in different areas of the same country.

Changing borders An ongoing fact of life for a number of tribal groups whose traditional territories have often been almost continuously invaded, occupied, controlled, sold, purchased, divided or amalgamated with a rival tribe's territory by a succession of nation states. Consequently, the exact geographic, ethnic and cultural relationship between the various tribal groups – as well as the names and national allegiances of the territories in which they live – have changed dramatically over the centuries, and, given the political uncertainty in some areas, this may continue.

The relationship between ancient and modern weaving regions Several modern nations now occupy territory that was either traditionally known by a different name (e.g. Persia/Iran) or have been formed from an amalgamation of smaller, independent states (e.g. Afghanistan from Ariana, Bactria and Drangiana), or alternatively seceded from a larger region (e.g. Kazakhstan, Kirghizstan, Turkmenistan, Tajikistan and Uzbekistan emerging from the vast, vaguely defined area traditionally referred to as Turkestan). The exact relationship between these modern nations and the ancient territories can be extremely confusing, and is often compounded by inconsistencies in the use of their names, especially the common practice of calling certain modern nations by their traditional names (e.g. contemporary Iranian rugs are often marketed as 'Persian', despite the fact that Persia officially changed its name in 1936).

The ancient weaving nations, territories and regions

Anatolia Traditional name for the Asian part of Turkey (i.e. east of the Bosporus). It is possibly derived from 'Andolu' – an older name for the region – which is a compound of two Turkish words, *ana* (mother) and *dolu* (full), implying 'pregnant mother' or 'fertile earth'. It was originally occupied by Kurds, Armenians and other Indo-Europeans, but was settled by successive waves of Turkic invaders. It was the centre of some of the earliest known agricultural societies (e.g. Phrygians, Hittites and Lydians), which flourished between the 3rd and the 1st millennium BC, and later came under the influences of Ancient Greece and the Roman Empire. Islam was introduced by the Arabs in the 7th century, and cemented by later Seljuk and Ottoman conquests and colonizations. In 1452, after the Ottomans captured Constantinople, it became the epicentre of the Ottoman Empire until 1923 when – its borders having receded to roughly their present positions – it renounced its Caliphate (Islamic spiritual) status and became a republic of Turkey. Turkish rugs are often referred to as Anatolian.

Ariana Ancient name for Afghanistan.

Armenia (ancient or ethnic) Corresponds to the Armenian Republic and parts of north-west Iran and eastern Turkey. The Caucasian part of the region was once the centre of the ancient Urartu civilization, but, during the 1st millennium BC, was occupied by ethnic Armenians, who (by the end of the millennium) had founded an empire that, for over a century, rivalled the power and influence of Rome.

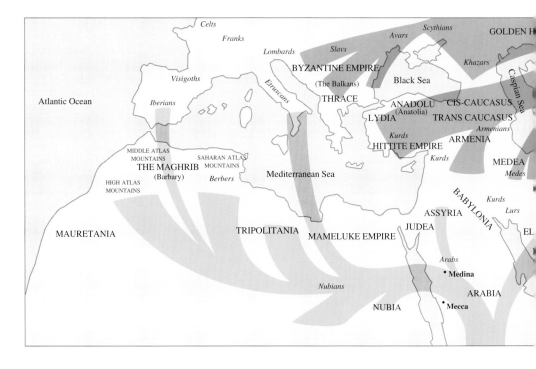

During the next 2,000 years, ethnic Armenia was invaded, conquered, divided, annexed and partially reunited by a succession of foreign powers. The Caucasian part of Armenia was incorporated into the Soviet Union (1922) and gained its independence in 1991.

Bactria Ancient region in Afghanistan that gave its name to the Bactrian breed of camels.

The Balkans Derives its name from the Balkan Mountains and is the most easterly of Europe's three southern peninsulas, encompassing Greece, Bulgaria, Albania, former Yugoslavia, Romania and the European part of Turkey.

Baluchistan (ethnic) Once used to describe a loosely defined area of Iran, Afghanistan and Pakistan that corresponded to the traditional territories of the Belouch. It is now the name of a province in south-west Pakistan.

Barbary Named after its indigenous inhabitants, the Berbers, and made famous in pirate tales of the Barbary Coast. It corresponds to the Maghrib region of North Africa.

Byzantium Ancient city in Thrace that gave its name to both the Byzantine Empire and the fusion of western and eastern art and architecture that became known as Byzantine Art. It was the site of Constantinople (now Istanbul).

The Caucasus Region lying north and south of the Caucasian Mountains that corresponds to the Armenian, Azerbaijan and Georgian Republics and Daghestan ASSR. It has the most varied and complex ethnic, cultural and religious mix anywhere in the rug-producing world – with around 350 different racial and tribal groupings, who speak over 90 different languages and dialects. The region to the north of the Caucasian Mountains is known as the Cis-Caucasus and the region to the south as the Trans Caucasus.

Central Asia Collective term for a vast region that encompasses the former Soviet Central Asian Republics, parts of Afghanistan and the Sinkiang Province of China. (*See* Turkestan)

East Turkestan Eastern territories of the Turkic tribesmen – also known as Kashgaria – now the Sinkiang Province (or Xinjiang Uighur Autonomous Region) of China. It centres on the vast arid regions of the Takla Makan Desert and the Tarim Basin – which many historians believe to be the cradle of tribal weaving – and is populated mainly by Uighurs and other people of Turkic or Turko-Mongol descent. It remains the only part of modern China that has not been heavily re-settled by the Han Chinese.

The Golden Horde Region in Central Asia, between the Urals and the River Irtysh that

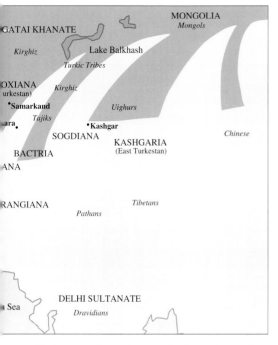

Ancient weaving regions, territories, nations and migratory routes. The Turko-Mongol invasion/migratory routes are dark orange and the Arab invasion/migratory routes are light orange

roughly corresponds to the former territory (or khanate) of the Turkic Kipchak tribe. Horde (or *ordas*) means district or specific tribal land and, during the reign of Ad Allah Uzbek Khan (r. *c.* 1313–40), the region became synonymous with the Islamic section of Genghis Khan's army.

Kashgaria *see* East Turkestan

The Maghrib Arabic word meaning land of the setting sun used for the western territories of the Arab Empire (i.e. Morocco, Algeria, Tunisia and western Libya). The region is dominated by Arabs – numerically, politically and culturally – although the indigenous Berbers are still a substantial minority. (*See* Barbary)

Persia Former name for Iran that is still widely used when referring to items currently produced in the country. The name was changed in 1935 and in this book Persia and Persian will be used when referring to events or rugs produced prior to this date. (*See* Iran)

Soviet Caucasian and Central Asian Republics After the Russian Revolution (*c.* 1917), the new Soviet authorities pursued a policy of dividing the old Russian Empire and the newly acquired Soviet territories into a number of separate,

quasi-autonomous regions based on the ethnic origins of the indigenous majority. This policy was formalized, in 1936, and resulted in the establishment of two distinct regional political structures: Soviet Socialist Republics (SSRs) – which were constitutional republics that had their own elected government, national representatives and fiscal and legal powers – and Autonomous Soviet Socialist Regions (ASSRs) – which were semi-governing regions within a larger SSR. In the Caucasus, the SSRs were Azerbaijan, Armenia and Georgia; and, in Central Asia, Kazakhstan, Kirghizstan, Tajikistan, Turkmenistan and Uzbekistan. The other ethnic regions of Daghestan, Tartary, Karakalpakstan, Chechnia, Nagorny Karabagh and Lesghistan became ASSRs within one of these Republics. On the dissolution of the Soviet Union, in 1991, the SSRs joined a loose federation of former Soviet States – called the Commonwealth of Independent States (CIS) – and, within the next two years, established themselves as fully fledged republics. The ASSRs have remained within their former SSRs; although several have attempted to gain independence or to be united with their kin in other republics.

Thrace Ancient name for the western (European) part of Turkey that extended into southern Greece and the Balkans.

Transoxiana Western part of Turkestan that extended from Kashgaria to the Amu Darya or Oxus river in modern Turkmenistan.

Turkestan Literally translated as 'land of the Turks or Turkmen' and was applied to a vast, vaguely defined area in Central Asia, extending eastwards from the Gobi Desert to the Caspian Sea. Today, it roughly corresponds to the Republics of Turkmenistan, Kazakhstan, Kirghizstan, Uzbekistan and Tajikistan and parts of northern Afghanistan and Iran. Turkic and Turko-Mongol domination of the region began with the Hun invasion (2nd century BC) and was firmly established, between the 11th and 15th centuries, after invasions by Genghis Khan and Tamerlane. Turkestan was effectively divided, during the early part of the 1st millennium AD, into East and West. China annexed Kashgaria (East Turkestan) shortly after the dissolution of the Hun Empire, leaving the White Huns (or Ephthalites) to rule Transoxiana. This division has remained relatively constant ever since, although, during the next 1,500 years, both East and West Turkestan were overrun by a succession of invaders who either displaced or absorbed most of the indigenous inhabitants (e.g. Indo-European Tokharians, Persian Yuen-chih nomads and other mainly tribal people about whom very little is known). Arabs introduced Islam into Transoxiana in the 8th century AD and laid the foundation for the conversion of the later Turko-Mongol tribes. A greater degree of political and ethnic stability was established in the 19th century when Transoxiana was conquered by Russia, becoming the province of Turkestan, and Kashgaria, the Sinkiang Province of China. *Note* It is common practice to refer to West Turkestan simply as Turkestan.

Contemporary weaving nations

The national boundaries and ethnic mix of some contemporary weaving nations are relatively stable. However, the former Soviet Caucasian and Central Asian Republics have only recently emerged as independent nations and other nations are still recovering from the aftermath of war or internal rebellion. Consequently, it may be some years before their borders, ethnic mix and weaving output reaches comparative levels of stability.

The major weaving nations in Asia and North Africa

Afghanistan The population (*c.* 15 million) is composed of Afghans (50%) – who are politically dominant – Tajiks (25%), Uzbeks (9%), Hazaras (9%), Turkomen, Aryans, Persians, Arabs and other ethnic minorities. In 1747 an Afghan tribal chief, Ahmed Shah, united the indigenous tribes (who inhabited the ancient kingdoms of Ariana, Bactria, etc.) and founded a dynasty that effectively lasted until a republic was formed in 1973. Afghanistan is a major centre for tribal rugs, especially Belouch, Uzbek and Turkoman. (*See* Chapter VII: Aimaq, Belouch, Kutchi, Labijar, Mushwani, Qala-i-Nau, Sar-i-Pul, Tartari, Timuri, Uzbeks)

Algeria Largest country in the Maghrib with a population of 25 million (74% Arab and 24% Berber) which became an Islamic socialist, one-party state in 1976. Algerian tribal rugs are produced by Berber and to a lesser extent Arab weaving groups – but political instability means that few now reach the west.

China Third largest country in the world, whose current borders include East Turkestan (Sinkiang Province), and the former independent countries of Manchuria, Inner Mongolia and Tibet which have all been heavily resettled by ethnic Han Chinese (94% of China's total population of over one billion). However, Sinkiang's population of *c.* 13 million is still predominantly made up of Uighur (75%) and other Turko-Mongol tribesmen. Chinese tribal rugs are confined to the items produced in the Sinkiang Province, and to a lesser extent those made in Tibet and Inner Mongolia. They occasionally reach the west, and may be sold under a variety of names. (*See* Mongolia and Tibet; and Chapter VII: Uighurs)

Iran Called Persia until 1935 and declared itself to be a Shi'ite Islamic Republic in 1979. Its population (*c.* 45 million) is mainly composed of the politically and culturally dominant Persians (63%), but there also significant minorities of Turkic and Belouch tribesmen (19%), Arabs (4%) and Kurds (3%). Iranian tribal rugs are made in a wider range of styles, and by a greater diversity of weaving groups, than in any other producing country. However, the full range of items available in Iran does not always find its way onto western markets, although most of the major groups are usually well represented. (*See* Chapter IV: Persian, Sassanian and Parthian Empires; and Persian Qajar and Persian Pahlavi Dynasties and Chapter VII: Afshar, Azerbaijani, Bakhtiari, Bebehan, Belouch, Bidjar, Borchalu, Bowanat, Hamadan, Kerman, Khamseh, Khorramabad, Khorassan, Kurds, Lurs, Meshed, Niriz, Owlad, Qashga'i, Senneh, Shahsavan, Shiraz)

Iraq Occupies most of Mesopotamia and is the site of the ancient Sumarian, Akkadian, Babylonian and Assyrian civilizations. Its population of *c.* 15 million is composed of Arabs (75%), Kurds (15%) and Turkomen (5%), who are reasonably evenly divided between Shi'ite (55%) and Sunni (40%) Muslims. Baghdad was an important centre of the Arab Empire and, in 1683, the region became part of the Ottoman Empire. Since the late 1960s Iraq has been ruled by decree as a one-party state under the *de facto* dictatorship of Saddam Hussein. In 1975, Kurdish rebels were heavily defeated by Government troops and, in common with other minorities (e.g. Marsh Arabs), have suffered genocidal persecution ever since.

Iraqi tribal rugs are mainly produced by Kurds and, to a lesser extent, Marsh Arabs. However, very few items reach the west, although some are smuggled into adjacent countries (mainly Iran) from where they are sold, often as Kurdish or Kurdistan rugs. (*See* Chapter VII: Kurds and Arab weaving groups)

Mongolia Socialist state whose current population of Mongol (83%) and Kazakh (8%) tribesmen gradually moved towards a more settled agrarian existence, during the course of the 20th century, although a significant number are still semi-nomadic. Mongolia shares a close ethnic, cultural and religious affinity with Tibet, and, despite atheism being the official doctrine, Tibetan Buddhism is still the country's main religious influence. It is one of the world's oldest nations and is also believed (by some historians) to be the original home of rug making. (*See* Chapter IV: Mongols)

Morocco Constitutional monarchy at the western boundary of the Maghrib. Its population of 24 million is composed of Arabs (65%) and Berbers (30%). Moroccan tribal rugs are produced by Berbers – and to a lesser extent Arabs – living nomadic, semi-nomadic or settled lifestyles in the Middle and High Atlas Mountains and the Tennsift coastal region. It is the largest exporter of rugs from North Africa. (*See* Chapter IV: The Caliphate and the Arab Empire and Chapter VII: Arab weaving groups, Berber weaving groups, Azrou, Boujaad, Glaoua, Klenifra, Taznakht)

Pakistan Islamic republic, which acquired dominion status, in 1947, as one of two (West and East Pakistan) Islamic areas of India that would form a single self-governing state after British withdrawal. However, conflict between the powerful West and the desperately poor East resulted in a war of secession that led to the formation, in 1971, of two totally independent states. East Pakistan became Bangladesh, and West Pakistan retained the name Pakistan. Its importance as a centre for tribal rugs only began during the Afghan–Russian War (1979–89) when over 2 million refugees flooded across the border, bringing with them their weaving traditions.

Pakistani tribal rugs are produced by indigenous Belouch (and other related) tribesmen in the Baluchistan Province and also by Aimaq, Belouch, Afghan, Turkoman, Uzbek and other refugees from Afghanistan who now live mainly in and around the frontier towns of Peshawar and Quetta. Their rugs are similar to those made by kindred tribal groups in Afghanistan, although more eclectic, commercialized tribal-style items are made as well.

Pakistan also acts as a centre for goods from Afghanistan, Uzbekistan and other neighbouring countries. (*See* Chapter VII: Baluchistan, Belouch)

Syria Theoretically a constitutional republic, which was the centre of the ancient Assyrian Empire. Its population of nearly 11 million is composed of Arabs (90%), Kurds, Armenians, Circassians, Assyrians and Turks – most are Sunni Muslims (70%), although there is a substantial Christian minority (13%). Tribal rugs are woven almost exclusively by nomadic and semi-nomadic Kurdish tribes, but very few reach the west. (*See* Chapter VII: Kurds)

Tibet Ancient country that is the traditional homeland of the ethnic Tibetans. It shares much of its cultural, religious and rug-making traditions with Mongolia but, since its annexation by China (1950), most forms of Tibetan cultural and artistic expression have been repressed. (*See* Chapter IV: Tibetans)

Tunisia Republic in the Maghrib with a population of *c.* 7 million, which is a well-integrated mixture of Muslim Arabs and Berbers (98%), and very small minorities of Jews, Turks and Europeans. The region was incorporated into the successive Byzantine, Arab and Ottoman Empires before becoming a republic in 1956. Tunisian rugs are similar to those produced in Morocco, but most are woven by both Arabs and Berbers and are generally more regional/tribal than authentically tribal. (*See* Chapter VII: Oudref)

Turkey Republic, straddling Europe and Asia, that combines the ancient territories of Anatolia (Asia) and the south-eastern part of Thrace (Europe). The current population of *c.* 50 million is composed mainly of Turks (85%) – who are a fusion of people of Turkic, Turko-Mongol and Mediterranean stock – and Kurds (12%). Turkish tribal rugs are largely confined to those produced by Kurds (in the east) and by disparate nomadic and semi-nomadic Turkic tribesmen who are generally referred to as Yuruks. However, there are a number of village weaving groups that produce items which are distinctly tribal in character and appearance. (*See* Chapter VII: Kars, Kurds, Manastir, Van, Yahyahli and Yuruks)

Former Soviet Caucasian Republics

Armenia (Republic of) Mountainous, subtropical region which has a population of over 3 million composed of Christian Armenians (90%), Sunni-Islamic Azerbaijanis (5%), Kurds

(2%) and Russians (2%). It was incorporated into the Soviet Union (1936) as a constitutional republic (SSR) and, on the dissolution of the Soviet Union (1989), Armenian demands for union with the Armenian enclave of Nagorny Karabagh, in neighbouring Azerbaijan, led to conflict between the two states. Armenia declared its independence (1991) as part of the CIS. Tribal rugs made by ethnic Armenians are normally sold under a regional designation (e.g. Kazakh), and those made by non-Armenians under the name of the tribal weaving group (e.g. Shahsavan). (*See* Chapter VII: Armenian weaving groups, Erivan, Karabagh and Kazak)

Azerbaijan (Republic of) Mountainous and semi-desert region with a population of *c.* 7 million made up of Sunni-Islamic Azerbaijanis (78%), Russians (8%) and Armenians (8%) – mainly concentrated in the Nagorny Karabagh ASSR – as well as isolated pockets of Kurdish and Shahsavan tribesmen. It was incorporated into the Soviet Union (1936) as a constitutional republic (SSR) and, in 1991, declared its independence and joined the CIS. Azerbaijan rugs produced by Azerbaijanis and Armenians are generally classified under regional designations (e.g. Shirvan, Karabagh), but those made by Kurdish or Shahsavan tribesmen are usually sold under the name of the tribal weaving group. (*See* Chapter VII: Azerbaijani, Armenian weaving groups, Kurds, Shahsavan and Traditional Caucasian weaving groups: Baku, Gianja, Karabagh, Kazak, Kuba, Shirvan)

Daghestan (ASSR) Mountainous valley region. Its population of *c.* 2 million is made up of over 30 identifiable national and ethnic groups who speak a multitude of different languages and dialects, and share a diversity of religious beliefs. Daghestan was annexed by Russia from Iran (1723) and is now within the Russian federation. Daghestan includes the Checheno-Ingush ASSR (Chechnia) which is inhabited mainly by ethnic Chechens (53%) and Ingushes (12%). Daghestan tribal rugs are produced mainly by ethnic Chechens, but are normally marketed as Daghestans. (*See* Chapter VII: Traditional Caucasian weaving groups: Daghestan and Derbends)

Georgia (Republic of) Fertile, predominantly agricultural region with a population of *c.* 5 million, composed of Christian Georgians (69%), Armenians (9%), and Russians (7%), as well as mainly Islamic Azerbaijanis (5%), Abkahazians (2%), Ossetians (2%) and other ethnic minorities. Georgia came under Arab, Khazar, Turko-Mongol, Turkic and Russian domination during the centuries preceding its incorporation into the Soviet Union as an SSR (1936). In 1991 it declared itself to be an independent republic within the CIS.

Georgian pile rugs were only woven (in any number) in the eastern part of the country – where there were substantial pockets of Armenians and Azerbaijanis – and were generally categorized as a sub-group of Kazakh or Gianja rugs. In contrast, ethnic Georgians produced numerous kilims and flatweaves (known locally as *pardaghis*), almost exclusively for their own use, which were rarely exported to the west and consequently have never been properly recorded and classified. However, all Georgian rugs are generally tribal in character and appearance, and, unlike elsewhere in the Caucasus, have never been commercially produced in any number. They share most of the common Caucasian design features – often incorporating Christian and naturalistic motifs – but are generally less colourful (e.g. dark blues, black, deep reddish orange and browns, contrasted with lighter blues, pinks, yellow ochre and white) and more primitive in character and appearance. Most Georgian items fall into the medium-to-high price bracket. (*See* Chapter VII: Traditional Caucasian weaving groups: Gianja, Kazak)

Lesghistan (ASSR) Small ASSR bordering Daghestan that is the official territory of the mainly nomadic, or semi-nomadic, Lesghi tribes whose rugs, although authentically tribal, are generally classified as a Daghestan sub-group. (*See* Chapter VII: Traditional Caucasian weaving groups, Daghestan and Lesghis)

Former Soviet Central Asian Republics

Karakalpak (ASSR) Semi-autonomous region, which was conquered by Russia (1867) and was designated as the official homeland of the Karakalpaks (1926) and finally attached (1936) to Uzbekistan. Its current population of 1 million is mainly Karakalpak, with minorities of Russian, Uzbek and other, mainly Turkic or Turko-Mongol, ethnic groups. Rugs are produced by Karakalpaks and other Turkic or Turko-Mongol groups and are usually sold under the name of the ethnic group. (*See* Chapter VII: Karakalpaks and Uzbeks)

Kazakhstan (Republic of) Vast region that occupies most of northern Turkestan. It was

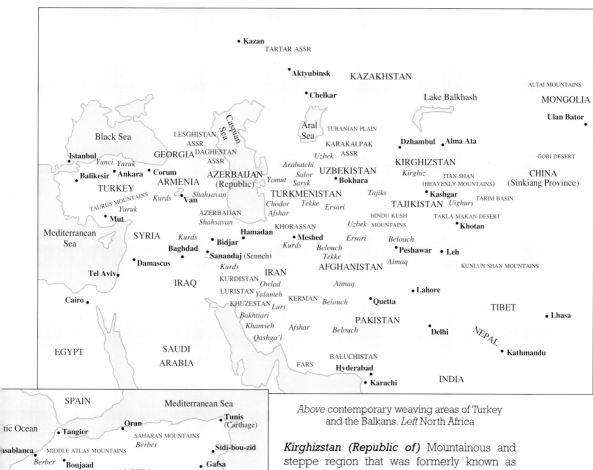

Above contemporary weaving areas of Turkey and the Balkans. *Left* North Africa

conquered by Russia in the 18th century, and (1936) became the official homeland of the Kazakhs as a Soviet Socialist Republic (SSR). Its current population (16 million) is comprised of Russians (41%), Kazakhs (36%), Ukrainians (6%) and other, mainly Turkic, minorities. Kazakhstan seceded from the Soviet Union (1991) and became an independent republic within the CIS. Tribal rugs are produced by Kazakhs and to a lesser extent other Turkic and Turko-Mongol tribal groups, and are usually sold under the name of the ethnic group. (*See* Chapter VII: Kazakhs)

Note Kazak is also a town in the Azerbaijan Republic that lends its name to one of the Traditional Caucasian weaving groups.

Kirghizstan (Republic of) Mountainous and steppe region that was formerly known as Kirghizia (the territory of the Kirghiz nomads) before being conquered by Russia, in 1864, and became an SSR in 1936 and an independent republic within the CIS in 1991. Its population of *c.* 4 million is made up of ethnic Kirghiz (52%), Russians (21%) and other, mainly Turkic and Turko-Mongol minorities. Tribal rugs are produced by ethnic Kirghiz and to a lesser extent other Turkic and Turko-Mongol tribesmen. (*See* Chapter VII: Kirghiz)

Tajikistan or Tadzhikistan (Republic of) Small republic that centres on the Bokhara region of West Turkestan. The area was designated the official homeland of the ethnic Tajiks in 1924 and became a SSR in 1929. Its current population (*c.* 5 million) is made up of Muslim Tajiks (59%) and Uzbeks (23%), and predominantly Christian Russians and Ukrainians (11%). It seceded from the Soviet Union, in 1991, and joined the CIS. Tribal rugs are produced by Tajiks and Uzbeks, and may be sold as either. (*See* Chapter IV: Tajiks)

Tartar or Tatar (ASSR) Quasi-autonomous region that was part of the Bulgar (Volga-Kama) state, during the 10th and 13th centuries, prior to being conquered by the Mongols, and then later (1552) by the Russians. Ethnic Tartars have inhabited the region for centuries and, in 1920, it became the Tartar ASSR. It now has a population of *c.* 3 million composed mainly of Tartars, but also with Russian, Uzbek and other minorities. Tribal rugs are produced in very small quantities and rarely find their way to the west. Items marketed as Tartar or Tartari generally refer to a style, rather than an ethnic or regional origin. (*See* Chapter IV: Tartars and Chapter VII: Tartari and Uzbeks)

Turkmenistan (Republic of) The official homeland of the Turkoman tribes, who have occupied the region since the 11th and 15th centuries. It was annexed by Russia and formed into a SSR in 1925 and seceded from the Soviet Union, in 1991, and joined the CIS. Its population (*c.* 3 million) is composed mainly of Turkomen (69%) – or Turkmenians as they are now officially called – Russians (9%), Uzbeks (3%) and Kazakhs (3%), who (excluding the Russians) are almost exclusively Sunni Muslims. Tribal rugs are produced by a number of individual Turkomen tribes and sub-tribes and are usually sold under the name of the weaving tribe. Almost identical regional/workshop items were also made during the Soviet era, and were normally marketed under the name of the *gul* used in the design. (*See* Chapter VII: Labijar, Turkomen)

Uzbekistan (Republic of) An area of valleys, mountains, deserts and oases that was conquered by Russia (1865–76), and, in 1925, became a SSR. It is officially designated as the Uzbek homeland, but also contains the Karakalpak ASSR. It has a current population of *c.* 19 million – Uzbeks (69%), Russians (11%), and Tajiks (4%), as well as Tartars (4%) and Mesketian Turks, who were forcibly relocated by Stalin, in 1944, from the Crimea and Georgia, respectively. Uzbekistan seceded from the Soviet Union, in 1991–92, and joined the CIS as an independent republic. Tribal rugs are woven mainly by Uzbeks – although some items are also woven by Tajiks and other minority Turkic groups – and are usually marketed under their tribal name. (*See* Chapter VII: Labijar, Sar-i-Pul, Tartari and Uzbeks)

The Americas

Bolivia South American republic that takes its name from Simon Bolivar – the Venezuelan-born revolutionary leader – and shares much of its pre-Hispanic history with Peru. Its official language is Spanish – although Quechua and Aymara are also widely spoken – and its population of just over 6 million is composed of Mestizos (31%), Quechua (25%), Aymara (17%), and Europeans (14%) – most of whom are Catholic. Tribal rugs are produced mainly by Quechua and Aymara weavers and often feature simple striped designs dominated by large areas of black. Workshop rugs in a wide range of designs are also made.

Canada Settled by the French and British in the 17th and 18th centuries, but severed its official ties with Britain (1982). The indigenous Amerindians did not suffer quite the same degree of genocide as in the USA, but a number of conflicts (especially with the British) and a harsh reservation policy substantially reduced their numbers to around 300,000 and undermined native culture. Tribal rugs were made by a number of Amerindian tribes inhabiting the Salishan region of the Pacific coast and are normally more overtly Totemic (similar to Innuit or Eskimo art) than Amerindian items produced in the USA. (*See* Chapter IV: Nootka, Salish, Tlingit)

Colombia Republic in South America whose indigenous inhabitants (the Chibcha) were conquered by the Spanish in the 16th century. Its population is Mestizo (58%), European (20%), Mulatto (14%), Negro (4%) and Amerindian (1%). Colombian rugs are generally regional, rather than tribal, and based on a fusion of Spanish, Catholic and native Amerindian influences.

Ecuador Republic that shares most of its history – prior to independence in 1830 – with Peru. It has a population of *c.* 9 million – Mestizo (55%), Amerindian (25%), Spanish (10%) and African (10%), most of whom are Catholic. The official language is Spanish – although Quechua and Jivaroan are also spoken. Tribal rugs are mainly produced by Otavalo and, to a lesser degree, Salasca and Quechua Amerindian weavers. They are similar to Peruvian rugs, but tend to employ a brighter, more vivacious palette, and often feature animals as well as mythological figures. Post-Hispanic subject matters (e.g. village life), Mestizo folk art (a fusion of Spanish and Amerindian), and other contemporary designs also feature quite prominently. Items in a similar range of designs are produced by individual artist/craftsmen weavers and in commercially run workshops and are often indistinguishable from many Amerindian tribal items. (*See* Chapter IV: Otavalo)

Mexico Federal republic that occupies most of the Central American Isthmus. It was the centre of a number of advanced Amerindian civilizations (e.g. Olmecs, Toltecs, Aztecs and Mayans) prior to the arrival of the Europeans (mainly Spanish) in the 16th century. The country was ruled by Spain until 1821, and the basis of the current constitution was established in 1917. Mexico's population (*c.* 80 million) is composed of Mestizo (55%), Amerindian (29%) and Spanish/European (10%) – most of whom are Roman Catholics. Tribal rugs are produced by a number of indigenous Amerindian groups – who mostly inhabit the south of the country – but similar items are also produced in commercial regional centres. Mexican tribal rugs usually feature either human and mythological figures, or symbolic geometric motifs, based on ancient Mayan, Aztec and other Amerindian rugs or illustrations. However, some items also reflect post-Hispanic culture, incorporating Christian or Spanish symbolism, as well as more realistic historical, social or environmental scenes. (*See* Chapter IV: Amuzgo, Maya, Mixtec, Nahua, Perpechua, Zapotec)

Peru Constitutional republic that was the centre of successive Amerindian civilizations (e.g. Chinchorro, Paracas, Nazca, Chancay, Wari, Cara, Chimu and Inca) that stretch back to the second millennium BC, and perhaps earlier. The last of these (the Inca Empire) – which extended from the town of Cuzco (in south central Peru) throughout Ecuador and Bolivia, and into large areas of Colombia, Chile and Argentina – was destroyed, in *c.* 1532, by the Spanish conquistador, Francisco Pizarro (*c.* 1475–1541). Peru gained its independence from Spain in 1824 and its current borders were finally established in 1942. It has a population of *c.* 20 million – Amerindians (45%), Mestizos (37%), Europeans (15%) and minorities of Africans and Asians. The official languages are Spanish and Quechua (Inca) – although Aymara is also widely spoken – and over 90% of the population are theoretically Roman Catholics.

Tribal rugs are produced mainly by Aymara and Quechua weavers – both for personal use and trade – and usually feature Inca, Paracas and other Amerindian mythological figures, geometric motifs and pictographs that are articulated mainly in earth colours (e.g. browns, beige, ochres, pale violets, blue and reds) although richer colours are also used. Some items featuring post-Hispanic subjects (mainly village scenes) are also produced. A similar range of regional/workshop rugs are also woven, by both Amerindians and Mestizos, in a number of regional centres. However, there has been little attempt to establish tribal or regional authenticity and most Peruvian rugs are marketed under the name of a regional centre or stylistic type. (*See* Chapter IV: Ayamara, and Chapter VII: Ayuchucho, Cuzco, San Pedro de Cajas)

United States of America European settlement began in the late 16th century and, by the 18th century, the country was effectively part of the British Empire. However, a series of small revolts culminated in the War of Independence (*c.* 1775–83) and British recognition of US sovereignty. Conflict between European settlers and native Amerindians began, after a brief period of mutual coexistence, as a result of the settlers' insatiable desire for land. The ensuing Indian Wars decimated the native population. Thousands were killed in military engagements and there were several massacres of unarmed people. Also the reservation policy was a catalogue of broken promises (giving birth to the expression 'Indian giving') and often proved to be little more than genocide by starvation and deprivation. The US population of *c.* 250 million includes *c.* 1 million Amerindians (around half live on reservations). Tribal rugs are produced almost exclusively by the Navajo, but a number of older (and occasionally contemporary) items made by Pueblo, Nez Perce and a few other tribes appear on the market. (*See* Chapter VII: Navajo; and Chapter IV: Pueblo, Nez Perce)

CHAPTER SEVEN

Weaving groups

This chapter contains all the major tribal weaving groups listed under their most commonly applied names and divided into general and specific classifications. Selection has been made based on current availability and collectability – and allowances have been made for localized variations in popularity. Some regional weaving centres (e.g. Shiraz) produce both non-tribal regional/workshop items and also act as marketing centres for authentic tribal rugs. The most important of these centres have been included in this chapter, and, where appropriate, a clear distinction has been made between regional/workshop and tribal items that may be sold under the same name. Information on general ethnic groups, or tribal groups whose rug production is limited, are contained in Chapter IV; and information on national rug production can be found in Chapter VI.

General weaving groups

This section outlines all the major ethnic and tribal confederacy general weaving groups throughout Asia, North Africa and the Americas. The sub-groups that are normally closely associated with a general weaving group – or whose rugs are largely indistinguishable from those made by kindred groups – are contained here.

Afshar (or Awshar) (pls 9, 13, 35)
Ethnic tribe, believed to be descended from the Oghuz branch of the Turkic tribesmen, who live a nomadic, semi-nomadic and settled lifestyle in four separate areas of Iran. They are also found in isolated pockets in other parts of Iran, the Caucasus and eastern Turkey. They were one of the seven tribes, who (in the 15th century) formed part of the Kyzylbash (redhead) federation – a military/political grouping, mainly of Dervish influence, who derived their name from their red turbans – credited with promoting the first Safavid Shah, Ismail, to the Persian throne. However, in the 16th century the Afshar leader tried to kill Shah Abbas's mother, and sections of the tribe were forcibly resettled from their traditional territories in the north west to remoter parts of the country. The Afshar are one of the most important and most influential tribal weaving groups in Iran.

Afshar rugs are arguably the most varied in quality, colour and design of all contemporary tribal items. At their best, they can rival the most prestigious urban workshop items in the fineness of their knotting and the intricacy of their designs, but they can also be fairly coarsely woven (e.g. 40–50 knots in^2) and sometimes employ rather kitsch or finicky compositions, usually when the weavers are trying to reproduce European-style floral or other workshop designs. However, the vast majority are compact, tightly woven (80–150 knots in^2), using good quality wool and cotton warps, and normally have a short to medium pile. Traditional designs employ amulet or pole-medallions (diamond Afshars), repeating *botehs* (Afshar *dejahs*), repeating all-over floral motifs (floral Afshars), repeating geometric motifs that are believed to resemble chickens (Afshar *morgi*), and an exceptionally dramatic scheme, based on a huge central motif, said to represent an animal skin stretched out for tanning (animal-skin Afshars). However, a wide range of other designs are also found. The palette is dominated by deep reds and blues, but burnt orange, brown and yellow ochres, rose, greens and cream are also common. Good quality kilims, bags and animal trappings are made. Afshar rugs are widely available in the west, usually retail within the low-to-medium price bracket (although the finer items are more expensive) and may be marketed simply as Afshars or under their regional association. (*See* Kerman, Niriz)

Azerbaijan Afshars Made by mainly settled tribesmen, who escaped the forced relocation of their kinsmen. They are very similar to other items woven in the region, and mainly feature medallions on open or sparsely decorated grounds in deep reds, blues, yellow and orange ochres, with hints of white. Kilims are also made in similar designs, usually in slitweave and occasionally double-interlock.

Bidjar Afshars (pl 13) Produced by settled tribesmen in and around the villages of Tekab and Tekkenteppe, near Bidjar in Kurdistan, and are considered to be the most technically accomplished of all tribal rugs. They are finely woven (sometimes in excess of 250–300 knots per in^2) and usually feature intricately articulated, floral medallions in a rich palette of reds, blues, yellow ochres, greens and creams. They span the medium-to-high and high price brackets, and may be sold as Bidjars.

Kerman Afshars (pl 9) Woven by the largest and most prolific of the major Afshar splinter groups. They were banished to this remote, mountainous region in the 16th and 17th centuries, and many have subsequently opted for a settled way of life, intermarried with other local inhabitants, and merged their weaving traditions with those of other groups in the area. However, a significant number have retained their tribal identity and lifestyle and continue to produce pile rugs, kilims, bags and animal trappings in traditional diamond, *dejah*, *morgi*, floral and animal-skin designs. A wide range of other medallion, repeating, all-over and banded schemes which often feature a plethora of tiny infill motifs (e.g. animals, people, talismen, small rosettes or floral heads and geometric forms) are also found. Deep reds, blues, yellow and orange ochres, white and occasionally green are the dominant colours. The fineness of the knotting varies considerably, depending largely on the demands of the design, but they are normally well made, compact and aesthetically accomplished. Kilims are usually rectangular and are woven in slitweave, double-interlock, weft wrapping and dovetailing. Kerman Afshars may be sold under the names of the specific marketing towns in the region (e.g. Sirjand, Jiruft and Baft), but, despite small, stylistic nuances, the vast majority are sold simply as Afshars or Kerman Afshars – the latter often being reserved for finer quality rugs. (*See* Kerman)

Khorassan Afshars Made by descendants of the tribes banished in the 16th and 17th centuries, who are now divided into settled and semi-nomadic groups. The former mainly produce items that conform to the general Khorassan style, but some of the semi-nomads weave a variety of pile rugs, kilims, bags and animal trappings that retain more distinctive Afshar characteristics. These are usually fairly small, compact (although not especially finely knotted) and employ a number of amulet/medallion and (mainly geometric) all-over designs. Kilims often incorporate small geometric motifs, usually crenellated or zig-zag, into medallion or banded designs, and are made using slitweave, double-interlock, weft wrapping and weft-faced patterning techniques. Deep reds and blues are the dominant colours.

Aimaq or Chahar Aimaq (pl 36)

Informal confederation of four Persian-speaking nomadic, semi-nomadic and sedentary tribes of mainly Turkic, Mongolian, Persian and Arab origins who inhabit a vast area in north-west and west central Afghanistan. Their name is derived from the Persian and Mongolian words for four (Chahar) and nomad (Aimaq). Most Aimaq rugs are very similar in character and appearance to those made by the neighbouring Belouch tribes, and it is fairly common for them to be sold in the west as Belouches. Aimaq rugs generally fall into the low price bracket. (*See* Sarmayie, Qala-i-Nau)

Firozkohi Semi-nomadic tribesmen – whose name means mountains of turquoise (probably an oblique reference to their territorial origins) – who are concentrated into two main groups, each with numerous sub-tribes and clans. The eastern group are more Mongolian in appearance than their Mahmud counterparts in the west, but there is very little difference in the character and appearance of their rugs. The Firozkohi do not have their own distinctive design repertoire, preferring to copy popular Taimani, Belouch and other tribal designs. Consequently, many Firozkohi items are sold in the west under the name of the weaving group whose design has been used. This is particularly true of pile rugs, which are generally of reasonable quality. However, their flatweaves, bags and animal trappings are rather more distinctive, and are produced mainly in balanced plainweave, with supplementary embroidery and inserts, in a variety of geometric patterns (frequently based on diamond motifs) in brown, orange, green, white and cherry red.

Hazara Tribal people of Mongoloid appearance, believed to be descendants of Genghis Khan's hordes, who are divided into two distinct groups. The first are Sunnite Muslims, who live in and around the town of Qala-i-Nau and produce good quality pile rugs (similar in appearance to Jamshidi items) and distinctive, high quality kilims which are usually marketed as Lagharis or Qala-i-Naus. The second group are Shi'ite Muslims, living in the central Hazarajat region, who are sometimes involved in the production of Belouch-style rugs.

Jamshidi Persian-speaking tribal group of obscure (possibly Arab and Persian) origins who are now divided into mainly sedentary farmers and traders (living in and around the city of Herat) and semi-nomadic clans scattered throughout the Badghis and Herat Provinces. They have no original designs and normally copy either Tekke (Mauri) Turkoman or Taimani and Belouch designs. Jamshidi rugs are generally fairly coarsely woven and loosely articulated and are often sold under the name of the tribe associated with the design.

Taimani (pl 36) Largest of the Aimaq tribes, divided into at least ten main clans, with several smaller sub-clans, who live a mainly semi-nomadic existence throughout west-central Afghanistan. They are among the most prolific and important tribal weavers in the region, producing a huge range of pile rugs, kilims, bags and animal trappings in a variety of designs – ranging from simple prayer rugs to more intricate pictorial items, including Afghan War Rugs. They are similar to Belouch items, but are usually less precisely articulated, possess a more primitive, folk-art quality and generally employ a brighter palette, which often includes orange, purple and small areas of yellow and green, as well as lighter shades of red and blue. Pile rugs are generally small to medium in size, not very finely woven, but they are fairly compact and use good quality wool. Flatweaves employ a number of techniques – including semi-pile, *soumak*, weft wrapping and weft-faced patterning. Taimani rugs usually fall in the low price bracket, but exceptional items (e.g. War Rugs) may cost more.

Arab weaving groups (sim pls 4, 5)
Arabs are an Indo-European people of Semitic origin, who constitute the largest – and the politically and culturally dominant – ethnic group in North Africa and the Middle East. They are also found – often in isolated tribal groups – in other parts of the weaving region. The earliest known Arab civilization existed, during the 2nd century BC, in the watered highlands of Yemen and gradually spread through Saudi Arabia and the Nile Delta. However, the flowering of Arab culture began in the 7th century when an Arab Islamic Empire emerged and extended its influence through North Africa, the Middle East and parts of Europe. The Arabs were originally a minority racial and religious group in their conquered territories, who treated Christians and other non-Muslims (and non-Arabs) as separate, self-governing 'Peoples of the Book' (the Koran). However, the tax, career and social advantages available to Muslims resulted in many of the subject peoples converting to Islam. Arab political dominance was gradually supplanted in most of its conquered territories, but it left behind a profound cultural, religious and artistic legacy, and established varying degrees of Arab settlement throughout western Asia and North Africa.

Arab rugs are made throughout North Africa and to a lesser extent in Iran, Afghanistan and other parts of Asia. However, most Arab rugs are classified as regional, rather than tribal, because they are either made in conjunction with other ethnic groups (e.g. Berbers) or else they are closer in character and appearance to the items produced by other groups in the region than to a homogeneous Arab style. However, there are a few Arab tribes, mainly in the Tennsift River region of Morocco, who are usually accepted as forming specific Arab weaving groups. Kilims are generally more common than pile rugs, and are usually large and rectangular, or long and narrow, brightly coloured, employ banded designs with repeating geometric (or *wasm*) infill motifs, and are usually woven in a combination of plainweave and slitweave – distinguishing them from Berber kilims, which rarely use slitweave. Pile and semi-pile items are often fairly coarsely woven and the designs are often simpler versions of those found on Iranian and Turkish tribal rugs. Red is the dominant ground colour, offset by fairly gentle shades of orange, yellow ochre and blue. Arab tribal rugs normally fall in the low price bracket and are not as common in the west as Berber rugs. (*See* Bowanat, Firdous, Nasrabad)

Chiadma Tribe neighbouring the Oulad Bou Sbaa, whose rugs share a number of features, but are often wilder and less symmetrical in their designs. Intense shades of red, burgundy, orange, black, white and other primary colours are common. Chiadma pile rugs are fairly coarsely woven and their kilims sometimes employ plainweave and pile insertion, as well as slitweave.

Marsh Arabs Collective term for the trìbes living mainly in the delta region of southern Iraq, who make brightly coloured, ornately patterned *namads* (felt rugs) and flatweaves (in a mixture of weaving techniques). However, their persecution by the Iraqi regime means that few of these items reach the west.

Oulad Bou Sbaa Tribe in the Tennsift region noted for their boldly decorated, brightly coloured items that often possess a rather primitive folk-art quality. Oulad Bou Sbaa pile rugs are often quite coarsely woven and usually feature a variety of repeating geometric motifs, sometimes interspersed with human and animal forms, based on red or orange grounds. Their kilims are woven predominantly in slitweave, employ a similar palette, but are more often made in banded designs.

Rehamna Tribe in the Tennsift region, who produce extremely distinctive rugs – using an unusual semi-pile technique – that feature numerous small monochrome diamonds and squares, juxtaposed in such a way as to create the impression of a totally abstract painting, reminiscent of the work of Mondrian.

Armenian weaving groups (pl 23, sim pl 24)

The Armenians are an Indo-European people whose exact origins are uncertain. Herodotus, the ancient Greek historian (*c.* 485–425 BC), believed that they were related to the ancient Phrygians, but most contemporary historians trace their genesis to the Urartian civilization that flourished in the Caucasus during the 6th century BC. The Armenians established a civilization (during the 1st century BC) that was powerful enough to challenge the Roman Empire, and (since adopting Christianity in the 3rd century AD) their cultural, religious and racial integrity has withstood nearly 2,000 years of conquest, subjugation, dispersal and persecution (culminating in the massacre and forcible expulsion of nearly 6 million ethnic Armenians by Turkey and Russia at the beginning of the 20th century). It is also generally accepted that the Armenians are among the world's finest weavers, and that they have had a profound effect on the evolution of rug weaving throughout most of western Asia. Today, Armenians can be found in the Armenian Republic and a number of countries throughout the Caucasus and the Middle East.

Armenian rugs are generally extremely well made, richly coloured in harmoniously contrasting reds, blues, green, yellows and other primary shades and feature bold, often overtly heraldic, central amulet/medallions set against intricately patterned fields, or equally dramatic repeating or all-over formats of naturalistic or stylized vegetal or geometric forms. They sometimes contain Roman inscriptions and elements of Christian imagery and Armenian folk art. However, they have invariably been classified according to their regional, or stylistic characteristics, although a number were probably made by semi-nomadic Armenian herdsmen. Some tribal confederacies contain ethnic Armenians. (*See* Kemereh, Traditional Caucasian weaving groups)

Azerbaijani weaving groups (sim pls 23, 24)

Azerbaijanis are a fairly homogeneous ethnic group of Turkic or Turko-Mongol origins who are now divided between the Azerbaijan Republic and the bordering province of the same name in north-west Iran. They live a predominantly settled existence, are mainly Shi'ite Muslims, and, despite an on-going conflict, share many of their weaving traditions with their Christian Armenian neighbours.

Caucasian Azerbaijani rugs Fall into two categories: contemporary items that are generally similar in price, character and appearance to Iranian Azerbaijanis; and older, more expensive Traditional Caucasian rugs.

Iranian Azerbaijani rugs Similar to Caucasian Azerbaijanis, but generally more primitive in character and appearance, and also reflect the design traditions of the other indigenous ethnic groups (e.g. Shahsavan). They usually employ bold, geometric motifs (e.g. amulet- and pole-medallions), often with various geometric or stylized animal, bird and floral motifs, and tend towards either a fairly sombre palette of deep reds and blues, or brighter interplays of red, blue, orange, ochres and occasionally greens. Sizes vary, but most are either small to medium, or long and narrow. Pile rugs are usually not very finely woven (e.g. 80–120 Turkish knots in^2), but they are generally compact and durable. Flatweaves are made using several weaving techniques and feature a range of banded, repeating and pile-rug designs. Bags and animal trappings are also woven. They are normally low to medium in price, and may be sold under the names of local regional/workshop centres (e.g. Ardebil, Meshkin, Sarab).

Bakhtiari (pl 31)

The Bakhtiari are a major sub-tribe of the Lurs, and are believed to be one of thirty tribes that migrated from Syria in the 14th century. They mainly inhabit a broad area on either side of the Zagros Mountains, and around the town of Shushtar and the Chahar Mahal Valley in western Iran. They are divided into a number of sub-tribes (e.g. Duraki), some of whom still practise a nomadic or semi-nomadic way of life and produce authentic tribal items. However, most of the rugs that western dealers sell as Bakhtiaris are regional items made by non-Bakhtiari weavers.

Bakhtiari tribal rugs (pl 31) Produced by nomadic and semi-nomadic Bakhtiari tribes. Kilims are usually long and narrow, woven in double-interlock and based on a wide variety of medallion, repeating, all-over and panelled designs, in different shades of deep red, blue, reddish brown, yellow ochre, cream and white. Pile rugs are not very finely knotted, small to medium in size, and are produced in a similar range of colours and designs. Bags and animal trappings are also made. Items marketed in Shushtar generally employ medallions and various rhomboid central motifs set against an open or sparsely decorated field, and those produced in and around the Chahar Mahal Valley usually feature a wider range of small geometric and naturalistic motifs; including *botehs* and tiny human and animal figures. Tribal Bakhtiaris are available in moderation and are normally low to medium in price.

Bakhtiari regional rugs Produced by Kurds, Lurs, Armenians, Bakhtiari and other, mainly Turkoman, ethnic groups in a number of villages in Chahar Mahal va Bakhtiari region. Panelled designs predominate, but the precise composition, internal motifs, colour scheme, structure, quality and the fineness of the knotting varies between villages. Chahal Shotur is generally acknowledged as producing the finest Bakhtiaris, and top quality items are also made in Saman and the Armenian village of Feridan (which often use parrots as infill motifs). Attractive, medium grade items are woven in Boldaji and Shalamzar; Shahr Kurd (which literally means Kurdish town) makes medium-to-good quality double-wefted rugs. Regional Bakhtiaris may be sold under the name of the weaving group or simply as Bakhtiaris, and vary in price between low to medium and medium to high.

Belouch (pls 1, 7, 21, 26, 32, 33, 37)

The Belouch are an informal tribal confederation of mainly Indo-European nomadic and semi-nomadic herdsmen who occupy a vast, largely inhospitable area that stretches from eastern Iran, through Afghanistan into western Pakistan. The name Belouch simply means nomad, and, although we know that they were established in most of their current territory by the 10th and 12th centuries, their precise origins are unclear. One of their myths alludes to their direct descent from Nebuchadnezzar, which may be taken as an allegorical reference to their origins in Arabia, Aleppo (Syria), or Iraq, although some historians argue that they were Persian nomads who were forced eastwards by the Turkic and Turko-Mongol invasions of the 10th and 11th centuries. Many of the larger Belouch tribes are Persian-speaking, but others (e.g. the Brahui) speak a Dravidian (south Indian) dialect, and include a number of Indian customs and practices in their otherwise orthodox Sunnite Muslim social and religious rites. It is possible therefore that the Belouch are a fusion of at least two separate, migratory groups – one moving eastwards from Persia, and the other travelling westwards from India – whose cultural differences have been largely eroded over the centuries, resulting in a relatively homogeneous group, who are among the most prolific, accomplished and generally underrated of all tribal weavers.

Belouch rugs, kilims, bags and animal trappings are produced by numerous individual tribes, sub-tribes and settled villagers throughout Afghanistan, eastern Iran and western Pakistan. The term Belouch is also used as a generic description for items made in the Belouch style by non-Belouch weavers. However, most Belouch and Belouch-style pile rugs are well made – normally with 60–100 Persian knots in^2 (although finer items are produced) – using good quality wool, in various sizes (mainly small to medium). Good quality flatweaves are also woven – using a mixture of weft wrapping, weft-faced patterning, weft twining, plainweaving and supplementary pile-insertion techniques. Designs are dominated by repeating geometric, prayer-rug, pictorial and banded compositions (often with intricate infill decorations), which are often articulated in a sombre palette of dark blues, reds, violet, blue-black, brown and orange ochres, with white, cream and yellow highlights, although brighter and more varied colours are also used – especially in pictorial items. Belouch and Belouch-style rugs are widely available in the west, and normally fall into the low or low-to-medium price category and are often sold collectively as Belouches. (*See* Bagdiz, Baluchistan, Chichaksu, Dokhtar-i-Ghazi, Farah, Firdous, Ghurian, Haft-Boleh, Jan Begi, Malaki, Maldari, Mushwani, Nishapur, Shirikhani, Timuri, Yakob Khani)

Herat (or Afghan) Belouch rugs (pls 6, 7, 21, 33) Generic term – derived from the city of Herat – often applied to any Belouch or Belouch-style item made in Afghanistan. However, it is often reserved for small pile rugs, usually around 5' x 3' (1.5 x 0.9 m), which employ a variety of prayer-rug designs. The fineness of the knotting varies, but the general quality of the wool and manufacture is normally good. Colour schemes range from a limited palette of dark blues and reds, with white highlights, to a much broader range of often lighter shades, including orange, brown and camel.

Meshed (or Iranian) Belouch rugs (pl 37) Generic term derived from the major town in north-east Iran for Belouch, or Belouch-style, rugs made in Iran by the Salor Khani, Ali Akbar Khani, Brahui, Khodadada'i, Husseinza'i, Rashin Khani and other indigenous tribes who generally market their wares in the towns of Shakhs, Torbat and Nishapur. However, the term is often reserved for good quality, reasonably finely knotted pile rugs that mainly feature repeating or pictorial designs.

Peshawar (or Refugee) rugs (pl 1) Generic term for items made by refugee Belouch and other tribesmen, who fled from Afghanistan during the Afghan–Soviet War and settled in and around the towns of Peshawar and Quetta in western Pakistan. They now produce a range of pile rugs and kilims in a number of traditional Belouch designs – generally echoing Meshed Belouches – often in a brighter, more varied palette.

Berber weaving groups (pls 4, 5)

The Berbers are an Indo-European people, who are the indigenous inhabitants of the Maghrib, and derive their name from the ancient Roman word *barbari* – which means not Greek or Latin and thus uncivilized, coarse, cruel and barbarous. The Berbers were overrun by the Arabs, in the 7th century, and despite periods of ascendancy (especially during the reigns of Saladin and the Fatimids)

they have been dominated, both politically and culturally, by the Arabs ever since. However, many Berbers have maintained their cultural and weaving identity and the vast majority of North African tribal rugs are made by Berber tribes – mainly in the Tennsift region, and the Middle and High Atlas Mountains of Morocco. Pile rugs are not very finely knotted, and may employ loop knotting or tassel insertions, as well as more orthodox Turkish, Persian, Spanish and Berber knotting techniques. Kilims, usually featuring banded designs, are normally woven in a mixture of plainweave and weft-faced patterning. Berber rugs are produced by a number of individual tribes and normally fall into the low price category.

Middle Atlas rugs can be roughly divided between the colourful, often thematically vivacious, items made in the west – which are sometimes based on completely wild interplays of pile, kilim and tassel insertion – and the extremely thick, mainly white or monochrome rugs – often containing small tracery motifs in slightly lighter or darker shades of the field colour – woven in the east and central areas, which are the origin of the western, machine-made, Berber fitted carpets.

High Atlas pile rugs are generally more restrained in structure, colour and design (often based on more orthodox oriental rug or diagonal lattice schemes) and usually only have a fringe at one end. Flatweaves generally employ banded and, less frequently, geometric repeating designs.

Ait Haddidou Tribe inhabiting a remote area of the High Atlas Mountains, noted for extremely tightly woven flatweaves in simple banded designs, which are dominated by black (or dark blue) and white (or cream).

Ait Quaouzguite High Atlas tribe who mainly produce flatweaves and semi-pile rugs in banded, panelled/compartmental, diagonal lattice and occasionally medallion, all-over and pictorial designs. Their palette is a curious mixture of fairly pastel reds, orange and brown ochres, blues, violets and greens, sharply contrasted with dark blue, black, white and cream. They are well made, and often sold as Glaouas.

Beni M'Guild and Beni M'Tir Two semi-nomadic tribes, inhabiting the Middle Atlas Mountains, who make pile rugs and flatweaves that often feature a variety of slightly asymmetrical checker-board, banded, panelled and repeating designs, either in fairly harmonious pastel reds, blues, browns, yellows and cream or a darker palette of blue, black and red, contrasted with white or cream.

Beni Quarain Tribe living north of the Middle Atlas Mountains noted for flatweaves in banded designs that use alternating monochrome plainweave and highly decorated weft-faced patterning in sharply contrasting light and dark colours.

Beni Saddene Small tribe, inhabiting the Middle Atlas Mountains, who are noted for their exuberant, primitive items – usually in warm colours and bold banded designs.

Zaiane Semi-nomads inhabiting the higher ranges of the Middle Atlas Mountains, who produce long-pile rugs in banded, repeating, skeletal medallion and expanding, concentric diamond formats. Red is often used as the ground colour, offset by blue, purple, yellow ochre and white. Kilims are woven in a variety of sizes, mainly in alternating rows of broad, intensely decorated bands separated by narrow monochrome strips.

Zair Middle Atlas tribe whose rugs are similar to Zaiane items, but are usually slightly wilder in appearance and often feature rows of tiny metallic disks or beads, or tassel insertions.

Zemmour Tribal confederation – originally from the Middle Atlas Mountains, but now inhabiting the northern extremities of the Tennsift region. They are prolific weavers, and produce both pile rugs and flatweaves in a variety of banded, all-over and panelled schemes (often with tiny geometric infill motifs) in different shades of red.

Khamseh (or Khamsa) (pl 10)

The Khamseh are a formal tribal confederation of five main tribes, primarily of Turkic, Luri and Arab ethnic origins, who inhabit the Fars Province of southern Iran. They take their name from the Persian word for five, and were formed (in 1862) by a wealthy merchant family (the Qavams of Shiraz) in order to guard their trade routes against Qashga'i raids. Today, most Khamseh tribesmen live a settled existence, but some still retain their traditional semi-nomadic and nomadic lifestyles.

Khamseh rugs are produced by each of five main tribes (the Ainallu, Baharlu, Bassira, Jabbareh and Sheibari), but – despite slight differences in their respective character and appearance, and regardless of the weavers' lifestyle – they are all normally marketed collectively as Khamsehs and are very similar in quality, size and design to those produced by the Qashga'i, Lurs, Afshar and other tribal groups in the region. There are, however, two specific compositions that are closely associated with the Khamseh. The first is known as the *si-murgh* (or thirty-bird) design – sometimes referred to as chicken rugs – which features a plethora of tiny birds, interspersed with stylized floral and other naturalistic forms – either in a simple all-over format or in conjunction with a cruciform diamond pole-medallion set within a crenellated surround. The second employs a similar pole-medallion set against a series of narrow, vertical stripes and is sometimes referred to as the cane design. A variety of amulet, medallion-and-corner, *boteh*, all-over and pictorial designs (often featuring lions) are also produced – usually in fairly light shades of blue, red, orange and yellow ochre, cream and white, although deeper colours are also used. Pile rugs are generally well made and sometimes quite finely woven. Kilims – woven in slitweave and double-interlock – bags and animal trappings are also made. Most Khamseh rugs are low to medium in price and are fairly widely available, but may be sold as Qashga'is or Luris. (*See* Shahsavan)

Kurds (pls 12, 20, 25, 26, 29, 38)

The Kurds are a culturally homogeneous Indo-European people who are among the oldest inhabitants of a vaguely defined area – stretching from the Iranian plateau through northern Iraq and into eastern Turkey – that is commonly known as ethnic Kurdistan. Their precise origins are obscure. Kurdish folklore traces their genesis to one of the 500 *jinns*, or *genies* (supernatural beings), who were sent by King Solomon to find 500 virgins for his harem. However, after hearing of Solomon's death, the *jinn* claimed the virgin bride for himself and settled in the Zagros Mountains (in southern Iran), where he fathered the Kurdish race. Taken as an allegory, this story reinforces the belief that the Kurds originated in Palestine and Syria, and then migrated to the north and east. We know that a tribe called the Kuti (or Guti) existed in ancient Assyria and Babylonia (Iraq, Syria, etc.) as early as the 2nd millennium BC, and that later Assyrian documents (*c.* 900–600 BC) make references to the Kurtie and later to the Kardu. However, the name Kurd was first used *c.* 640 AD to describe a number of tribes who inhabited western Persia and the southern Caucasus. It is from this point that a more precise picture of Kurdish history begins to unfold. The Kurds (in common with the Armenians, with whom they formed an alliance against the Ottomans during the 16th century) have maintained their cultural identity, despite centuries of conflict, subjugation, persecution and forced migration. Today, most Kurds still live in ethnic Kurdistan, but there are pockets of settlement in other parts of Iran (especially Khorassan), the Caucasus, Iraq and Syria. Many Kurds have now adopted a settled lifestyle, but some still retain a nomadic or semi-nomadic existence.

Kurdish rugs are made in such a diversity of qualities, designs and overall characteristics that it is impossible to categorize all the items woven by ethnic Kurds into a homogeneous group. Several specific weaving groups, which are composed mainly of ethnic Kurds, make rugs that are clearly regional (or workshop) in character, appearance and manufacture. Some of these (e.g. Hamadan) are classified as regional, whereas others (e.g. Bidjar) are still viewed as essentially Kurdish. There are also a number of nomadic, semi-nomadic and settled groups that are generally accepted as being authentically tribal, and whose rugs share a number of overall characteristics. Pile rugs are generally well made – although the fineness of the knotting varies considerably – employ good quality wool, and feature a range of amulet- and pole-medallion, *herati*, *boteh*, repeating geometric, panelled and banded designs. Good quality kilims (usually made in slitweave, with the occasional use of supplementary weft wrapping or weft insertion), bags and animal trappings are also produced. The Kurdish palette varies from either predominantly dark reds, blues, orange, brown and yellow ochres – offset with greens, creams, beige and white – to much lighter shades of the same colours. Sizes and shapes differ, although small, medium and long and narrow items predominate. Kurdish tribal rugs are fairly widely available in the west, and may be sold under the name of the tribe, marketing centre, region or simply as Kurdish, and generally fall into the low or medium price bracket. (*See* Bakhtiari, Bidjar, Khorassan, Quchan, Senneh, Van)

Barzani Tribe in Iraq, but often used as a generic term for rugs made by a number of tribes in the region. Barzani rugs are usually coarsely woven, employ wool, goat and mohair in the pile, and feature a number of fairly dramatic, simple geometric designs – including primitive copies of workshop items – in a limited range of moderately bright colours.

Dizai Mainly settled tribe in the Erbil Plain (Iraq), who make pile rugs and kilims in a mixture of predominantly Iranian and Caucasian designs. Items made by other local tribes (e.g. Surchi/Mantik, Girdi, and Khailani) may be sold as Dizais, or Erbil Plain rugs.

Goyan (pl 20) Large tribe, living around the Iraqi–Turkish border, who are closely associated with the Hartushi and produce a significant number of pile rugs and flatweaves in repeating geometric, lattice and banded designs in a mainly dark palette of red, blue, orange, brown and green, contrasted by white, pink and lighter shades of the same colours.

Hartushi (pl 20) Large tribe, divided into 12 to 16 sub-tribes, in eastern Turkey and northern Iran, who are primarily noted for good quality kilims that are similar to Goyan and Herki items.

Herki (pl 20) Prolific weaving tribe, who inhabit eastern Turkey and northern Iraq, noted for a variety of pile rugs, flatweaves, bags and artefacts featuring mainly repeating hooked diamonds, *guls*, amulet/medallions and banded designs in either dark or light browns, orange and yellow ochres and blues, reddish brown and white.

Jaff Large and important tribe, inhabiting a vast area of ethnic Kurdistan in Iraq and Iran, who weave numerous pile rugs, kilims, bags and animal trappings. Designs vary, but are usually based on repeating geometric (often hooked-diamond) motifs in fairly bright reds, blues, burnt orange and white.

Kakaberu (sim pl 28) Nomadic and semi-nomadic tribe, living near Senneh (Iran), who make sturdy, double-wefted rugs in amulet/medallion, *herati*, geometric and stylized vegetal motifs in repeating and all-over formats and the lightning design. They are similar to Kolyais, but are generally darker. They may be sold as Hamadans and usually fall into the low-to-medium price bracket.

Kolyai Mainly semi-nomadic tribe in Iranian Kurdistan, who normally market their rugs in the town of Sonqur. They are generally well made (although not especially finely woven), small to medium or long and narrow in size, and feature mainly amulet- and pole-medallions, repeating geometric and, less frequently, stylized floral and animal all-over designs. Colours vary, but reds, blues, burnt orange, cream, white, green and yellow, brown and orange ochres dominate.

Kurds of Khorassan (pls 25, 38) Generic term for items made by a number of Kurdish tribes (e.g. Shadlu, Zafaranlu and Rashwan) in the Khorassan Province of eastern Iran. They are generally well made, and feature designs that have a close affinity with north-western Iranian traditions (the area from which they were deported during the 17th century) and also contain Belouch, Turkoman and more universal Kurdish elements. Two of their most famous compositions are of an Ersari-influenced panelled format (housing individual scarab-like motifs) and a Caucasian-influenced pole-medallion – often inwardly decorated with stylized floral motifs – known as the *hawz*, or water tank, design. Kilims and bags – often based on hooked lozenges within banded and latticed schemes – are also made. Colours vary from bright to sombre, but usually contain burnt orange, golden yellow and a range of ochres, blues, reds and white.

Senjabi Southern-most Kurdish tribe in Iran, but often used as a generic term for items (in *herati* or repeating geometric designs) made by several tribes in the Kermanshah region.

Lurs (pls 2, 28, 31)

The Lurs are an Indo-European people, who are believed to be among the earliest inhabitants of south-western Iran. However, little is known about them until the 8th century BC, when they were prominent in the Elamite Kingdom, which stretched eastwards from Babylon to the Zagros Mountains (Iran) and is credited with producing the famous Luristan Bronzes (a number of whose designs still feature, in modified forms, as motifs in Luri and some other Iranian tribal rugs). For much of their history, they were divided into the Great Lurs (who inhabited the southern territories) and the Little Lurs (who lived in the north). However, this division had largely disappeared by the 15th century, and today they are generally viewed as a homogeneous ethnic group, divided into a number of sub-tribes – the most important of which is the Bakhtiari. Some Lurs now have settled lifestyles – or belong to tribal confederacies – but a substantial number still live nomadic and semi-nomadic lifestyles in their traditional territories – throughout Luristan and southern Kurdistan, across the Zagros Mountains into the Fars Province – where they are known locally as the Kuhi (mountain people) and still speak a language closely related to Persian. Luri rugs are

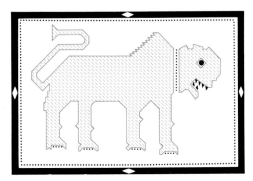

Lion, taken from a Luri or Qashga'i rug

generally not very finely knotted – employing 50–80, usually Turkish, knots in^2 – but they are normally well made, using good quality wool, and extremely sturdy. They are sometimes indistinguishable from Qashga'i and Khamseh rugs – especially those that employ complex, intricately detailed designs – but most are based on simple pictorial, pole-medallion and repeating geometric formats often using large areas of undyed wool or a few primary (or mellowed) shades of red, blue, orange, yellow ochre and brown. Kilims, bags and animal trappings are also made. Luri rugs are widely available and generally fall into the low and low-to-medium price brackets. (*See* Bebehan, Khorramabad, Nasrabad, Owlad)

Navajo (pls 39, 44–47)

The Navajo, or Dineh (meaning people), are an Athapascan-speaking tribe who migrated from Canada to the south-west USA (e.g. Colorado, Arizona, New Mexico) some time between the 10th and 13th centuries. On arriving in their new territories, the Navajo initially raided Pueblos settlements for food and occasionally slaves (usually women), but gradually forged a mutually cooperative relationship, absorbing a number of Pueblo customs and skills, including weaving. The Navajo were primarily nomadic hunter-gatherers, who had a rich spiritual and mythological heritage, but few agrarian, husbandry or practical craft-making skills. Their main deity is an hermaphrodite Creator (Ahsonnutli, or Turquoise Man-Woman) who stationed twelve men at strategical places around the Earth to hold up the sky. They share with the Incas (and other more southerly Amerindian peoples) a belief in the four cardinal points. In Navajo mythology they are guarded by a Great White Swan, which conjures the winds, and are each governed by a specific colour (i.e. white – east, blue – south, yellow – west and black – north; white and black also hold sway over the lower world, and blue over the upper or ethereal realm). These beliefs possibly underpin the Navajo sacred ceremonies (or chants) which usually involve the creation of sand paintings that are scattered (to the wind) when the ceremony is over.

Navajo rugs can be traced back to the 17th century (although they were possibly made slightly earlier), but it was not until the first half of the 18th century that their unique characteristics began to emerge. Unlike Pueblo weavings, Navajo rugs were produced by women and made from wool (the Spanish had introduced sheep into the region during the 16th century). At first, they were made primarily from undyed wool (augmented by a few local vegetable dyes) and featured simple geometric patterns, based mainly on Pueblo designs. However, around the mid-18th century, dyes became increasingly available and Navajo weavers were exposed to more sophisticated Peruvian and Mexican Hispanic-Amerindian items and European cloth (which they unravelled and re-wove into their rugs). This resulted in a rapid evolution in the technical and aesthetic quality of their rugs that reached its zenith during the Classic Period (1850–75). Most were made for use as wearing blankets or ponchos, which were often traded to the Plains Indians (e.g. Cheyenne, Arapahoe and Sioux), and usually featured simple bands, stripes, zig-zags, diamonds, crosses and rectangles in a limited palette of mainly blue, red, black and white. However, European clientele soon began to demand floor-coverings and wall-hangings in a wider range of colours and designs. Today, Navajo rugs are produced in a number of centres throughout the Navajo Reservation. They are invariably flatwoven (using a number of techniques) in banded, striped, amulet/medallion, repeating, all-over and pictorial (including *yei'is* and sand painting) designs. Zig-zag, swastika, diamond, cruciform, latch-hook and triangular motifs are common, and the Navajo palette ranges from undyed wool, offset by one or two primary colours, to dazzling interplays of a dozen or more shades. Sizes vary, but most items are small to medium. Navajo rugs are sold mainly in North America, but a few reach Europe and elsewhere. Prices range from medium to high. They may be sold simply as Navajos or under their stylistic, period or regional attributions.

Chief's Blankets (pls 44, 45) Generic term for items – which are not blankets and were not woven for chiefs – made in the latter half of the 18th century that are usually divided into four design groups: First Phase, which has only horizontal bands; Second Phase, which employs both horizontal and vertical bands that may form rectangles or squares; Third Phase, which sets diagonal strip or diamond motifs against horizontal bands; and the Variable Phase, which employs a mixture of the previous three designs. They are usually wider than they are long, employ a limited palette of blue, red, black and white, and are expensive.

Saltillo serapes *Serape* (meaning man's blanket in Spanish) is derived from the Aztec name for a woven shawl (*tzalanpepechtli*). They were originally made by Peruvian and Mexican Hispanic-Amerindian weavers in the town of Saltillo and were tapestry woven, worn as ponchos, and featured vertical stripes, zig-zags and columns of tiny stepped-diamonds in natural reds, blues, yellows, greens and white. This basic design was adapted by the Navajos for their round-the-shoulder blankets – which did not require the central slit – and was reproduced (often without the central diamond) on subsequent items. Both Mexican and Navajo Saltillo *serapes* are highly collectable and fall into the high price category.

Germantown weavings Generic term for early items made by Navajo weavers using mainly synthetic yarn obtained from Germantown, Pennsylvania. They often echo Saltillo *serape* and Chief's Blanket designs and normally fall into the high price category.

Chinle Regional weaving centre near the Navajo holy retreat at Canyon de Chelly, which produces thick, sturdy, textured rugs. Designs are often based on stepped diamonds, and the palette is dominated by earth colours (frequently obtained from vegetable sources). They usually fall into the medium price range.

Coal Mine Mesa Regional weaving centre, near Tuba City, that specializes in twilled saddle blankets and sculpted (or raised outline) weavings – which insert an extra weft around the motifs to accentuate their form – in mainly geometric designs. They normally fall into the low-to-medium or medium price brackets.

Crystal Regional weaving centre associated mainly with simple banded formats in earth colours. They are well made, use mostly vegetable dyes and are medium in price.

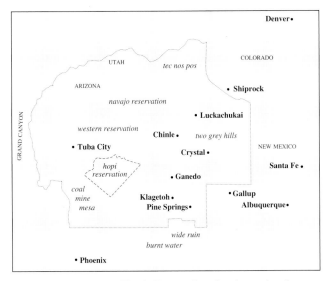

Navajo Reservation, showing regional
weaving centres

Gallup Regional centre noted mainly for small throw rugs – often coarsely woven on cotton warps, brightly coloured and featuring geometric, pictorial and stylized floral motifs, although some finer items are also made. They are low to medium or medium in price.

Ganado and Klagetoh Adjoining regional weaving centres. Ganado is noted for simple, bold medallion and repeating geometric designs (often serrated diamonds, stars or crosses) set against monochrome or sparsely decorated fields in vivid reds and other primary shades. Klagetoh employ similar (often simpler) schemes based on diamond medallions in a palette of natural grey, black and red. Both are generally medium in price.

Luckachukai Regional weaving centre noted for *yei'is* and pictorial designs. They are similar to Shiprock rugs, but use darker colours (e.g. brown, red, grey, black, pink, turquoise and tan), have a slightly coarser weave and fall into the medium price range.

Shiprock Town and regional weaving centre noted especially for *yei'is*, *yei-be-chais*, sand paintings and other pictorial items, often on beige or white grounds. They are generally well made, very collectable and medium or medium to high in price.

Tec Nos Pos Regional weaving centre (meaning circle of cottonwood trees) whose designs are quite similar to those used in Two Grey Hills, but have smoother less agitated edges and use slightly warmer muted reds, orange,

beige, tan, blue and white. They are generally well made and are usually medium in price.

Two Grey Hills Regional weaving centre that produces tightly woven contemporary items, often featuring bold, usually fairly large stepped or latch-hooked medallions, set within echoing corners or serrated linear surrounds against a sparsely decorated field containing stars, swastikas, latch-hooks and other (largely jagged-edged) motifs. A high proportion of undyed wool – supplemented by red, blue, black and tan dyes – is common. They are fairly widely available and usually fall into the medium price category.

Western Reservation Large area – incorporating a number of individual weaving centres – noted for traditional geometric schemes, articulated in black, grey, white, brown and red. It is especially associated with the Storm Pattern design, which is based on a central square or diamond (symbolizing the centre of the world) connected by zig-zag lines (lightning) to smaller echoing motifs in the four corners (representing the four houses of wind in the four sacred mountains). Swastikas and stylized water beetles are common infill motifs. They normally fall into the medium price bracket.

Wide Ruin, Pine Spring and Burnt Water Three adjoining regional weaving centres noted especially for their use of natural dyes. Designs often feature horizontal bands, zig-zags and connecting diamonds, without borders, in autumnal umbers, ochres and sepias, offset by pale blues, grey and white. They are finely woven and usually fall into the medium and medium-to-high price range.

Qashga'i or Kashgay (pls 8, 11)

The Qashga'i are an informal tribal confederation of nomadic, semi-nomadic and settled tribesmen, mainly of Turkic origin, who live primarily in the Fars Province (south-west Iran). However, their exact origins are unclear. Some authorities trace their arrival in the region to Genghis Khan's Turko-Mongol army, which conquered Persia during the 13th century and left behind either an established tribe or disparate mercenaries (who later formed a culturally homogeneous group). Others suggests that they were part of the Seljuk Turkic invasion in the 11th century, and there is also a body of opinion that argues that they arrived at a much earlier date, possibly as part of a Ephthalite (White Hun) incursion during the 5th or 6th century. The Qashga'i themselves are equally divided – some claim that their name is a direct reference to their original homeland in Kashgaria (East Turkestan), whereas others use the same evidence to argue for direct descent from a famous tribal leader, Jani Agha Qashga'i, who exercised authority over the tribes of the Fars Province during the Safavid Dynasty.

Qashga'i rugs are arguably the most aesthetically vivacious of all Iranian tribal items, and, regardless of the basic composition, are usually imbued with a dazzling variety of tiny, delightfully articulated floral, animal, bird, human and geometric infill motifs. Amulet/medallions are especially common, but pictorial, *boteh* and other repeating and all-over formats are also frequently employed. The Qashga'i palette is based mainly on primary shades of red, blue, cream, white, yellow and orange ochres, and hints of green. Pile rugs vary considerably in quality, ranging from extremely well made, compact items (with over 150 Turkish knots in²) to more loosely constructed examples (with 60–100 knots in²). Kilims (often in repeating, panelled or banded designs), bags and animal trappings are also woven. The Qashga'i confederation has a number of sub-tribes (e.g. Kashguli, Shishboluki, Farsimadan, Darreshuri and Amaleh), but their rugs are normally sold simply as Qashga'is. They are usually marketed in the town of Shiraz, and range between the low/medium to medium price bracket. (*See* Shiraz)

Shahsavan (pls 3, 12, 16, 19, 34)

The Shahsavan (meaning those loyal to the Shah) are a formal tribal confederation of mainly ethnic Turkic, Kurdish, Tajik and Georgian tribesmen. It was formed by Shah Abbas, at the beginning of the 17th century, as a buffer against the rebellious Kyzylbash (Dervish) movement in the north-west of Persia. Several tribes maintained their confederation after the rebellion was quelled and gradually evolved into a culturally homogeneous group. Some Shahsavan tribesmen are now settled among the Bakhtiari (near the Zagros Mountains) or have amalgamated with other tribal groups in the Fars and Khorassan Provinces, but most still maintain a nomadic or semi-nomadic lifestyle throughout north-west Iran, Armenia and Azerbaijan.

Shahsavan rugs are among the most attractive and diverse tribal items on the market today. They are generally well made –

averaging between 60 and 120 Turkish knots per in² – and employ a variety of amulet/medallion, repeating, all-over, banded, striped and lattice designs, which often include rows of tiny, highly stylized animals and birds (especially camels, horses, deer and the mythical two-headed bird), as well as abstracted floral, tree-of-life, and (often hooked or crenellated-diamond) geometric motifs. The palette is based on harmonious combinations of vibrant reds, blues, burnt orange, yellows and greens, balanced by cream, white and more subdued shades of the same hues. Kilims are usually long and narrow, or occasionally rectangular, and woven in slitweave (often supplemented by other weaving techniques). A wide range of *jajims*, *vernehs*, *soufrehs*, *rukorssis*, bags and animal trappings (especially *mafrashes* and horse blankets) are also made. Most Shahsavan rugs fall into the low-to-medium and medium price brackets. They are fairly widely available and are usually sold simply as Shahsavans, or prefixed by the region or marketing centre. (*See* Kharaghan)

Bidjar Shahsavans Woven mainly by settled tribesmen in several small villages around the town of Bidjar. They are similar to either Mogan Shahsavans, or local Kurdish items, but often use lighter shades of orange, reddish orange, yellow, blue, brown and pink.

Hastrud Shahsavans Produced mainly by the Duvayran tribe – who live semi-nomadic and settled lifestyles in and around the town of Hastrud in north-western Iran – and are sometimes referred to as Amroulahs. Kilims (often fairly loosely woven in slitweave), bags and animal trappings, as well as decent quality pile rugs, are made in a range of mainly banded and repeating designs, which often feature Caucasian, Turkic or *herati* infill motifs. Large hooked or crenellated medallions are also common, and the palette tends towards slightly pastel reds, blues, greens, pink and brown.

Khamseh Shahsavans Made by the Amir Afshar Shahsavan and other settled and, to a lesser extent, semi-nomadic tribes in the northern Iranian districts of Khamseh and Zanjan. Designs are influenced by both Caucasian and Kurdish rugs and often feature slightly more restrained repeating geometric and animal (mainly two-headed bird/beast) motifs in muted or dark reds, blues, browns and yellow ochres. Kilims are especially common, but some pile rugs are made.

Mianeh Shahsavans Generic name, derived from a town close to Hastrud, used for the top quality items (mainly kilims) made in the region. They are similar to Hastrud Shahsavans, but are generally larger, more finely woven and articulated, and use brighter colours.

Mogan Shahsavans (pls 3, 16, 19, 34) Made by settled, nomadic and semi-nomadic tribes who inhabit the Mogan Plain (straddling Azerbaijan Province and Azerbaijan Republic) and are generally considered to be the most tribally authentic of all Shahsavan weavings. Kilims are especially common and are usually long and narrow, and tightly woven – but good quality pile rugs, bags and animal trappings are also made. They employ banded, striped, all-over, repeating and amulet/medallion designs – which usually have a distinctive Caucasian flavour – in a varied palette of reds, blues, greens, browns, yellows, cream and white. Linear rows of tiny stylized animals (e.g. camels), birds and floral (e.g. tree-of-life) motifs, often set against contrasting light or dark grounds are also common.

Qasvin Shahsavans Mainly kilims made by settled and semi-nomadic tribes in and around the town of Qasvin (north central Iran). They are usually long and narrow, finely woven in slitweave, with supplementary dovetailing and feature a variety of typical Shahsavan, Kurdish and other tribal designs in fairly muted colours, often enlivened by turmeric yellow.

Saveh Shahsavans (sim pl 12) Produced by nomadic, semi-nomadic and settled tribesmen living in and around the town of Saveh in north central Iran. Pile rugs are generally well made, and mainly feature amulet/medallion, medallion-and-corner and, to a lesser extent, all-over and repeating designs – often containing extensive floral or *herati* infill decorations – as well as variations on the lightning design. The palette is usually fairly dark, rich and harmonious – dominated by blues, reds, browns and ochres, beige and cream – although lighter colours may be employed. They are not unlike local Kurdish and Hamadan (regional/village) items, and are sometimes marketed as such. Kilims are similar to those made in Qasvin, but are normally stiffer and more coarsely woven, often on cotton warps.

Veramin Shahsavans Made by nomadic, semi-nomadic and settled tribes in and around the town of Veramin. Kilims are especially common – although some pile rugs are made – and usually feature Caucasian-inspired, banded formats, often with rosette or 's' pattern infill decorations. (*See* Veramin)

Traditional Caucasian weaving groups (pls 14, 24)

The pile rugs and flatweaves produced in the Caucasus from the 18th to the mid-20th centuries are generally considered to be among the finest tribal and tribal-style regional items ever produced and, although the vast majority are no longer made, they remain of major importance. They were woven by Armenians, Azerbaijanis, Georgians, Chechens, Lesghis, Kurds, Lurs, Ossetians and other ethnic and tribal groups in and around hundreds of villages throughout the Caucasus. Each village (or area) was associated with the production of rugs that conformed to an overall style, regardless of where or by whom the individual items were actually made. For example, Daghestan rugs were woven mainly by Chechens, Karabaghs by Armenians and Shirvans by Azerbaijanis, but they are rarely, if ever, classified according to the ethnic group. Similarly, the traditional method of classification makes no attempt to separate trbal (e.g. Lesghi) from regional (e.g. Derbend) items. Traditional Caucasian rugs are extremely collectable and normally fall into the high price bracket.

Baku Town in Azerbaijan mainly associated with medium quality pile rugs in reds, blues, yellows, greens, browns, burnt orange and cream; often set against a blue-black ground. The main sub-groups are: Chila (*botehs* and small, repeating amulet/medallions in rich colours); Saliano (finer quality, featuring *botehs*, often in diagonal rows); and Surahani (more ochred colouring, in lattice, amulet/medallion, all-over and repeating designs).

Daghestan (pl 14) Generic term for tribal rugs produced in the region mainly by semi-nomadic Chechens and to a lesser extent Lesghis. Daghestan is most closely associated with small, quite finely knotted prayer rugs (usually based on a skeletal *mihrab*), featuring a lattice arrangement of tiny repeating stylized floral motifs in fairly pastel yellow and brown ochres, blue, red, green, and white. More primitive, usually less finely knotted, pile rugs, flatweaves, bags and artefacts are also made in amulet/medallion, repeating geometric, banded and striped designs. These include large, elongated flatweaves (known as *davagh-ins*) that normally feature a series of large, complex geometric motifs, articulated in red and set against a dark blue ground. Tribal Daghestans are still made, although only a few reach the west and usually fall into the medium-to-high price category.

Derbends (pl 24) A city on the Caspian Sea that lends its name to regional/workshop items made in Daghestan in a range of Caucasian designs.

Erivan (or Yerevan) Capital of Armenia sometimes used as a generic term for both unattributed Armenian rugs and items made by Kurdish nomads in the region that are often distinguished by the extensive use of burnt orange and yellow and brown ochres.

Gianja (or Gianje) Village in Azerbaijan, on the eastern edge of the Kazak region, that lends its name to items made in the area – mainly by Armenians. They are similar to Kazaks, but are less consistent in quality and usually have paler and softer colours and feature repeating all-over (star, tarantula, *boteh*, stylized floral and geometric, etc.) motifs in panelled, latticed or diagonal-striped formats.

Karabagh Quasi-independent Armenian ASSR in southern Azerbaijan noted for excellent quality pile rugs and kilims in European-style floral, amulet/medallion, repeating, all-over, *boteh*, *herati*, prayer-rug and striped designs in almost every conceivable shade of red, blue, green, yellow, brown, burnt orange, cream, white and black. They were produced by both settled and semi-nomadic (mainly Armenian) weavers. The main sub-groups are: Chelaberd (large, turreted-diamond medallions, often referred to as Eagle Kazaks); Chondzoresk (large, uneven octagonal medallions, inwardly decorated with distinctive undulating linear forms, commonly known as Cloudband Kazaks); Shushas (Persian-influenced designs, often with monochrome or sparsely decorated fields); Channiks (repeating *boteh* and small floral motifs on blue-black grounds); Goradiz (all-over designs, often featuring scorpion and vegetal motifs); Kasim-Ushag (complex amulet/medallion schemes, woven by Kurdish nomads); and rugs from the adjoining Karadagh region (Persian-inspired medallion and repeating designs) also known as Lampa-Karabaghs.

Kazak Village in north-western Azerbaijan that lends its name to pile rugs and kilims made in a region that stretches into western Armenia and southern Georgia. Kazaks are most closely associated with large, overtly heraldic central medallions, although repeating, prayer-rug, all-over, floral, tree-of-life and other (both geometric and naturalistic) designs are also found, mainly in rich reds, blues, yellow ochres, greens and whites. Kazaks were woven predominantly by settled Armenians, but semi-nomadic Armenian shepherds, and both settled and nomadic Kurds, Georgians, Lurs and Azerbaijanis are associated with specific sub-groups. The most important are: Borchalu (possibly woven by Georgians) and usually feature repeating geometric motifs or two or three hooked-diamonds set within a broad border decorated with latched-hooked zig-zags); Lori-Pambak (simple amulet/medallions and geometric motifs, often set against sparsely decorated fields, in fairly muted, ochred shades; possibly made by Lurs); Fachralo (amulet/medallion based on a superimposed large diamond and square, with horns extruding from both vertical axis); Karatchoph (rectangular and octagonal medallions; often set against a green field).

Kuba Town in north-east Azerbaijan associated with good quality pile rugs and kilims, featuring amulet/medallion, naturalistic floral all-over and repeating formats (employing geometric and stylized floral motifs) in a muted palette of rich reds, blues, burnt orange and yellow and brown ochres. They were woven mainly by settled Azerbaijanis and divided into sub-groups that are closely associated with specific designs: Perepedil (ram's horn motif), Konagkend (amulet/medallions), Karagashli (all-over geometric and stylized floral schemes), Chichi (complex repeating and all-over schemes probably made by Chechen semi-nomads), Sejshour (naturalistic all-over floral schemes).

Lesghis Made by Lesghi nomads in the Lesghistan and Daghestan ASSRs. They are often very similar to Daghestans – especially prayer-rug and all-over lattice designs – but generally employ a brighter palette of blues, reds, white and cadmium yellow, offset by chrome green, olive, burnt orange, cream and yellow and brown ochres. Lesghis are also associated with a specific amulet/medallion (composed of overlapping, forked rectangles), which is often referred to as the Lesghi Star, and other (usually complex) amulet/medallion and all-over stylized floral schemes. Similar items are still made, but very few reach the west. They are usually medium to high in price.

Mogans Made in the Mogan Steppe region, southern Azerbaijan, which contains several different ethnic and tribal groups (e.g. Azerbaijanis, Shahsavans). They are generally finely knotted, employ a fairly subdued palette of reds, blues, orange, cream, white and yellow and brown ochres, and feature mainly all-over repeating designs (e.g. small octagon, tarantula, star, hooked cruciform, swastika and other motifs); often on a narrow field within a large multiple border.

Shirvan District in central Azerbaijan, mainly inhabited by settled Azerbaijanis, associated with excellent quality pile rugs and flatweaves in (mainly geometric) repeating, amulet/ medallion, all-over, banded and striped designs. Colours are either rich or fairly dark shades of red, blue, green, yellow and brown ochre and cream. The two most important stylistic sub-groups are: Marasali (small, all-over repeating geometric, stylized floral and *boteh* motifs, often in a striped or prayer-rug format); and Akstafa (repeating amulet- or pole-medallions, usually formed from a superimposed cross, diamond and rectangle, which almost invariably feature large, stylized mythical birds, commonly known as the Akstafa bird).

Talish Region in south-east Azerbaijan, close to the Iranian border, which lends its name to quite finely knotted rugs that usually feature tiny stars, stylized floral and geometric motifs set against a fairly narrow field within a large, multiple border. Bright colours – mainly blues, reds, burnt orange, cream, white and yellow and brown ochres – and monochrome fields are common. The main sub-group is Lenkoran (usually three large, octagonal horned-medallions set against a dark blue field).

Turkomen (pls 15, 17, 18)

The term Turkomen (or Turkmen) is sometimes used as a collective description for all the Turkic and Turko-Mongol tribes of Central Asia. However, in rug weaving it is normally reserved for specific groups of eastern Turkic tribes (belonging to the south-western branch of the Turkic language group), who lived an almost exclusively nomadic or semi-nomadic existence until the early 20th century. Many have now been assimilated into the general population, but some still retain their individual tribal identity as nomadic or semi-nomadic herdsmen, or as settled farmers. Some of the major Turkomen tribes have several sub-tribes, or less clearly defined associated groups, whose exact inter-tribal connections are unclear. It is also common practice for villages to adopt the name of the dominant sub-tribe, and vice versa, so it is sometimes unclear whether the name of a specific weaving group (e.g. Kizil Ayak) refers to a distinctive sub-tribe, or whether it is a generic term for several different clans who inhabit the same location and whose rugs conform to uniform characteristics. (*See* Chapter IV: Turkic Tribes)

Turkoman rugs are made in the Turkmenistan Republic, Afghanistan and to a lesser extent north-eastern Iran and other parts of Central Asia. They are normally based on all-over, linear rows of repeating *guls*, set against red grounds and highlighted by dark blue, yellow, green, brown ochre and white secondary colours – although yellow ochre (or gold), white and cream may also be used as ground colours. Each tribe, or major sub-tribe, has its own distinctive range of *guls* and slight variations on the basic colour scheme, which gives their rugs their subtly unique appearance, but a tribe may borrow someone else's *gul* for purely aesthetic or commercial reasons. Consequently, a rug featuring a traditional Tekke *gul*, for example, although most probably made by Tekke weavers, may have been produced by another tribe. Some sub-tribes also veer towards non-*gul* repeating geometric and floral forms, and a few items featuring *hadklu* (*enssi*), lattice, banded, panelled and (occasionally) prayer-rug designs are also found. Turkoman pile rugs are normally extremely well made, using very good wool and can be exceptionally finely knotted (sometimes over 300 Persian knots in^2), although quality can vary both between different tribes and sub-tribes, and also between individual items from the same group. Common structural features are the frequent use of very fine wefts, which result in roughly twice as many knots along the vertical as the horizontal axes, and having extended kilim fringes at both ends. Flatweaves, bags and animal trappings – usually in the same range of colours and designs – are also made. Sizes vary, although runners are rare, and prices range between the low-to-medium and medium-to-high categories. Some tribes have now either ceased to be significant rug producers, or have had their weaving identity subsumed by another tribe or into a generic regional style, but the following are still important tribal weaving groups. (*See* Labijar, Mandali)

Chodor (or Chaudor) Major tribe, found mainly in Turkmenistan, noted for extremely attractive rugs that often feature a distinctive equilateral diamond *gul*, with a crenellated or saw-tooth perimeter, contained within a zig-zag lattice. Other *guls*, *hadklu* and repeating geometric or stylized floral designs are also found. They are similar to Yomuts, but not always quite as finely knotted and often employ larger amounts of pale yellow ochre or cream. They are quite rare and are usually medium and medium to high in price.

Ersari (pl 17) Large tribe with several sub-groups found throughout Turkmenistan, Uzbekistan and especially Afghanistan, where rugs featuring the Ersaris' large, octagonal elephant-foot *gul* are often referred to simply as Afghans. The Ersari employ a variety of other *guls* and produce most of the Turkoman items woven in *hadklu*, prayer-rug, medallion, lattice, banded, and repeating geometric and stylized floral designs. Colours also vary and cream, yellow ochre and light brown grounds are not uncommon. Pile rugs are generally compact and well made – although the knotting is rarely as fine as in Tekkes, Saryks or Yomuds. Good quality kilims are also made. Prices vary, but usually span the low-to-medium and medium price brackets.

The majority of Ersari rugs reaching the west originate from Afghanistan, where many Ersaris have now settled in villages and towns: some of which produce both regional/workshop rugs and also lend their names to authentic tribal items made in the area – consequently, it is often unclear whether rugs sold as Andkhoys, for example, have been woven by the individual Suleiman, Kizil Ayak, Chaker, Charchangi or Ghaba Saqal sub-tribes or are regional items that conform to the generic Andkhoy style. This is also true of rugs named after the following towns: Daulatabad (Charchangi and Farukh Qaraish clans), Alti Bolagh (Qara), Kundoz (Dali), Sherberghan (Kizil Ayak) and Mazar (Kazan). However, the following sub-tribes generally market rugs under their tribal name.

The Arabatchi mainly inhabit the border region between Turkmenistan and Uzbekistan. Pile rugs are quite finely knotted, favour a darkish palette of red, reddish brown, blue, yellow and orange ochres, and employ *gul* and repeating medallion and geometric forms – especially a fairly elongated stepped *gul*, an overlaid diamond and square *gul*/medallion

and a highly stylized flying moth or bird. Their production has declined in recent years.

The Beshir inhabit the southern border region of Turkmenistan and Uzbekistan, and parts of Afghanistan. They are usually classified as an Ersari sub-tribe (although their exact origins are unclear). Pile rugs are not especially finely knotted, but they are well made, compact and often extremely attractive. Design and colour schemes are similar to other Ersari items, but they usually favour stylized floral and vegetal motifs, rather than *guls*.

The Jangalarik are a small tribe, mainly in Afghanistan, who make sturdy, fairly coarsely knotted rugs that feature a small *gul* with two white quarters as well as prayer rugs, often with dark blue *mihrabs* on plum-red grounds.

The Kizil Ayak (pl 17), which means red foot, are mainly found in Turkmenistan and Afghanistan and are generally considered to be an Ersari sub-tribe. They are noted for excellent quality pile rugs that feature a number of distinctive *guls* in fairly light reds, yellow ochres and blues. Afghan and former-Soviet regional/workshop items in these designs are often sold as Kizil Ayaks.

Salor Generally accepted as being the finest of all the Turkoman weaving groups until their production declined at the beginning of the 20th century. Pile rugs are very finely knotted (sometimes in a mixture of wool, cotton and silk) and employ *gul* and repeating geometric and stylized floral designs in harmonious interplays of red, blue, yellow, orange, green, white and pink. A huge variety of exceptional bags (mainly *chuvals* and *torbahs*) and animal trappings (e.g. *asmalyks*) were also made. Today, Salor weaving has largely subsumed into that of the Saryks, but authentic Salor rugs occasionally appear on the market. Older items are very expensive and sought-after.

Saryk (or Sarukh) Large tribe, living mainly in Turkmenistan and to a lesser extent Afghanistan, who make very compact, often finely knotted rugs (sometimes in silk). The main Saryk *gul* is a medium-sized, delicately patterned hexagonal lozenge, set within a larger saw-tooth (or anchor pendanted) hexagonal surround. It is often articulated in a deep brownish or purplish red against a fairly open dark blue ground, although dark green and unbleached, white cotton are also sometimes used. The Saryk are closely associated with the Salor tribe and sometimes weave items using traditional (or variant) Salor *guls*. The name Pendi (a corruption of the Penjdeh Oasis) was used as a generic description for the best quality Soviet regional/workshop items based on Saryk designs. Saryk tribal rugs sometimes reach the west and are usually medium or medium to high in price.

Tekke The largest and most important Turkoman tribe in the 19th century, but whose influence has declined in recent years. They live mainly in Turkmenistan and to a lesser extent in north-eastern Iran, northern Afghanistan and Uzbekistan. Tekke rugs are generally finely knotted in good quality wool (occasionally silk) and often have extensive kilim fringes. Designs are based on linear rows of medium-sized major *guls* – usually slightly elongated, stepped octagons, with rounded edges, divided into quarters – set against off-set rows of smaller, hooked-cruciform minor *guls*. They often have wide borders, with a plethora of tiny geometric and stylized vegetal motifs. Colours range from pale reds (usually with an orange or rose tinge) to darker reddish browns and reddish purples, offset by blue, blue-black, yellow ochre and cream. Kilims, bags and animal trappings are also made. Tekke rugs are generally believed to be the model for generic Bokhara items produced in workshops throughout Central Asia, Pakistan and Afghanistan and are sometimes referred to as Tekke Bokharas. Rugs made in the Afghan towns of Barmazit and Sharkh were originally woven by Tekkes, but today many items marketed under these names are made by a mixture of Pashtuns, Uzbeks, Tajiks and Aimaqs. Tekke rugs are reasonably widely available and generally fall into the medium and medium-to-high price brackets.

Yomut (or Yomud) (pls 15, 18) Large tribe inhabiting Turkmenistan, Afghanistan, north-eastern Iran and Uzbekistan. They are divided into several sub-tribes (e.g. Ogurjalis), but their rugs are almost always marketed simply as Yomuts. Designs are dominated by the classic Turkoman *gul* format based on three medium-sized, major *guls*: a pendanted, elongated form, dissected by vertical cross-pieces, known as the *kepse gul*; a flattened hooked-diamond (*dyrnyk gul*); a quartered square, with thinner, horizontally extending central sections (*chuval gul*). They also employ a large, rounded star form, with complex external serations, as well as *hadklu*, all-over (often serrated zig-zags) and repeating geometric and stylized vegetal (mainly tree)

designs. Their palette contains diverse shades of red, blue, yellow and brown ochre, burnt orange, cream, green and white (yellow ochre, cream and white are sometimes used as grounds). Pile rugs can be very finely woven, using good quality wool (and sometimes silk), and often have extended end sections (either kilim or pile), which are frequently decorated with serrated zig-zags. They are generally comparable in quality and price to Tekke and Saryk rugs, but are more widely available. Kilims, bags and animal trappings, especially *iolem* (tent bands) are also made.

Uzbeks (sim pl 15)

The Uzbeks are a relatively homogeneous, Turkic-speaking tribal group believed to be a breakaway faction of one of the Turko-Mongol (possibly Uighur) tribes that first moved westwards into Central Asia during the 1st millennium. They later formed part of the Turkic and Turko-Mongol invasions of Asia and eastern Europe that took place between the 11th and 16th centuries. Their name is derived from one of their leaders, Uzbek Khan (*c.* 1313–40), who is credited with converting them to Islam, and became a collective term for the Muslim section of Genghis Khan's army. Most Uzbeks live in the Uzbekistan Republic, but a significant number are found in Afghanistan and other parts of Central Asia.

Uzbek rugs are probably the most varied in colour, design, and weaving techniques of all the rugs woven by Turkic-speaking Central Asian weaving groups. Designs range from Turkoman-style *gul* formats to a variety of banded, panelled, zig-zag, prayer-rug, all-over geometric and stylized floral schemes. Their palette runs the gamut of traditional Central Asian deep reds, blues, brown and yellow ochres (with lighter highlights) to more pastel shades of the same colours on white, cream or pale brown grounds. Pile rugs are not particularly finely woven (averaging around 50–80 knots in^2), but they are generally well made in a variety of shapes and sizes. Kilims, *ghudjeris*, *namads*, *suzanis*, *ikats*, bags and animal trappings are also made. Uzbek items are fairly widely available and normally low to medium in price. (*See* Sar-i-Pul, Tartari)

Yuruks

The Yuruk are primarily nomadic and semi-nomadic tribesmen – in the Yuncu and Taurus Mountain regions of western and southern

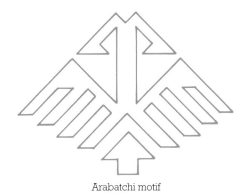

Arabatchi motif

Turkey – who derive their name from a Turkic word for nomad. They are believed to be direct descendants of a Turko-Mongol people (closely related to the Hungarians, Finns and Samo-yeds), who migrated southwards during the 6th century AD. The vast majority were absorbed into the general population, but a small number retained their traditional way of life and (in the 9th century) were known as Turkomen, and later (during the Ottoman Empire) acquired the name Yuruks. Today they are sometimes divided into *gocebe* (nomadic) and *yerli* (semi-nomadic) tribes. Yuruk rugs are usually small to medium in size, employ good quality wool (often with substantial additions of camel and horse hair) and often exude a rough-hewn vitality and charm. They vary considerably in quality and appearance, ranging from coarse, loosely woven, shaggy pile items – which are often riddled with abrashes and based on minimalistic, primitively articulated geometric designs – to more finely knotted, medium pile items that feature bold amulet- and pole-medallions, concentrically expanding hexagons and other geometric motifs in reds, blues, yellows, purples and violets, with hints of orange and green. Kilims are usually quite finely woven (using slitweave) in mainly banded and all-over designs – often based on interlocking *perepedil* (ram's horn) motifs. Bags and animal trappings are also made. Yuruk rugs are usually marketed simply as Yuruks, but, depending on the area of origin, may be sold as Yuncu or Taurus Yuruks, or Balikesirs or Muts (their respective marketing towns) or as Dag (mountain) rugs.

Minor weaving groups

Adraskand (pl 21) Village in Afghanistan that is a major centre for Belouch-style rugs which are now produced mainly by local Pashtun tribes (e.g. Alizai, Nurzai, Bobakza'i), who learned their craft from the Belouch. Adraskands are similar to Mushwanis – they tend to be fairly long-piled, employ a darkish palette of deep red, blue, purple, brown ochre and green, and favour repeating or concentrically expanding, hooked-diamond designs.

Ardebil Town in Iranian Azerbaijan noted for regional/workshop rugs in Caucasian-influenced designs. Other villages in the area (e.g. Meshkin, Karaja, Lamberan, Georavan and Sarab) make similar, tribal-style regional items.

Ayuchucho (pl 40) Large town and weaving centre in Peru that lends its name to flatwoven items made by Quechua, Ayamara and other ethnic and tribal groups. Ayuchuchos are quite tightly woven (on both backstrap and treadle looms) and usually feature a range of pre-Colombian motifs (mainly Paracas, Chancay, Nazca and Inca) in panelled, banded, pictorial and repeating formats. Mythological figures (especially the flying man of the Paracas), ideograms and agricultural calendar motifs predominate, although more abstract geometric forms (e.g. zig-zags) are also found. The palette is generally based on fairly pastel light greys, browns, mauves, reds and blues, yellow and orange ochres, and white. Ayuchuchos are usually small to medium in size and fall into the low price bracket.

Azrou (pl 4) Village in the Middle Atlas Mountains, in Morocco, that is a major centre for settled and semi-nomadic Berber pile rugs, mainly in banded and repeating designs (sometimes with tassel insertions). Good quality flatweaves, which are often large, intricately patterned and mainly white, are also made.

Bagdiz Small tribe in Afghanistan, probably of Arab origin, who produce reasonable quality Herat Belouch-style rugs.

Baluchistan (pl 32) Arid province in southeastern Pakistan inhabited by Belouch and other related tribal groups. Pile rugs are rare, but simple, sometimes brightly coloured kilims, bags and artefacts often reach the west.

Bebehan Town in Iran between Hamadan and Shiraz that acts as the marketing centre for the mainly Luri tribes in the area. Bebehans tend to have fairly sombre colours (reddish mauve, blue-black and greyish blue), often enlivened by bright orange, and generally feature variations of the Luri latch-diamond motif in repeating or pole-medallion formats. They are usually quite coarsely knotted, fairly long and narrow, employ mainly natural dyes and are in the low and low-to-medium price brackets.

Bidjar (pl 13) Town in Kurdistan (Iran) that acts as the marketing centre for local tribes, and also produces expensive finely knotted, extremely hard-wearing workshop/regional rugs, which often feature precisely articulated *herati* designs, set within a large diamond or hexagonal skeletal medallion, in reds, blues and creams. (*See* Afshar, Kurds, Shahsavan)

Borchalu (pl 22) Tribe of Mongol descent, who inhabit the remote fringes of the Hamadan district (Iran), near the villages of Khumbajin and Khumbazan. Pile rugs are often quite finely knotted, and usually feature neatly articulated, often sharply pinnacled, variations of amulet/medallion, *herati* and floral motifs – including a version of the American Sarouk scheme (large, fairly naturalistic floral bouquets) – in quite rich reds, blues, white or cream, with hints of green, orange and ochres. They are among the finest items from the Hamadan region and normally fall into low-to-medium price brackets.

Boujaad (pl 5) Village on the edge of the Middle and the High Atlas Mountains (Morocco) that acts as a centre for local Berber tribes. Boujaads are similar to Zairs, but are often wilder and more eccentric in appearance, and may include sewn-on coins, beads and synthetic fibres, etc.

Bowanat Town in southern Iran that acts as a marketing centre for local (mainly Arab) nomadic tribes. They are similar to Qashga'is, but tend towards hexagonal pole-medallions (with saw-tooth edges), set against more sparsely decorated fields, in deep reds and blues, highlighted by white. They are normally quite coarsely knotted, long-piled, soundly constructed and low or low to medium in price.

Charakasur and Sarhadi Villages in western Afghanistan associated with quite finely knotted, good quality Belouch-style rugs, which feature mainly repeating and prayer-rug designs in predominantly sombre reds and blues. Most are woven by the settled Pashtun (mainly Rukhshani) and Belouch tribes, but some (especially Sarhadi items with a distinctive, skeletal prayer-rug format, in reddish maroon against a cream field) are associated with the Zurhuris, a tribe believed to be of Arab descent. Excellent quality kilims are also produced. Charakasur and Sarhadi rugs are

among the best Herat Belouches and normally fall into the low-to-medium price bracket.

Chichaksu Village in Afghanistan associated with the finest quality Herat Belouch rugs. They are woven by several ethnic and tribal groups – in a range of Belouch and, more recently, non-Belouch designs – but are most closely associated with the *Haft-Boleh* design; often in a fairly warm palette of orange, brown and yellow ochres, offset by darker blues. They are normally low to medium and, occasionally, medium in price. (*See* Haft Boleh)

Cuzco (pl 41) Town in central Peru (at the entrance of the Sacred Valley of the Incas) often used as a generic term for Quechua, Ayamara and other local tribal weavings. They are made for domestic use, employ fairly simple repeating patterns, in reds and browns, and are among the most tribally authentic of all South American weavings. They are quite rare and normally medium priced.

Dokhtar-i-Ghazi Large Belouch tribe in Afghanistan, whose name can be translated as judge's daughter. They are closely associated with a distinctive prayer-rug design – featuring a fairly squat, rectangular head-and-shoulder *mihrab* set against a latticed field decorated with tiny stylized floral motifs, often in deep reds and blues offset by white. Dokhtar-i-Ghazi is also used as a generic term for rugs woven in this design – mainly by Taimanis in and around the town of Shindand – and it is often unclear whether the name refers to the tribe or the design. Both are usually of good quality and low to medium in price.

Farah Town in Afghanistan noted for low-priced Belouch-style kilims – woven primarily by Pashtuns – that employ very dark reds, blues and greens (with hints of white or yellow) in banded, prayer-rug and repeating designs. Fairly coarsely knotted pile rugs are also made.

Firdous Village in the Khorassan Province (Iran) occupied mainly by Arabs who produce decent quality, low priced Belouch-style rugs that generally favour dark (often autumnal) colours in banded and repeating designs.

Ghurian (or Ghorian) Generic term for reasonable quality Belouch-style pile rugs woven (mainly by Taimanis) in Ghor Province (Afghanistan) in mainly prayer-rug and pictorial designs. Charchangan, the provincial capital, gives its name to finely woven kilims.

Glaoua Region in the High Atlas Mountains, in Morocco, used as a generic term for items made by several local Berber tribes.

Haft Boleh Means seven demons and is the name of a small Pushtu-speaking (probably Pashtun) tribe, in north-west Afghanistan, who are associated with a distinctive prayer-rug design, featuring seven (intricately decorated) ascending columns that support the *mihrab*. They are generally quite finely knotted and low to medium in price.

Hamadan (pl 12) Major town, district and weaving region at the northern edge of Kurdistan (Iran) that encompasses dozens of small villages – which produce a huge variety of mainly tribal-style regional items – and also acts as a centre for local tribal items. Pile rugs vary in fineness and quality, but are generally well made and usually feature amulet/medallion, pole-medallion, repeating geometric or *herati* designs – in reds, blues, deep pink, burnt orange, dark brown and yellow ochre, beige and white – and often use warp-loop fringes at one end. Kilims are also made, although they are sometimes sold as Harsins. Hamadans are widely available, and usually fall into the low-to-medium and medium price categories. Kurdish, Borchalu and Shahsavan tribal rugs may be sold as Hamadans.

Jan Begi Very small, Persian-speaking tribe, mainly living a settled lifestyle in north-west Afghanistan, noted for good quality carpets that feature distinctive repeating floral motifs.

Karakalpaks (sim pl 15) Turkic-speaking people who inhabit the former Tartar ASSR and other parts of Central Asia, especially Uzbekistan. They are closely related the Kazakhs, but contain people of Bulgarian extraction, and are sometimes referred to as Tartars. Karakalpak rugs often employ an octagonal (or elephant-foot) *gul* – very similar to the one associated with Afghan (Ersari Turkoman) rugs – in repeating, all-over formats on a predominantly red ground, as well as a variety of repeating geometric and lattice motifs, often on pale beige or white grounds. Pile rugs average 60–120 Turkish knots in², but are generally well made, using good quality wool. Flatweaves, bags and animal trappings are woven in a similar range of colours and designs. Most Karakalpak items fall into the low-to-medium and medium price brackets, but comparatively few reach the west.

Kars Town in eastern Turkey that lends its name to Kazak-style regional items (made primarily by settled Kurds), as well as acting as a marketing centre for rugs made by semi-nomadic and nomadic Kurdish tribes, which

Mixtec spinner, taken from Codex Vindobonensis

feature amulet- and pole-medallion, prayer-rug, repeating geometric and banded designs in mainly darkish reds, browns, blues and yellow and orange ochres. Kilims are also made, almost invariably in slitweave using natural brown woollen warps (often in two halves), in a variety of shapes and sizes. Kars tribal items are available in moderation, and are usually low to medium in price.

Kazakhs (sim pls 15, 18) Turkic-speaking people of Mongoloid appearance, generally believed to be a fusion of Turkic tribesmen (belonging to the Kipchak group) and Mongols, who invaded and settled in Transoxiana during the 8th and 13th centuries, respectively. Kazakh mythology traces their origins to the three sons of a single progenitor, who divided the Kazakh territory into three Hordes, or Ordas – the eastern (Great), central (Central) and western (Little) regions – which were each bequeathed to one of his sons. Today, most Kazakhs live in Kazakhstan, Mongolia and Sinkiang Province (China), but isolated pockets can be found in other parts of Asia. Kazakh rugs are similar to Turkoman rugs except that they normally employ a range of diamond and hooked geometric forms, rather than *guls*, as their main decorative motifs. Pile rugs are generally well made, although not very finely woven (average 50–70 knots in²) and employ the standard Central Asian palette of deep red and dark blue with yellow ochre, orange and white highlights. Kilims, bags and animal trappings are also made. Kazakh rugs are usually small to medium in size, and low to medium in price, although only a few reach the west. *Note* Kazak (Kazakh) is also a town in the Azerbaijan

Republic that gives its name to a Traditional Caucasian weaving group.

Kemereh Small area on the outskirts of the Hamadan district, containing an Armenian enclave, noted for attractive, quite finely knotted pile rugs in an intricate, all-over floral scheme in muted crimson or rose, commonly known as the American Sarouk design. They are often sold either as Lillihans (the principle village) or Armenibaffs (i.e. woven by Armenians) and are medium to high in price.

Kerman Province in south-eastern Iran that gives its name to the sophisticated workshop rugs produced mainly in and around the city of Kerman, and is a generic term for items made in the region by Afshar (mainly Jahanshahi and Amu'i clans), Qashga'i, Luri and a number of smaller tribes of uncertain origin (e.g. Buchaqchis, Suleimanis, Qutlus, Qara'is and Shuls). However, the Afshar are the largest and most influential tribe in the region, and it is common practice for Kerman rugs to be marketed as Afshars (or Kerman Afshars). They often employ blue grounds, are sometimes very finely knotted, and vary in price between the low and medium brackets.

Khamseh A generic description for fairly basic, Hamadan-style, regional pile rugs produced in the Khamseh district (northern Iran) and should not be confused with Khamseh Shahsavans or Khamseh tribal items.

Kharaghan Group of villages at the northern edge of the Hamadan region noted for low-to-medium grade rugs, mainly in pole- and amulet medallion designs (often with birds, animals and stylized vegetal secondary motifs). They are sometimes attributed to the Saveh Shahsavan or Kurdish Kolyai tribes and vice versa, and are usually low in price.

Khorassan (pl 26) Province in north-east Iran that lends its name to unattributed rugs made by local Kurdish, Belouch, Turkoman (mainly Tekke and Yomut) and Afshar tribes – especially ones that conform to a distinctive fusion of Kurdish and Belouch characteristics (e.g. bold amulet/medallion and repeating geometric motifs in a muted burnt orange, brown and orange ochres and blue). They are generally well made and low to medium in price.

Khorramabad Town, north-west of the Zagros Mountains (Iran), that lends its name to thick-pile, hard-wearing rugs made primarily by indigenous Luri tribes. They employ mainly fairly primitive, hooked-diamonds and amulet/medallions in darkish greys, browns, reddish

mauve and orange set against sparsely decorated fields. They are sometimes sold as Gebbehs and are low to medium in price.

Kirghiz (sim pl 15) Turkic-speaking ethnic group who live in the Kirghizstan Republic and to a lesser extent other parts of Central Asia and Sinkiang Province (China). Their exact origins are unclear, but they are generally associated with the Turanian Turks (or Tartars) who inhabited the Steppe country of southern Siberia and northern Mongolia. Today, the Kirghiz are increasingly gravitating towards a settled existence, but some still practise a nomadic or semi-nomadic lifestyle. Kirghiz rugs share a close affinity with both Central Asian and Sinkiang items. Pile rugs are generally well made, using good quality wool, but are normally coarsely knotted (averaging only 40–70 Persian knots per in^2). Flatweaves, bags and animal trappings are also produced. Designs are normally based around stylized floral and geometric motifs in all-over or panelled formats. Their palette is generally softer than that of most Central Asian weavers, and is dominated by muted reds, blues, yellow and orange ochres, highlighted with darker blues and white. Kirghiz rugs are made in a variety of shapes and sizes (although large carpets are rare). They are not widely available in the west and are usually low to medium in price.

Klenifra Berber village in the High Atlas Mountains noted for good quality kilims that are similar to those woven by the Zaiane.

Koudani Small tribe or clan (probably an offshoot of the Jamshidi Aimaq), inhabiting the Herat region of Afghanistan, who are associated with excellent quality, finely articulated Belouch-style rugs, featuring intricately patterned tree-of-life and architectural/mosque prayer-rug designs in mauvish brown and orange and yellow ochres. They usually fall into the low-to-medium price bracket.

Kutchis Mainly Indo-European nomadic tinkers and traders – often called the gypsies of Central Asia – whose name is frequently used as a term of derision, implying that something or someone is shoddy, worthless or not to be trusted, and appears to reflect the general opinion of the Kutchis as a people, rather than being a comment on their rugs. Kutchi pile rugs, kilims, bags and animal trappings are similar to many Belouch and Aimaq items, but are generally more coarsely woven and limited in design to relatively simple medallion and repeating geometric motifs (often embellished with glass beads, small coins, pieces of metal, synthetic threads and cowrie shells) articulated in bright (sometimes quite garish) reds, reddish browns, blues, orange, yellow ochre and white. However, Kutchi rugs often possess a considerable rough-hewn charm and may be sold as Taimanis or Belouches, or under the name of their marketing town (Mukkur). They normally fall into the low price bracket.

Labijar Generic name (meaning next to the canal) for two types of kilims made in a group of small villages – near the Darya Safidi River (Afghanistan) – inhabited mainly by Uzbeks, and Ersari and Saltuq Turkomans. Uzbek Labijars generally favour panelled, zig-zag and inter-locking poplar leaf designs in a soft palette of reds, blues, browns and white. Ersari Labijars often feature squares with internal double-arrowhead motifs, employ a darkish palette of deep reds, blues, yellow and white, and are usually large and rectangular. However, this ethnic division is somewhat arbitrary. Both types of kilim are normally tightly woven and fall into the low price bracket.

Malaki Generic term for flatweaves made by Belouch (and possible other) nomads inhabiting the vast Dasht-i-Margo (Desert of Death) in south-western Afghanistan. They employ a mixture of weaving techniques (including pile insertions), a dark palette (usually reds, blues and black, offset by touches of white, cream and pale yellow), and mainly feature intricately patterned banded and prayer-rug designs. They are among the finest Belouch flatweaves, and are usually low to medium in price.

Maldari Term – meaning sheep or goat owner – used as a generic description for kilims and semi-pile rugs (made by Taimani, Belouch and Pashtun tribes in Afghanistan) based on simplified, crudely executed Belouch designs, which often possess a charming naivety and are among the cheapest Belouch-style rugs.

Manastir Generic name for good quality items (mainly kilims) woven by Balkan expatriates in the Mihaliccik area of northern Turkey. They feature bold (usually sparsely decorated) prayer-rug and repeating designs in primary colours and are low to medium in price.

Mandali Persian-speaking tribe (possibly Belouch), who inhabit Herat Province (Afghanistan) and produce fairly good quality rugs in Ersari (mainly elephant-foot) designs.

Meshed Major city in Khorassan Province (Iran) noted for large, workshop carpets – mainly in medallion-and-corner designs on deep red grounds – that also acts as a centre for local tribes. (*See* Khorassan and Belouch)

Mushwani (sim pl 21) Semi-nomadic and settled tribesmen of Indo-European, probably Pashtun ancestry, who speak Farsi (Persian) and mainly inhabit western Afghanistan. They were noted especially for kilims and fairly long flatwoven and semi-pile *dastarkans*, but also now produce Belouch-style pile rugs, featuring a wide range of designs in a palette dominated by black or blue-black, dark red, deep brown, and yellow and brown ochres, offset by paler reds and blues. They are closely associated with an all-over scheme based on concentrically expanding hooked-diamonds or zig-zags. Mushwani rugs are generally of excellent quality, fall into the low-to-medium price bracket and may be sold as Adraskans.

Nasrabad Generic term for low-to-medium priced, robust, solidly constructed, although fairly coarsely knotted, rugs produced – mainly by Luri, Qashga'i and possibly Arab tribes – in the fringe desert area south-east of Isfahan (Iran). They usually employ Luri-style pendanted amulet-medallions in fairly light reds, blues, camel, and yellow and brown ochres and often use goat hair for the warps.

Niriz (pl 35) Town between Shiraz and Sirjand (Iran) inhabited by settled Afshars who produce finely knotted, superbly articulated pile rugs in a variety of designs, which usually fall into the medium or medium-to-high price bracket. The town is also associated with basic quality Shiraz rugs, some of which are probably woven by nomadic Arab tribes.

Nishapur Town in north-eastern Iran associated with good quality – usually quite finely knotted – Belouch rugs that are similar to Meshed Belouches, but generally employ brighter colours (e.g. ultramarine and cobalt blue) and feature complex all-over or repeating vegetal and animal motifs. They are normally low to medium or medium in price.

Oudref Region in northern Tunisia noted for Bedouin saddle blankets (*bost*) and animal trappings. Kilims and pile rugs are also made.

Owlad Word meaning clan or tribe applied to a small group of Luri or Bakhtiari tribesmen, living near Naghun in the Zagros Mountains (Iran), who are noted for sturdy, well-constructed rugs. They usually feature either Bakhtiari-style panelled designs, or repeating and pole-medallion formats (based on Luri hooked-diamond or hexagonal motifs) in dark reds and blues. They are sometimes called

Pashkuhis and are low to medium in price.

Qala-i-Nau Generic term for items made in and around the small towns of Qala-i-Nau and Laghari in north-west Afghanistan by settled, nomadic and semi-nomadic Hazara Aimaq, Mushwani and other tribal groups. Good quality kilims, semi-pile and pile rugs are made mainly in intricately patterned banded and Belouch-type designs in cherry red and gold, as well as more typical darker shades. They are usually low to medium in price.

Quchan (pl 29) Village in north-eastern Iran that lends its name to the rugs made by Kurdish tribesmen in the region. They are fairly coarsely knotted, sometimes employ goat-hair warps and generally feature repeating and all-over formats based on geometric (e.g. octagonal, hooked-cruciform and star) and stylized vegetal (e.g. tree-of-life) motifs that are reminiscent of Caucasian, Turkoman and Belouch designs. Colours are more traditionally Kurdish dark or muted burnt orange, red, blue, yellow and brown ochres, and pinkish white. They are low to medium in price.

San Pedro de Cajas Village in the Andean foothills, directly inland from Lima (Peru), that produces distinctive wall-hangings – woven in the wadding technique – featuring pastoral scenes of contemporary village life (usually including women in bowler hats) in fairly pastel shades of red, blue, yellow, green, orange, brown and white. They are usually small and fall into the low price range.

Sar-i-Pul Town in Afghanistan, on the fringes of the Hindu Kush, that lends its name to distinctive kilims that often employ broad monochrome sections, usually in cream or white, separated by smaller bands of coloured patterning. They are associated with Hazara Aimaqs and Uzbeks, and are usually low or low to medium in price.

Sarmayie Generic name for items – mainly kilims – made by Chahar Aimaq tribes, who live in and around the town of Charchangan (Afghanistan). They normally feature banded compositions – often with diamond-shaped inner decorations – in fairly muted shades of brown, yellow, burnt orange and brick red and are usually low or low to medium in price.

Senneh or Senna Former name for the capital (now called Sanandaj) of Kurdistan Province (Iran) that is noted for finely knotted regional/workshop rugs. They usually feature small flowers (or *botehs*) arranged in an all-over, repeating format – often within a skeletal medallion on variegated grounds – in rich reds and blues, highlighted with white, yellow ochre and green. Senneh also occasionally acts as a marketing centre for a number of mainly Kurdish tribes in the region (e.g. Jaff, Senjabi) who sometimes employ similar, although usually less sophisticated, versions of this design.

Shiraz (sim pl 8) Major town in Fars Province (Iran) that is the focal point for low-priced regional/workshop rugs made in numerous villages in the area, which are based mainly on Qashga'i designs, but are often more coarsely knotted and cruder in articulation. It also acts as a marketing centre for local Qashga'i, Luri, Khamseh, Arab and other tribal groups.

Shirikhani (pl 6) Semi-nomadic, Persian-speaking tribe (possibly of Alizai Pashtun origin) who produce Belouch-style rugs that are similar to Koudanis, although are rarely as fine.

Sinkiang (pl 27) Generic term for items, made by a number of groups throughout Sinkiang Province (China) and the border region of Central Asia, that conform to East Turkestan design traditions. They are usually well made (although not especially finely knotted) and employ variant Turkoman and other Central Asian designs in a more Chinese palette of muted reds, blues, orange, yellow and brown. They may be sold under the names of several towns – which are associated with specific designs or general styles – the most important of which are Khotan, Yarkand and Kashgar.

Tartari Generic term often used to describe two distinctive styles of kilims produced, mainly in Afghanistan, by Uzbek (and to a lesser extent other tribal weavers). Safid (or white) kilims are synonymous with Sar-i-Pul and Ranghi (or red) kilims are usually finely woven in double-interlock, in a variety of all-over diamond grids, or zig-zags. (*See* Sar-i-Pul)

Taznakht Village in the High Atlas Mountains (Morocco) that acts as a centre for settled Berber tribes in the region. It is mainly noted for good quality kilims and semi-pile rugs that are long and narrow, and usually based on horizontal or vertical repeating designs.

Timuri Nomadic and semi-nomadic tribes of uncertain origin who make pile rugs, kilims and artefacts that are almost identical to those woven by the neighbouring Taimani and Belouch in Afghanistan. They are fairly common and fall into the low price bracket.

Uighurs (or Uygurs) (sim pls 15, 27) A fairly homogeneous ethnic group of Turkic-speaking tribesmen, who established an empire during the 8th century from the ashes of the eastern Turkic Khanates (which had earlier split from the western Turkic territories), and later assisted the Tang Dynasty (in China) in combating the An Lushen Rebellion (*c.* 755–63). In the 9th century, they were overthrown by the Kirghiz and split into two groups – one moving to the Hexi Corridor (northwestern China), where they founded the Kingdoms of Dunhuang and Zhangye, and the other migrating to the south of the Heavenly Mountains (Tian Shan) in Sinkiang Province (China). The Uighurs are believed to be ethnically and culturally related to the Uzbeks and the Mongols and were converted to Islam in the 10th century – although Buddhist, Manicheist and Shamanist influences are still present in their cultural and artistic expression. Uighur rugs are a fusion of Central Asian (Islamic) and Far Eastern (Taoist/Buddhist) traditions, and generally employ slight variations on Kirghiz and to a lesser extent Uzbek motifs and designs, usually in a more Chinese palette of muted reds, blues and yellow and brown ochres. Pile rugs are usually well made, although not especially finely woven. Good quality kilims (usually slit-woven) and bags are also made. Uighur rugs are not widely available in the west, and are often sold under generic attributions (e.g. Kashgaria, Sinkiang) and normally fall into the low-to-medium and medium price categories.

Van (pl 20) Major town, near Lake Van, in eastern Turkey that produces regional items (mainly flatweaves), and also acts as a marketing centre for nomadic and semi-nomadic Kurdish tribes. However, it is often extremely difficult to distinguish between the two. Kilims are usually square or rectangular, medium-sized, and woven (often in two halves) in fairly tight slitweave; sometimes with additions of metallic and synthetic thread. Pile rugs are often slightly longer and narrower, and generally compact and well made, although fairly coarsely knotted. Banded and repeating designs are common and are normally based on hooked- or crenellated-diamonds – articulated in dark reds, blues, browns and occasionally greens, offset by tracings of yellow, brown and orange ochre, and white – amulet/medallions are also found. Van rugs (whether regional or tribal) generally fall into the medium price bracket.

Veramin Town close to Tehran (Iran) noted for extremely good quality, finely knotted workshop pile rugs – mainly in sophisticated *herati* and *mina khani* schemes – as well as brightly coloured, good quality regional kilims that often feature eye-dazzler designs. The area is heavily populated by Kurds, Lurs, Shahsavans, Arabs, Qasgha'is, Turkomen and other Turkic-speaking tribes who market their rugs in the town and whose unattributed pile rugs, kilims, bags, *soufrehs*, *rukorssis* and animal trappings – which often use undyed brown wool for the warps (and sometimes wefts) – may be marketed as Veramins and are usually low to medium or medium in price. Garmsar, a nearby town, is associated with similar items, but is especially identified with large kilims featuring diagonal rows of small hexagons.

Yahyahli Village in south-eastern Turkey that takes its name from the local (probably Turkic) tribal inhabitants. Yahyahli pile rugs are sometimes quite coarsely knotted, but they are well made, use good quality wool (normally also employed for warps and wefts) and often feature heraldic, hexagonal amulet/medallions – which are frequently pendanted with stepped or serrated edges – set against an open or sparsely decorated field. Deep reds, blues and brown and orange ochres, offset by green, golden yellow and white are the dominant colours. They occasionally reach the west and are normally low to medium in price.

Yakob Khani Small, semi-nomadic Persian-speaking tribe (probably related to the Timuris), whose name literally means House of Jacob. They inhabit Herat Province (Afghanistan) and are noted for good quality, low-to-medium priced rugs that often employ narrow, elongated panels set against an indigo field.

Yalameh (pl 30) Semi-nomadic tribe (probably of Luri origin) who inhabit the Bakhtiari region of Iran, near the town of Shah Reza, and usually market their rugs in Talkunncheh or Isfahan. Pile rugs are quite finely knotted, employ good quality wool (which is also normally used for the warps and wefts) and tend to be fairly long and narrow. Kilims, bags and artefacts are also made. Designs are usually based on repeating hooked-diamonds, or other geometric motifs – although amulet/medallion, panelled and latticed formats are also found – in an often dazzling interplay of contrasting reds, blues, greens, yellow, orange, cream and white. They are reasonably widely available and normally fall into the medium price category.

Public collections of tribal rugs

A number of museums throughout the world have tribal rugs as part of their overall oriental rug collections. In Europe, these include: the Victoria and Albert Museum, London, England; the Whitworth Art Gallery, Manchester, England; the Burrell Collection, Glasgow, Scotland; the Berlin Gallery, Berlin, Germany; the Osterreichisches Museum für angewandte Kunst and the Museum für Völkerkunde, Vienna, Austria; the Statens Museum, Stockholm, Sweden; the Poldi Pezzoli Museum, Milan, Italy; the Osterreichisches Museum für angewandte Kunst, Frankfurt, Germany; Linden-Museum, Stuttgart, Germany; and the Muraltengut and the Museum Rietberg, Zürich, Switzerland.

In North America, these include: the Metropolitan Museum of Art, New York, USA; the Philadelphia Museum of Art, Philadelphia, USA; the Textile Museum, Washington, DC, USA; the Museum for Indian Heritage, Indianapolis, USA; the Elkus Collection, California Academy of Sciences, San Francisco, USA; Glenbow Museum, Clagary, Canada, and the Royal Ontario Museum, Ontario, Canada.

In the former Soviet Union, these include: the Hermitage and the Museum of Ethnography and the Russian Museum, St Petersburg, St Petersburg, Russia; the Museum of Azerbaijan Carpets and Handicrafts, Baku, Azerbaijan; the Makhachkala Art Museum, Daghestan; the Museum of Georgian Architecture and Daily Life, Tbilisi, Georgia; and the Museum of the History of Armenia, Erivan.

In the Far East, there are a number of collections of tribal rugs, mainly from East Turkestan, eastern China and Mongolia, and the Shosoin Treasure House, Nara, Japan has a remarkable collection of antique items from these areas.

Shipibo tribal design illustrating rivers and settlements
(Pucalpo region of the Peruvian Amazon)

Index